SPQR

A ROMAN MISCELLANY

ANTHONY
EVERITT

with

RODDY
ASHWORTH

First published in 2014 by Head of Zeus Ltd
This paperback edition first published in 2015 by Head of Zeus Ltd

1 3 5 7 9 10 8 6 4 2

A CIP catalogue record for this book
is available from the British Library.

ISBN (PB) 9781781859414
(E) 9781781855683

Designed by Ken Wilson | point918
Printed and bound in the UK by Clays Ltd, St Ives Plc

Head of Zeus Ltd
Clerkenwell House
45–47 Clerkenwell Green
London EC1R 0HT
www.headofzeus.com

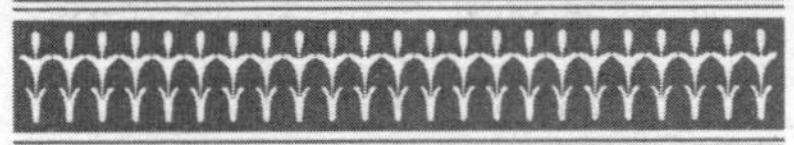

CONTENTS

WHAT THE ROMANS ACHIEVED

ROME CREATED ONE OF THE LARGEST EMPIRES IN WORLD HISTORY. In its heyday, under the emperor Trajan in the second century AD, it governed up to 60 million people in an area of about 5 million square kilometres. It stretched from Spain to Turkey, from the Black Sea to the Maghreb, over what are now more than forty modern countries. Even so, in population and extent the Roman empire was easily surpassed by others—among them, the empires conquered by the British, the Mongols, the Russians, the Muslim Caliphs and the Spanish.

Where Rome wins out is in staying power. Its empire lasted as a single entity for more than 500 years, and its eastern half survived another millennium until the fifteenth century AD, when Muslim invaders brought it down. How did it manage this feat? The Romans were the most aggressive of people, and as they built their power, hardly a year passed when they were not at war with somebody. They acquired most of the then known world through conquest.

One would have thought this would have aroused resentment against their rule. But, having beaten up their victims, Romans shook them by the hand and invited them to join them as partners in the imperial project. Eventually every adult male living inside the frontier of this multicultural world became a Roman citizen. He was a stakeholder and stakeholders seldom revolt.*

Also, the Romans governed those who agreed to be governed with a light, decentralized touch. As a result they brought peace and prosperity. Although Roman officials tended to be arrogant and patronizing, it was in everybody's interest to maintain the status quo. Even the barbarian invaders who eventually destroyed the empire did not do it on purpose. They wanted to join it rather than destroy it.

The consequence of longevity was that Roman institutions and assumptions sank deep into Europe's psyche. Roman law profoundly influenced the legal systems of the West. In architecture and town-planning the language of pediments and pillars, arches and vaults, survived into the twentieth century; the characteristic spaces and places in Roman towns that were open to all—the square, the temple, the racetrack and the baths—became the foundation of the modern democratic city. For better or for worse, the entente between church and state launched Christianity on its way to becoming one of the world's great religions. Rome's forms of constitutional government influenced legislators in Europe and the United States.

Latin has not been a living language since its transformation into modern tongues such as Italian and Spanish, but it has cast a long shadow forward. The Roman Catholic Church conducted its services in Latin until the 1960s. Plants, stars, constellations and anatomical terms are also still catalogued in Latin.

But what were the Romans actually like? In these pages I give a flavour of their world. Here are stories that aren't usually told: stories that are interesting, instructive, funny—and sometimes disgusting. Incidents of daily life rub shoulders with great events, fine-dining recipes with barbarian invasions. I profile great men and women, criminals and eccentrics. Also, I correct inaccurate clichés about the Romans and how they lived. Non-Roman voices make themselves heard too, for people of many different

* The Jews were an exception and their two uprisings were put down with maximum force and cruelty.

nationalities inhabited an empire which they felt belonged to them just as much as it did to its founders.

Despite its distance from us, we can still see aspects of the Roman way of life mirrored in our own. The crowded and noisy amenities of urban life, the state's cultivation of high culture, the brutal excitements of mass entertainment, sports celebrities, a rising divorce rate, seaside resorts and second homes in the country, the miseries of civil war, the misdemeanours of the young, political dinner parties, fast-food bars, economic globalization (at least within the empire's boundaries), disastrous wars in what is now Iraq—all these, among many other things, have their modern resonance. The basic message is that while social landscapes differ markedly on the surface, the deep core of human nature changes little over time.

I make no claim to be comprehensive; this is simply a personal selection of items that have caught my eye. There is plenty that has been left out.* But I hope that, taken altogether, this anthology will sketch a portrait, warts and all, of the originators of our Western civilization.

* For readers who want to gain their bearings, I give a coherent albeit abbreviated narrative of Rome's history in a timeline at the end of the book (see page 305).

I

FOUNDATIONS

1

ROME'S FABULOUS FOUNDATION

THE ROMAN STATE was founded on a fiction: a legend that forged a link between Rome and Troy, the famous and once powerful city on the coast of Asia Minor. The complicated story told how a Trojan prince, Aeneas, accompanied by his young son and aged father, escaped from the smoking ruins of Troy, which had finally been destroyed by the Greeks after ten years of fighting. He then sailed around the Mediterranean with a group of survivors looking for somewhere to establish a new city. Finally he settled in Italy, and from him sprang the Roman nation.

The link between Troy and the Romans was largely invented by Greek historians, who liked to bring interesting up-and-coming foreign powers within their net. The fullest version of Aeneas' escape from Troy and his subsequent adventures can be found in Virgil's national epic, the *Aeneid*.

For their part, the Romans were flattered by the attention. They suffered from a pronounced inferiority complex vis-à-vis Greece. They were not at all impressed by latter-day Greeks, whom they had invaded and annexed in the second century BC. They regarded them as decadent and incompetent, the cheese-eating surrender monkeys of their day. But they were lost in admiration for the classical Hellenic past—the architecture of Ictinus, the tragedies of Aeschylus, Sophocles and Euripides, the philosophy of Socrates, Plato and Aristotle, the sculpture of Pheidias. There was nothing in Roman culture that could compare. Even when in due time Rome produced its own stock of geniuses, such as the poets Virgil and Horace, they tended to imitate Greek originals.

In the second century AD the emperor Hadrian did his best to reinvigorate Hellenic culture and presented it as an essential ingredient of Rome's imperial ideology. When Rome itself was sacked and the western empire collapsed at the end of the fifth century AD, the eastern half, governed from Constantinople, remained in place for another 1,000 years. Its official language, its *lingua franca*, was Greek, and although its people called themselves Romans, they used the Greek word *Romaioi*.

ii

THE RELUCTANT HERO

IN THE COURSE of the Trojan hero Aeneas' wanderings around the Mediterranean, one port of call was Carthage, the great entrepôt recently founded on the coast of north Africa. Here he fell in love with Dido, the Carthaginian queen. However, his destiny was to found the Roman race in Italy, and Jupiter, king of the gods, sent him a sharp message reminding him of his duty. He lost no time in jilting Dido and resuming his travels. It is not my fault, he protests, but I do have to leave! 'I really don't *want* to go to Italy'; or, in the famous words that Virgil gives to Aeneas as he ends his affair: *Italiam non sponte sequor.** Dido, bereft, then kills herself, thereby giving cause for the subsequent visceral hatred between Rome and Carthage.

After leaving Carthage, Aeneas settled in Latium. His son Ascanius founded the city of Alba Longa, and from him descended a long line of kings as fictional as he was. These culminated in the father of the twins Romulus and Remus, who left Alba Longa to found Rome.

iii

THE TROJAN WAR

THE STORY of the war between the Greeks and the Trojans is one of the greatest tales ever told. The seed of strife is sown when handsome young Paris, prince of Troy, seduces and abducts Helen, the beautiful queen of Sparta. Her husband Menelaus and his brother Agamemnon, king of Mycenae, assemble an expeditionary force to sail across the Aegean Sea and get her back. The Greeks then spend ten fruitless years in front of Troy's walls. Such heroes as Ajax, Diomedes and—most famous of all—Achilles do their best but fail to capture the city. Eventually the wily Odysseus (the Roman Ulysses) devises a cunning plan.

* Aeneas has a habit of being somewhat graceless in his relations with women. As well as behaving badly to Dido, he lost his first wife by his inattention while leaving Troy and stole another man's fiancée on his arrival in Italy.

The Greeks pretend to sail off home, leaving behind as a peace offering a large wooden horse, which in fact conceals a party of Greek warriors. The Trojans are fooled and pull the horse inside the city walls. At night the Greeks return and the men in the horse open the gates to them. Troy is sacked.

In ancient times, this tale was widely supposed to be historical. Two epic poems by Homer, the *Iliad* about the anger of Achilles, and the *Odyssey* about Odysseus' journey home from Troy, acquired a quasi-biblical authority and showed Greeks all that it meant to be Greek and civilized. The salient point, from the Roman perspective, is that Rome's foundational figure Aeneas—originally, at least—plays a minor part in this great tale.

Modern archaeology has shown that there actually was a Troy, which was burned down at about the time supposed by legend—the closing years of the second millennium BC. However, we can be pretty sure that Achilles, Helen and all the rest of them never existed.

iv

ROMULUS AND REMUS

ROMULUS and his twin brother Remus were the infant sons of a small-time king in central Italy, who was deposed by his brother. The boys were abandoned in the countryside to die. A she-wolf found them and gave them suck, and they were watched over by a friendly woodpecker.* A passing shepherd came across them and brought them up, and they grew to become fearless, hot-tempered young men who ran local gangs. As is the way with such legends, their true identity was eventually discovered, and Romulus and Remus helped replace their father on his throne. They then decided to go off and establish a city and kingdom of their own.

A group of hills on a bend in the river Tiber seemed ideal for the future site of Rome. The brothers agreed to fortify one of

* If you're thinking that 'being raised by a wolf' sounds unlikely, it might be useful to know that the Latin word for 'she-wolf', *lupa*, was also common Roman slang for 'prostitute'. It probably wasn't a good subject to raise with the twins, though.

the hills, but not *which* hill. To resolve the dispute, each stood on his chosen spot and watched for the flight of birds: the decision would go to the one who saw the most auspicious kind of bird. Remus struck lucky first, for six vultures flew past him. Romulus, not to be outdone, lied that he had seen twelve vultures. His brother did not believe him and challenged him, whereupon twelve vultures did in fact put in an appearance. Remus claimed victory because he had been the first to see vultures; Romulus, because he had seen the larger number of vultures.

Remus jumped scornfully across a trench his brother had dug, whereupon Romulus attacked and killed him. Romulus immediately realized the gravity of his offence: he had founded his new state on the crime of fratricide. This did not prevent him making himself ruler, however. He welcomed immigrants and won wars, and the state thrived. Then, after a long and successful reign, Romulus mysteriously vanished in a thick mist.

v

REWRITING HISTORY

MANY famous cities and states boast founding fathers, or at least great unifiers, from the early centuries of their story. Gilgamesh built the walls of Uruk; Theseus destroyed the Minotaur and established Athens as a leader of Greece; Arthur was a chivalrous king who defended Britain from foreign invaders. Although these men are allowed their faults, they are at heart noble and benevolent. They deserve their status as national heroes.

There is one big exception: Rome. The character of its founder Romulus—a fratricide and tyrant—leaves much to be desired. Why did the Romans make up such a disagreeable tale? Like Romulus himself, the answer has dematerialized—on this occasion into the mists of time. But there are some clues.

The 'official' version of Romulus' end was that he had disappeared from view in a cloud of mist. But another more plausible account spread quickly. This was that the members of the Senate, Rome's governing committee, had struck him down during a meeting. They then cut him up into pieces and each senator hid a body part under his clothes when leaving the meeting: hence his mysterious disappearance.

Can it be an accident that another notorious Roman, Julius Caesar, was struck down in similar circumstances? Both men became despots, for which they were assassinated in the Senate. A coincidence indeed: perhaps the Romans tailored their past to fit later events in their blood-stained history.

vi

THE RAPE OF THE SABINE WOMEN

AT FIRST Rome had a tiny population and more citizens were urgently needed. Romulus established a policy of offering all-comers the gift of Roman nationality, a welcoming approach to foreigners that was to last a thousand years. He opened a sanctuary for criminals, vagrants and every kind of rogue, and a miscellaneous rabble soon gathered. It rapidly became clear, however, that there were far too few women to go round among the growing number of male citizens. Something decisive had to be done.

The king staged a great festival at the racecourse, the Circus Maximus. Many people attended, including families from the neighbouring Sabine tribe. At a signal from Romulus, a large force of armed Romans kidnapped all the unmarried Sabine women they could find. Their menfolk were left unharmed and encouraged to make good their escape. The infuriated Sabines demanded the return of their women. Romulus refused and war broke out. Three indecisive battles followed, and finally, under a general called Titus Tatius, the Sabines invaded Rome itself. A fight ensued in the marshy valley between Rome's hills (later to become the city's forum or main square).

At this point a remarkable event occurred. The Sabine women came pouring down into the valley from every direction. They had been abducted and forcibly married, but they now accepted their fate and insisted on peace. A treaty was drawn up, acknowledging that the Roman husbands had treated their Sabine spouses with respect. All who wished to maintain their marriages were allowed to do so. Most of the women stayed where they were. Romulus and the Sabines took an even more radical decision. They agreed a merger of their two states. All Sabines would be awarded Roman citizenship and equal civic rights. Tatius shared the throne with Romulus.

This legend—the so-called rape of the Sabine women—reveals one of the secrets of Rome's success.* Throughout its history it encouraged immigration and conferred citizenship on many of those whom it conquered. In this way it won consent for its rule as well as increasing the manpower needed for its legions.

[vii]

THE SURPLUS HILLS OF ROME

According to tradition, Rome is built on seven hills, but the claim calls for some creative accountancy. One plausible count gives the Eternal City thirteen hills, but you could choose a variety of different numbers: it all depends what you mean by a hill.

Some named hills could be seen as spurs or rises attached to larger eminences. Also, as the city grew, it took in more hills. From Romulus' point of view, the Janiculum hill was on the far side of the river Tiber and had nothing to do with Rome, although later it became an integral part of the city. During the long centuries of the Roman Republic the Vatican hill lay outside the city walls beyond the Campus Martius ('Field of Mars', god of war), a small plain of about 500 acres on which military exercises were held.

For the record, the traditional septet are the Aventine, the Caelian, the Capitoline, the Esquiline, the Palatine, the Quirinal and the Viminal. Other qualifying elevations are the Cispian, the Janiculum, the Oppian, the Pincian, the Vatican and the Velian.†

* The word 'rape' here is, of course, a conventional translation of the Latin word for seizure or abduction; it does not carry the modern connotation of sexual violence.

† As well as Rome, numerous other cities across the world claim to be built on seven hills. They range from Athens and Jerusalem to Brussels, Budapest and Bath.

viii

LONG-LIVED KINGS

ROMULUS was followed by Numa Pompilius, Tullus Hostilius, Ancus Marcius, Lucius Tarquinius Priscus, Servius Tullius and Lucius Tarquinius, nicknamed Superbus or the Proud. The last three were probably historical, at least in name. The dates of the foundation of Rome (753 BC—the Romans' favourite date) and of the Roman Republic (509 BC) were taken as read, and as there were only seven kings to cover the interval of time, basic arithmetic meant that each monarch had to reign for an implausibly lengthy thirty-five years. Perhaps there had been other kings whose names were forgotten? It was a mystery.

Then modern archaeologists excavating the Roman Forum and its environs discovered that the earliest settlement had been one hundred years later than the traditional date, and so everything fitted easily into place.

ix

ROMAN DATES

THE ROMANS had their own dating system, which took as its starting point the city's supposed foundation year: 753 BC (in modern terms). To them, 44 BC, the year in which Julius Caesar was assassinated, was AUC 709, where AUC stands for *ab urbe condita*, 'from the city's [i.e. Rome's] foundation'. The system of dating we use today was invented in AD 525. It is based on the presumed date of Jesus Christ's birth; BC signifies 'Before Christ' and AD *Anno Domini* ('in the Year of the Lord'). The year zero is left out,* so 1 BC is immediately followed by AD 1. Instead of BC and AD, some people today prefer BCE and CE, 'Before the Common Era' and the 'Common Era'. But the system still depends on the Christian division of time, so it is hard to see what advantage it brings.

* The usefulness of the zero had not been established: how can nothing be something? people asked.

[x]

A YEAR OUT OF STEP

For centuries the Roman year was 355 days long. Because this is much shorter than the solar year, the Romans had to add a corrective (intercalary) month every other year. During the civil wars of the first century BC this was not done, and by 46 BC the inaccuracy extended to two-and-a-half months. Julius Caesar, in his capacity as head of the College of Pontiffs (*pontifex maximus*), introduced a new calendar based on a 365-day year with one extra day intercalated every four years.

Our calendar today shows signs of its classical heritage. For many centuries the Romans began their New Year in March, as we can tell from the Latinate names of some of our months: September means the seventh month, and so on to December, the tenth. Julius Caesar and Augustus gave their names to July and August.*

[xi]

DAYS OF THE MONTH

The Romans never feared pointless complexity, witness their handling of the days of the month. The first of a month was called the Kalends. Depending on whether it was a long month (31 days) or a short one (29 days, except for February, which was 28 days), the Ides fell on the fifteenth or the thirteenth day of the month. The Nones was eight days before the Ides and fell on the fifth or seventh day of the month, depending on the position of the Ides. Dates were counted backwards (inclusively) from these three special days. So, for example, 2 May (a long month) was Six Days before the Nones of May and 8 May was Seven Days before the Ides of May.

* In Britain, the Julian calendar lasted until 1752, when it was replaced by the slightly amended Gregorian calendar; this meant that the date had to be advanced by eleven days. Legend has it that people rioted under the slogan 'Give us back our eleven days'. In fact, this was the satirist William Hogarth's little joke. The phrase is inscribed on a placard in his satirical painting *An Election Entertainment*.

[xii]

EXEMPLARY TALES

THE TALES we make up about ourselves are as telling as the histories that describe (or attempt to describe) events that actually took place. The Romans are no exception. They crammed the times before memory with instructive legends.

Among other qualities, a citizen of the Roman Republic measured himself and others by *virtus*: a word whose meanings included manliness, self-sacrifice, strength, moral excellence and military talent.* The nineteenth-century historian and politician Lord Macaulay evokes these qualities in his *Lays of Ancient Rome*:

> To every man upon this earth
> Death cometh soon or late.
> And how can man die better
> than facing fearful odds
> for the ashes of his fathers
> and the temples of his gods.

Some stories exemplified simple courage and had a happy ending. But many told of old, unhappy, far-off things. There is a grimness in the traditional Roman idea of goodness.

[xiii]

THE DUEL OF THE CURATII AND THE HORATII

THE THIRD of the Kings of Rome, Tullus Hostilius, was even more war-like than Romulus. His reign was marked by a long struggle with Alba Longa, the city from which Romulus and Remus had emerged to found Rome. This was, in effect, Rome's first civil war.

The two sides made a treaty according to which the loser of the conflict would agree to unconditional surrender. To avoid a full-scale battle with all the attendant casualties, a duel was arranged between two sets of triplet brothers: the Curatii for

* From *virtus* comes our own softer 'virtue'.

Alba and the Horatii for Rome. In the fight all the Curatii were wounded, while two of the Horatii were killed. The survivor, Publius Horatius, then reversed the fortunes of battle by killing all the Curatii. He had been able to tackle them one by one when they became separated from each other because of their injuries.

The hero of the hour, Publius marched back to Rome carrying his spoils, the three dead men's armour. At the city gates he was greeted by his sister. It so happened that she was engaged to one of the Curatii, and when she noticed that Publius was carrying his blood-stained cloak, she let down her hair, burst into tears and called out her lover's name. In a fit of rage Publius drew his sword and stabbed his sister to the heart. 'Take your girl's love and give it to your lover in hell,' he shouted. 'So perish all women who grieve for an enemy!'

Publius was condemned to death for the murder, but reprieved by the people, who refused to countenance the execution of a national hero. However, something had to be done to mitigate the guilt of such a notorious crime. The Horatius family was obliged to conduct some expiatory ceremonies. Once these had been performed, a wooden beam was slung across the roadway under which Publius walked with his head covered as a sign of submission. His sister was buried on the spot where she had fallen.

Two ancient memorials survived which were believed to mark the event. Livy, the great historian of Rome, writing at the end of the first century BC, observed:

> The timber is still to be seen—replaced from time to time at the state's expense—and is known as the Sister's Beam. The tomb of the murdered girl was built of hewn stone and stands on the spot where she was struck down.

For many of its citizens, the city of Rome was a stage where great and terrible deeds had been done. People of the present were energized and uplifted by the legendary actors of a glorious past. Publius Horatius did a very Roman thing: he committed a crime which, counter-intuitively, was a good deed—in this case, it displayed the noble rage of valour.

Were these people, the Romans, men or wild animals? enquired Dionysius of Halicarnassus, a civilized Greek historian of Rome's beginnings.

[xiv]

THE RAPE OF LUCRETIA

WOMEN had an uncomfortable time of it throughout Rome's history. Even the morally excellent could come to a bad end.

One evening in the late sixth century some young soldiers were chatting in camp. One of them was Sextus Tarquinius, son of King Tarquin the Proud. Everyone was drinking heavily. The conversation turned to the men's wives; each man extravagantly praised his own. Whose was the best?

Sextus proposed that they ride at once to town and see what their wives were doing. It turned out that they were all having a good time at a party, except for Lucretia, spouse of a certain Collatinus. Beautiful and virtuous, she was found at home spinning in company with her maids. It was unanimously agreed that she had won the contest for female virtue hands down.

Sextus was smitten. A few days later, unbeknownst to her husband, he called on Lucretia and asked to be put up for the night. In the small hours he crept into her bedroom and woke her up. If she would not let him sleep with her, he whispered, he would kill both her and a slave, whose naked body he would place in her bed. He would say he had killed them *in flagrante delicto*. The lady cared for her reputation and to preserve it conceded her charms. Sextus had sex with her and rode back to camp.

In the morning Lucretia summoned her husband and other relatives, and revealed what had taken place. 'My body only has been violated. My heart is innocent. But I must take my punishment.' Whereupon she drew out a knife concealed in her dress and stabbed herself to death.*

The scandal was immense. A meeting of the people's assembly called for an end to the monarchy, and the Tarquins were driven from Rome.

* Ungallant modern scholars have suggested that the story was made up to conceal the fact that a historical Lucretia had been caught in adultery and condemned to death by a family council. There is no evidence to support this attack on the lady's good name.

[xv]

HORATIUS AND THE BRIDGE

AFTER the monarchy had been overthrown and replaced by a republic, the exiled king Tarquin persuaded a friend of his, an Etruscan ruler called Lars Porsenna, to invade Rome and restore him to his throne.* This was a serious threat to the young republic.

When the enemy appeared on the far side of the Tiber, Romans in the fields ran back into the city, which was soon surrounded. The river had been thought a strong enough barrier in itself and no defences had been built along its bank, so Rome's only bridge was a weak point. If Porsenna's men could cross it, the war would be lost and Tarquin back in power.

The officer on guard at the bridge was a patrician named Horatius Cocles. He had lost an eye in battle—hence his last name Cocles, meaning 'one-eyed'. The enemy suddenly captured the Janiculum hill on the far side of the Tiber and ran down towards the bridge. All the guards panicked and fled except for Horatius and two companions. They strode to the head of the wooden footbridge on the Janiculan bank and prepared to mount a defence. Their aim was to buy time for men behind them to dismantle the timbers. The bridge was too narrow for more than a few of Porsenna's soldiers to advance across it at once, so the three men hoped they would be able to hold them up.

They had pluck and luck, and fighting at close quarters, killed many Etruscans. Horatius ordered his companions to save themselves, and he struggled on alone despite a spear having passed through one of his buttocks. At last he heard the crash of the falling bridge behind him, and with a prayer to the god of the river he dived into the water and swam back to the Roman shore.

The city was saved.

* The Etruscans lived in today's Tuscany.

[xvi]

THE FLAMING HAND

After he had been thwarted by Horatius on the bridge, King Porsenna settled down to a long siege. Time passed. A young nobleman, Gaius Mucius, decided to take the initiative. Having obtained the Senate's permission for an attempt to assassinate Porsenna, he slipped into the enemy camp, with a sword concealed on his person, wearing Etruscan clothes and speaking Etruscan fluently. Unfortunately, he did not know the king by sight and dared not risk his cover by asking someone to point him out. But he saw the royal dais and joined a large crowd surrounding it.

It was pay day and a well-dressed man on the platform, sitting beside the king, was busy handing out money. This was the treasurer. As most people addressed themselves to him, Mucius could not be certain which was the man and which the master. He made the wrong choice. He jumped up onto the platform and stabbed the treasurer to death. He tried to make his escape through the crowd, but was caught and brought back before a furious Porsenna.

Mucius betrayed no hint of fear. 'I am a Roman,' he said. 'My name is Gaius Mucius. I can die as resolutely as I can kill.' He then hinted that there were many other would-be assassins who would follow in his footsteps.

In rage and alarm, Porsenna ordered the prisoner to be burned alive unless he revealed full details of the plot to which he had alluded. Mucius cried out: 'See how cheap men hold their bodies who fix their eyes on honour and glory!' He then put his right hand into a fire that had been lit for a sacrifice, and let it burn there as if he felt no pain. The king was deeply impressed and had his guards pull Mucius from the altar. He then set him free, as a worthy enemy.

Mucius had no intention of letting Porsenna off the hook. Lying with conviction, he said: 'I will tell you out of gratitude what you could not drag from me with threats. There are 300 young Romans in your camp, disguised as Etruscans, all of whom have sworn to attempt your life. I happened to draw the shortest straw!' The king, shaken, decided to give up supporting Tarquin and go home. Mucius was given the additional name (*cognomen*) Scaevola, meaning 'left-handed'—an indirect reference to the fact that his right hand was now unusable.

Mucius' exploit was self-sacrifice, with a twist. In principle, Romans disparaged trickery in war. They were realists, though, and regularly practised deceit without always admitting it even to themselves. Here, Mucius, though in agony from his charred hand, had the sang-froid to lie about the number of Roman assassins lurking in the Etruscan camp. An unchivalrous response, one might think, to Porsenna's generosity in freeing him, but truly Roman.

[xvii]

GOD-LIKE OR BRUTISH?

THE DEPOSED king Tarquin sent an embassy to the city to announce his abdication and to ask for the return of his and his family's money and effects. The plea was allowed, and the envoys, under cover of cataloguing, selling or despatching the former monarch's property, suborned some highly placed young men, including two sons of the consul Lucius Junius Brutus.* Their project was to overthrow the new state. To prevent their plans from leaking out, the conspirators decided they should swear a fearful oath of secrecy and, after killing a man, pour his blood out as a sacrifice.

A slave chanced to be in the room one night when the conspirators entered. He hid behind a chest and heard everything they said. They agreed that they would kill the consuls and write letters to Tarquin announcing their plan. The slave reported what he had seen and heard to the authorities. The young men were arrested and the damning correspondence discovered.

What was to be done with the criminals, coming as they did from such important families? At a people's assembly there was general embarrassment, although some citizens, wanting to please Brutus, proposed exile.

* Two consuls headed the young Roman Republic; see page 24.

But the consul refused to be pleased. Having considered the evidence, he called each of his sons by name. 'Come, Titus, come Tiberius, why don't you defend yourselves against the charges?' They said nothing, and so he asked them the same question two more times. When they still held their tongues, Brutus turned to the consular bodyguard, the lictors, and said: 'It is now for you to do the rest.' They stripped the boys on the spot, tied their hands behind their backs and beat them with their rods. Brutus watched the scene with a fixed, unflinching gaze, even when his sons were then thrown to the ground and had their heads chopped off.

Belief in the rule of law, taken to the point of an almost inhuman severity, was a typical Roman quality. Self-esteem was the melancholy reward for this kind of self-sacrifice. The pragmatic and puzzled Greeks found Brutus' behaviour incredible. Plutarch, whose biographies of Greek and Roman generals and politicians explore the ethics of public life, was taken aback, though too polite to protest. Brutus, he wrote, had 'performed an act which is difficult for one to praise or to blame too highly... [it] was either god-like or brutish'.

II

THE REPUBLIC

1

A TALENT FOR COMPROMISE

IN 494 BC, not long after the expulsion of the kings, the young and inexperienced Roman Republic very nearly came to grief. One day the mass of common people—the plebeians or plebs—streamed out of the city and encamped on a nearby hill. There they sat, doing nothing. This was a 'secession'—in effect, a general strike. It came as a devastating blow to the nobles, or patricians, who suddenly found they had no one to rule.

Even more serious than the withdrawal of labour was the fact that the common people set up institutions of their own that mirrored those of the Republic. They created their own assembly and elected their own officials, the tribunes of the people. In effect, they made themselves a state within a state.

The plebs had two main grievances. Its members were excluded from public office, which was the traditional monopoly of patricians. Also, an economic crisis had created poverty, indebtedness and, worst of all, bond (debt) slavery. There was a war on at the time and an enemy army was approaching the city. The patricians needed soldiers and gave in: bond slavery was banned and the tribunes were given state endorsement. The secession had been a success.

More than just legend, the secession seems to have been an historical event. It was only the first of a number of such protests, the last taking place in 287 BC. Step by step over the years the patricians abandoned their privileges, and eventually the consulship and other public offices were opened to plebeian candidates. The old aristocracy was joined by a new plebeian nobility. Of course, the poor remained poor, but at least a lucky few could better themselves.

What was most remarkable about this long struggle was that there was no bloodshed. Elsewhere in the ancient world violent revolutions were the norm. A capacity for compromise, for avoiding extremes, for doing deals, was one of Rome's greatest political strengths.

[ii]

A PLAIN-LIVING PATRIOT

WHEN his son jumped bail on a capital charge, Cincinnatus had to pay a huge fine. Almost bankrupt, he sold his estate and retired to a small four-acre farm on the far side of the Tiber, where he lived and worked in the simplest of circumstances. He did not repine.

One day in 458 BC a delegation of senators arrived at the farm and found him at his plough. They invited him to accept the emergency post of dictator (see page 26) with full executive powers. A neighbouring tribe, the Aequi, was threatening the survival of the young Republic. Cincinnatus agreed, led an army out and cut the enemy to pieces in a great battle. The survivors were condemned to walk under a yoke—three spears set up as an arch—as a symbol of their humiliation. After only sixteen days Cincinnatus resigned his dictatorship and went back to his farm. Some years later he was appointed dictator for a second time and put down a domestic conspiracy.

For Romans Cincinnatus stood for simple country living, patriotism, modesty and disdain for power and riches. They held him up as a model, even though few copied him.*

[iii]

SACRED GEESE TO THE RESCUE

ROME FELL to Gallic raiders from the north in 390 BC. The citadel, an almost self-sufficient walled fortress on the Capitoline hill, was the only part of the city that the Gauls did not occupy. It stood authoritatively on a tall plinth of rocky cliffs. No catapult could harm it, and before the time of trebuchets and other advanced siege weaponry, it presented a daunting target.

One starlit night, a Gallic scout was sent to see if there was any

* Americans saw in the incorruptible George Washington, their first president, a latter-day Cincinnatus, and it was with him in mind that the city of Cincinnati in Ohio received its name.

remote chance of finding a way up the steep ascent without alerting the citadel's elite guards. He was astonished to find a point at which the rocky precipice could be climbed without too much difficulty. He returned with an armed scaling party and, according to the Republic's national historian Livy, the group managed to inch slowly up the vertical cliff below the citadel and then climb over its walls. When one of them reached the top and clambered down the other side, he found himself standing next to a huge building. It was the Temple of Jupiter Optimus Maximus (Best and Greatest): the invaders had discovered an unguarded way into the very heart of Rome itself.

Unfortunately for them, this was the cue for the humble goose to get its big moment in ancient history. The bird was sacred to Juno, a goddess who, through a complicated divine arrangement, was both sister and wife of Jupiter. As soon as the first Gaul appeared, a nearby gaggle of geese cackled, squawked and flapped so suddenly and so loudly that they woke up a former consul, Marcus Manlius. A distinguished and much decorated ex-army officer, Manlius seized his sword and shield, and yelling at the top of his voice, rushed outside to find out what the geese were so alarmed about.

'He hurried,' writes Livy, 'without waiting for the support of his bewildered colleagues, straight to the point of danger. One Gaul was already up, but Manlius, with a blow from the boss of his shield, shoved him headlong down the cliff.' The falling man's body clattered down onto the Gauls climbing below him, toppling many to their deaths. In the chaos, others had to drop their weapons so they could grab hold of the rocks, only to be cut down from above by Manlius' sweeping sword. 'Soon more Roman troops arrived,' adds Livy, 'knocking the climbers down with javelins and stones, until every one of them was dislodged and sent hurtling to the foot of the cliff.' Thanks to Juno's geese, the Gauls never took the citadel.

The Gallic invasion was only a temporary setback for the city, but it had been a big scare. For many generations monstrous hairy invaders remained just beyond the range of a Roman's peripheral vision, their possible return an abiding nightmare. And, every century or so throughout Rome's history, Celts, Gauls and other nomadic tribes *did* pour down again into the peaceful Italian peninsula or break through the Rhine and Danube frontiers of the Roman empire.

iv

THE DANGERS OF DEMOCRACY

WHAT EMERGED in Rome after several centuries of trial and error was a system of checks and balances: a form of governance that comprised a bit of monarchy, a bit of oligarchy and a bit of democracy.

Two consuls were elected as heads of state and government. They could do just about whatever they wanted, but there were brakes on their power. They were voted in for twelve months only and could be taken to court for illegal acts after leaving office. Also, each consul could veto whatever the other one might decide. Beneath the consuls were other groups of elected officials, also with twelve-month terms and the right to veto their colleagues.

The Senate, an advisory committee of present and former office-holders, debated policy. While consuls came and went, the Senate was a permanent body and so built up considerable influence. Roman citizens, meanwhile, met in a democratic assembly, elected all the officials and passed laws; discussion was forbidden, however, and they were only allowed to cast their votes. And then there were ten tribunes of the people whose job was to stick up for the ordinary Roman; they could veto any decision anybody took. They could even veto each other's vetoes.

v

THE LONG SHADOW OF ROME

IN THE eighteenth century politicians on either side of the Atlantic Ocean, all of them brought up on the classics, found the Romans' three-part balanced or mixed constitution very much to their taste. In their eyes a complete democracy would bring with it the potential chaos of mob rule.

In Great Britain, after the Glorious Revolution of 1688, the king naturally represented monarchy, the unelected House of Lords oligarchy, and the elected House of Commons democracy—although it would not be until the twentieth century that universal suffrage was introduced.

When the United States won independence from Great Britain, its founding fathers also opted for a balanced constitution. The president was a secular king: he was appointed by an electoral college, not directly by vote of the people. The US Senate was modelled on the Roman Senate, and its members, too, were not elected but appointed by state parliaments. The House of Representatives was seen as the People's House, and in this case members *were* directly elected. Over the years the system has been fully democratized, but the principle of checks and balances remains.*

vi

THE GREASY POLE

TO THE modern eye, the oddest feature of the Roman way of doing politics was a general spirit of interfusion. Senior statesmen doubled up as priests and as army generals. A consul might be Rome's high priest, *pontifex maximus*, as well as joint commander-in-chief.

Under the emperors officials continued to be elected, but over time their powers dwindled. Election came to be replaced by imperial nomination. The executive authority of the consuls was appropriated by the emperors.

Overleaf will be found a list of elected officials of the Roman Republic in the first century BC, according to the *cursus honorum* or 'honours race'. In practice, the minimum age rules were often bent or broken.

* In the United States the old Roman veto also survives in two limited but effective ways: the president can veto legislation that has been passed by less than a two-thirds majority, and members of the Senate have the right to filibuster and so talk out bills laid before them—effectively a prohibition.

CONSULS	2	Heads of government and state; also commanders-in-chief. Minimum age: 42 years.
PRAETORS	8	Law officers; also commanded armies. Minimum age: 39 years.
AEDILES	4	Responsible for public administration in Rome; festival organizers. Minimum age: 36 years.
QUAESTORS	20	Finance officers. Minimum age: 30 years.
TRIBUNES OF THE PEOPLE	10	Defenders of the common people. Their persons were sacrosanct. They could propose legislation.
CENSORS	2	Former consuls, they were elected for five years. They maintained a census of citizens, reviewed membership of the Senate and purged senators for misbehaviour. Also responsible for public works.
DICTATOR		Replaced the consuls in a state emergency for a maximum of six months (in theory) and held full powers. Could not be vetoed. Nominated by the consuls.
PROCONSUL OR PROPRAETOR		Governor of a Roman province or army commander; former consul or praetor.

[vii]

SPQR

SPQR is short for *Senatus Populusque Romanus*, meaning the 'Senate and People of Rome'. The acronym is generally used as short-hand for the Roman Republic, as it encapsulates the mix of democracy and oligarchy ('rule of the few') that characterized the state. The people passed the laws and the Senate was the advisory committee which embodied the ruling class. The term appeared on coins, inscriptions and dedications.* It continued to be used under the emperors on the pretence that the Republic was still in being.

* Even today the municipal authorities in Rome deploy SPQR on manhole covers and the like.

[viii]

DEALING WITH ROME'S UNDERCLASS

A PERENNIAL challenge facing the Roman authorities was what to do about Rome's underclass. The city was a magnet which attracted many thousands of unemployed immigrants from the countryside, who wanted to better their lot. But there were too few jobs and too many faces to feed.* And all this brought a danger of rising public expenditure.

Grain was imported from Sicily and Egypt to feed the urban population, but prices were high. From time to time there were riots. Something had to be done. Elected tribune of the people in 123 and again in 122 BC, the younger of the two Gracchus brothers, Gaius, subsidized the price of grain for citizens. In 58 BC Publius Clodius Pulcher, raffish brother to the disreputable Clodia,† made a career as a radical politician. As tribune of the people, he introduced free grain distribution for the poor, a hugely popular policy.

Politicians such as Julius Caesar and Augustus tried to reduce state spending and limited the scheme, but with little long-term effect. The emperor Septimius Severus added olive oil to the distribution, and Aurelian issued free bread instead of grain and added salt, pork and (even) wine to the handout. With so much coming for free, why should the jobless bother to look for work?

The world changes, but political issues remain stubbornly the same. And emperors found it no easier than modern governments to enforce financial cuts.

* For more on subsidizing the masses, see page 28; and for 'bread and circuses', see page 164.

† For an account of the colourful life of Clodia, see page 224.

[ix]

THE DOOM OF THE GRACCHI

A WIDENING chasm between the rich and the poor in the first century BC heralded the death of the Roman Republic and its replacement by the rule of emperors. The rich enjoyed vast estates and often encroached illegally on state-owned land, while many of the poor were landless. Someone eventually decided to act.

In 133 BC Tiberius Sempronius Gracchus was elected a tribune of the people, one of the officials whose job it was to speak for the rights of the masses. He had a radical land reform bill passed into law. His idea was to redistribute public land to those without smallholdings of their own. This greatly offended owners of real estate, especially those who were to be forced to disgorge their ill-gotten gains. Infuriated senators rioted, and in the mêlée Tiberius was killed. Ten years later his younger brother Gaius decided to enter public life too, and his attempt at introducing populist measures brought him a similarly violent end.

For centuries Romans, however fiercely they disagreed with one another, had done deals with their political opponents. No longer so: a terrible precedent had been set. When Appian wrote his history of the civil wars, it was no coincidence that he chose to begin his story with the death of the Gracchus brothers:

> No sword was ever brought into the assembly, and no Roman was ever killed by a Roman, until Tiberius Gracchus... became the first man to die in civil unrest... From time to time some elected official would be murdered... Undisciplined arrogance soon became the rule, along with a shameful contempt for law and justice.

With the violent deaths of the Gracchi, Rome entered a hundred years of violent feuding.

[x]

THE POPULAR VERSUS THE BEST

THERE WERE no organized political parties in Rome. All the politicians belonged to Rome's ruling class, but they came in two distinct varieties. The *populares*, the 'men of the people', spoke up for bettering the lives of ordinary citizens—although many of them did so only to advance their own careers. Their opponents were the *optimates*, the 'best people' (from *optimus*, 'best'), who liked the way things were and saw no need for change. The *optimates* usually controlled the Senate and the *populares* the assemblies.

[xi]

MARIUS AND SULLA

IN THE 80s BC, two great generals clashed. One was a respected *popularis*, Gaius Marius, who had been victorious over the Gauls. The second was one of the *optimates*, Lucius Cornelius Sulla. In 88 BC Sulla marched his army, loyal to him personally and to no one else, into the city of Rome to fight against Marius and his friends. Such an attack was completely illegal and had never happened before in the history of the Republic. Sulla's action set a very bad example for ambitious Romans in later years, as violence among politicians became more common.

One after another, Marius and Sulla staged massacres of their political opponents. Marius soon died, old and mad, while Sulla had himself elected dictator with supreme emergency powers. Then the bloodletting was effectively legalized. He launched what was called a 'proscription'. He posted in the Forum a list of his political enemies who were to be killed without trial. Anyone who killed a man on the list received a cash prize. At least forty senators and 1,600 wealthy men outside the Senate died.

Sulla brought in some reforms to strengthen the power of the Senate and weaken that of the people, and then in 80 BC he retired into private life for a final couple of years of debauchery.

He seems to have had a wonderful time, lying about drinking all day with his glitzy friends. Curiously, when he walked about the city as an ordinary citizen, nobody arrested or physically attacked him. The worst he had to endure were the insults of a teenage boy who once trailed him all the way to his house. Sulla put up with this patiently, only remarking: 'This lad will stop anyone else from laying aside such power.'

He was right. Nearly four centuries were to pass before another ruler of Rome voluntarily abdicated—the emperor Diocletian. Both men suffered from health problems, but they also had a life beyond politics. They believed, as Shakespeare's Coriolanus puts it, that 'there is a world elsewhere'.

Most of Sulla's reforms were quickly overturned after his death. Both he and his bitter rival Marius won power, but failed to make good use of it. There was one sad lesson to be learned from their careers. To its ruin, Rome was getting accustomed to the use of violence to settle political arguments.

[*xii*]

CIVIL SWORDS

THE LAND problem would not go away. But if civilian reform was blocked by vested interests, the poor found another, military solution. Peasant recruits were the backbone of the army and they gave unswerving loyalty to generals who promised them small farms when their terms of service were over.

During the first century BC the Roman constitution collapsed under the strain of military crises abroad and quarrels at home. Unscrupulous army commanders used force to win political power and rewarded their soldiers with the farms they sought. Senators who had resisted reason in the days of the Gracchus brothers now yielded to threats, but only at the last minute and with bad grace.

The most successful of these dynasts was Gaius Julius Caesar. Born in Rome in 100 BC, he had blue blood but no money. During his youth he was always heavily in debt. A left-wing politician, he was popular with the people and was good at winning elections.

Reactionaries in the Senate hated and feared him. Impatient with constitutional rules, he formed an alliance with two other ambitious politicians, Pompey the Great and Marcus Crassus; this was the first triumvirate, or in plain English, the Group of Three.*

As a result, Caesar was easily elected to Rome's top job, the consulship, in 59 BC. The combination of concordat and conspiracy proved irresistible; Pompey was enormously popular, Crassus was enormously rich and Caesar was enormously clever. The new consul enacted all their demands. The Senate was powerless.

[xiii]

RICHEST BUT NOT LUCKIEST

CRASSUS was said to be the richest man in Rome. He made his money through real-estate speculation. Rome was a crowded city, but had no police force or fire service. Fires often broke out and jerry-built apartment blocks collapsed. Crassus would send his agents immediately to the scene and buy up the properties at rock-bottom prices. He would then rebuild and resell at a large profit.

Crassus liked to say that nobody should claim to be rich who could not afford to pay an army's wages. And an army was what he wanted from the first triumvirate, when it was renewed in 56 BC. His ambition was to conquer the Parthian empire (in what is now Iran and Iraq), and the following year he set off with a large expeditionary force of more than 40,000 men.

In the summer of 53 BC, he came spectacularly to grief, tricked into defeat and death. A performance of the *Bacchae*, a tragedy by the Greek playwright Euripides, was staged at the Parthian court. At the end of the play the protagonist is decapitated, and Crassus' head was used as a grisly prop.

* The term 'first triumvirate' was coined by modern scholars. There was a later, second triumvirate; see page 36.

[xiv]

POMPEY THE GREAT

POMPEY thought he was a great soldier and liked to be compared with Alexander the Great. He was mistaken: he was only a competent general, but he *was* a great administrator.

Pompey was given a number of special commands which suited his talents. He cleared the Mediterranean Sea of the scourge of pirates and successfully reorganized the eastern half of the empire, after presiding over the conclusion of a long war in the Middle East (a task in which his predecessor had done the spadework).

To begin with, he got on well with Julius Caesar and joined the triumvirate on his return to Rome. This was because he wanted resettlement land for his veterans, which the Senate, with typical short-sightedness, was refusing to grant.

Pompey married Caesar's daughter Julia, and until she died in childbirth, the two men saw eye to eye. But with her death and that of Crassus, their relationship cooled. Jealous and fearful of Caesar's achievements in Gaul (see below), Pompey began to side with the Senate against his one-time partner and father-in-law.

[xv]

ROME'S SELF-PUBLICIST SUPREME

FOR THE MOST PART Julius Caesar has had a very good press.* He doesn't altogether deserve it, however. The fact is that he was guilty of mass murder. And he doesn't qualify as a criminal simply by today's standards: he was seen as such by his contemporaries.

Caesar wasn't just a clever politician, he was also a brilliant

* In the Middle Ages Caesar joined that most exclusive of clubs, the Nine Worthies, sharing pride of place with Alexander the Great and Kings Arthur and David. One of the finest modern scholars speaks of him as 'scintillating and many-sided' and the 'greatest genius produced by Rome'. Today, even the dimmest school student has heard of him.

general. He arranged for a long provincial command to follow his consulship and spent ten years conquering Gaul (roughly today's France and Belgium), for no very good reason except that he needed money and glory, and believed that the hapless Gauls would provide both (he was right). A series of spectacular campaigns added a vast new territory to the Roman empire and made him phenomenally rich. There was a downside: by his own estimation, one million Gauls lost their lives and another million—men, women and children—were sold into slavery.

To ensure that the right 'spin' was put on events, Caesar published a set of elegant literary masterpieces in which he gave his own account of his campaigns in Gaul and of his role in the ensuing civil war. Winston Churchill said that history would be kind to him, for he intended to write it himself. In this he was taking a leaf out of the books that Caesar had written 2,000 years earlier.

[xvi]

THE RUTHLESS CHARMER

CAESAR was a charmer—witty, fashionably dressed, cultivated, a generous friend. He was also an enthusiastic lover (with a special eye for the wives of his political rivals). But if you got in his way, he was ruthless; he rose to power on a hecatomb of corpses and ruined lives. That said, Caesar was not naturally cruel: once he had crushed his opponents, he was happy to be magnanimous.

Having completed his work in Gaul, he wanted to pass immediately from his governorship to a second consulship in 49 BC. If there was an interval of unemployment, he would lose his immunity from prosecution as a public official and his enemies would be able to bring criminal charges against him for some of his actions when consul in 59 BC. And that would be the end of his political career, perhaps even of his life. Once Caesar saw that he would not get his wish, he invaded Italy at the head of his legions.

Pompey and many senators abandoned Italy for Greece, where Caesar won an apparently decisive victory at Pharsalus. Pompey, out-generalled, fled the field, but he was assassinated in Egypt, where the authorities wanted to curry favour with the victor. A disgusted Caesar had those responsible put to death. It was not for foreigners to punish his enemies.

Despite Pharsalus, hostilities continued, with resistance in north Africa and Spain. But once he had won the war in 45 BC, Caesar was liberal with pardons. He wanted the support of his senatorial opponents and welcomed them back into public life in Rome. This policy of clemency and reconciliation failed, but it was not through want of effort on Caesar's part. The one thing for which people could not forgive him was his forgiving them.

[xvii]

A KING BY ANY OTHER NAME

AFTER Caesar's victory in the civil war, it was obvious that constitutional reform was urgently needed. Somehow the state had to be renewed, but any return to the messy hurly-burly of republican politics was out of the question. Caesar introduced a flood of useful and imaginative reforms, but what could he do about the way the Republic was governed? Its complicated checks and balances made Rome incapable of running an empire efficiently.

What was needed, Caesar saw, was a more streamlined and authoritarian system of government. He already had full executive powers, and he meant to keep them. Even if he had wanted to retire, he knew that he would not be left in peace as Sulla had been. Most Roman politicians were dyed-in-the-wool constitutionalists and would never accept him as king.

Realizing that his opponents would not make any compromises, he lost patience. He had himself deified and made a louche lieutenant of his, Mark Antony, his special priest.* Then, on 9 February 44 BC, in order to entrench his powers, he had himself appointed dictator for life.

For upper-class Romans, this was all too much. Senators who

* For more on deification, see pages 96–7; and for more on Mark Antony, see pages 38–9 and 229.

had survived the civil war found it unacceptable, simply beyond the pale: something had to be done to knock Caesar off his high horse.

[xviii]

THE IDES OF MARCH

ABOUT sixty elite Romans, led by Marcus Junius Brutus and Gaius Longinus Cassius, joined a conspiracy to rid Rome of the tyrant. Many were his supporters and high in his favour. Caesar was warned, but he had dismissed his Spanish bodyguards and refused to rehire them. 'There is no fate worse than being permanently under guard,' he commented. 'It means you are always afraid.' He mingled unprotected among all comers. At a dinner party on 14 March 44 BC—the day before the Ides—he remarked that the most pleasant death was a sudden and unexpected one.

Caesar couldn't believe that his enemies would be so stupid as to remove him. 'It is more important for Rome than it is for me that I survive,' he observed on more than one occasion. Throughout his life he had always been lucky, and he trusted he would be so again.

However, it is hard to avoid the impression that Caesar was knowingly courting death at this time. In the months since the final battle of the civil war at Munda in Spain, his health had been noticeably deteriorating. He seems to have been epileptic and was suffering from increasingly frequent dizzy spells. He had been under ceaseless psychological and physical strain for many years, and this had taken its toll.

At a Senate meeting on the morning of 15 March—the Ides of March—a crowd of members gathered round the dictator and struck him down. Ironically, the object of the conspirators' rage may have found his death a merciful release.

[xix]

MEETING IN NO MAN'S LAND

One of the problems facing Roman politicians was that there were no obvious safe spaces where they could discuss matters with their enemies when at war.* The ancient world was a very dangerous environment for kings and consuls. How could they be certain that they would not be ambushed, kidnapped or even killed while discussing a peace treaty? The answer was they could not.

The first task of a negotiator, then, was to find a location where risk was minimized. This was a challenge facing the three men who governed Rome as duly elected triumvirs after Julius Caesar's murder: Octavian, Julius Caesar's adopted son and heir (later to be Rome's first emperor, Augustus); Mark Antony, who believed *he* should have been Caesar's heir; and a makeweight called Lepidus.† They disliked one another, but knew that they had to make an alliance if they were to defeat armies raised by Caesar's assassins.

They selected an island on a river outside Bononia (today's Bologna) as a meeting place. The two protagonists, Octavian and Antony, arrived with 5,000 troops each on opposing banks of the river, and Lepidus went over to the island with a small taskforce to check it for weapons or hidden assassins. Only when he waved an all-clear did Octavian and Antony leave their bodyguards and advisers behind and cross to the island themselves. Here the three men met alone but in full view of their forces and spent two days reaching an agreement.

* The United Nations in New York had not been invented, and Brussels, Geneva and Strasbourg did not yet offer neutral committee rooms where agreements could be hammered out without risk to life or limb.

† This is the so-called 'second triumvirate'; for the first triumvirate, see page 31.

[xx]

THE EMPEROR THAT WASN'T

AFTER Caesar's killers had been comprehensively defeated at the battle of Philippi in 42 BC, and had committed suicide, Octavian and Antony divided the Roman world between them.* Sextus Pompeius, son of Julius Caesar's great opponent Pompey the Great, raised a fleet and ravaged the coastline of Italy. Unable to destroy him, the triumvirs (as they were still called, even though there were now only two of them) asked him for a meeting to work out a peace treaty.

They met at Misenum, a headland at the northern end of the Bay of Naples. The two sides sailed there with their fleets and moored at some distance from one another. Two wooden platforms had been erected in the sea, one for each group of negotiators. These were just far enough apart to allow private talk on each platform and public communication, if shouted, between the platforms. Unfortunately megaphones had not been invented, and by the time a deal had been struck voices will have been hoarse.

Goodwill and trust broke out and the participants asked each other to dinner parties on successive days on their various flagships. When it was Sextus' turn and everyone was comfortably drunk, his admiral Menodorus whispered in his master's ear: 'Shall I cut the cables and make you master of the Roman empire?' 'If only you had done it,' replied Sextus sadly, 'and not asked for my permission. As it is we must be satisfied with things as they are. I am a man of my word.'

If Sextus *had* accepted the offer, the history of the world would have taken an altogether different course. Nobody would have been talking about the emperor Augustus (as Octavian became), but the emperor Pompeius.

* By this time the third member of the triumvirate, the incompetent Marcus Aemilius Lepidus, had been sent packing. For more on Lepidus see pages 231–32.

[xxi]

ANTONY'S DEFEAT AT ACTIUM

THE SECOND of September 31 BC has long been a red-letter day for connoisseurs of the world's decisive military encounters. For this was the date of the battle of Actium, in which the man who was to be Rome's first emperor eliminated his last rival for absolute power, Mark Antony.

Antony, well known as the greatest soldier of the age, shared government of the Roman world with the youthful Octavian. When their alliance broke down and civil war beckoned, it looked a fairly safe bet that Antony would come out on top. His best strategy was to invade Italy, but he laboured under a great disadvantage. This was Cleopatra, Egypt's female pharaoh, with whom Antony was in league, sharing both her bed and her bank account. She insisted on joining Antony on campaign and he gave way to her wishes. But she was very unpopular with the Roman public and he knew that the legions would not follow him if he tried to lead them to Italy with her at his side.

So he had to think up a new approach. Rather than occupy all of Greece before sailing across the Adriatic Sea to the motherland, Antony decided to base his fleet and army at Actium, a sandy promontory on the west coast, leaving the north empty of his troops. He hoped that this would tempt Octavian to transport his army to Greece without apparent risk. It was a trap, for Antony's plan was to blockade the enemy while keeping open his own supply lines to the Mediterranean and Egypt. At leisure he would then proceed to fight the crucial battle, with every prospect of victory.

Unfortunately, Octavian's brilliant admiral Agrippa also knew something about traps. In a daring move he sailed right down the western seaboard of Greece, bypassing Actium and capturing fortress after fortress. All at once, the blockader was blockaded.

With their fleet and army stuck at Actium, Antony and Cleopatra's supplies dwindled. The almost non-existent tides of the Mediterranean failed to wash away the excreta of many thousands of men occupying a cramped space with few facilities. During the long hot summer months an epidemic ravaged

Antony's camp—perhaps dysentery or malaria. Men died and morale fell.

Somehow Antony's ships had to storm their way to freedom. On a fine autumn day they sailed out, but the enemy blockade held firm and a sea battle commenced. Then, in a carefully planned manoeuvre, a small flotilla, headed by Cleopatra's flagship, slipped through a gap in the opposing line and headed for the open sea and Egypt. Antony immediately followed. His sailors could not believe that their commander had abandoned them, but once they realized he had, they surrendered; so a day or two later did the soldiers at Actium. Throughout the empire support for the fugitive couple collapsed. Nobody appreciates betrayal.

This was a lesson Antony and Cleopatra themselves learned the following year when almost all their remaining friends made their excuses and left them to humiliation and suicide in the grand palace at Alexandria.*

* For more on the death of Antony and Cleopatra, see pages 143–44.

III

THE EMPIRE

1

SMOKE AND MIRRORS

THE CIVIL WARS were finally over and Octavian was the last man standing. As victorious war leader, he held Rome in his hands. Nevertheless, he faced an apparently insoluble problem. In spite of their defeat, senators—the traditional ruling class—remained devoted to the republican constitution and would not accept Octavian as tyrant or king. He knew he could not rule the empire on his own—he needed their co-operation. And somehow he must avoid Julius Caesar's violent fate.

In 27 BC Octavian, now thirty-six years old, entered his seventh consulship with Agrippa again as his colleague. On 13 January he made an extraordinary speech to the Senate—perhaps the most important of his life. 'I lay down my office in its entirety,' he said to universal amazement, 'and return to you all authority absolutely—authority over the army, the laws and the provinces.' While he was speaking, senators broke in with shouts and interjections. No one knew exactly how to react. Republicans were pleased by the abdication, but should they believe their ears? Men who were disillusioned with the old constitution and wanted change were alarmed.

When Octavian sat down, the protests continued. With a great show of reluctance, he allowed himself to be persuaded to accept an unusually large provincial command for ten years, consisting of Spain, Gaul and Syria. Conveniently, these happened to be the regions of the empire where most of Rome's legions were based. All other provinces were to fall under direct senatorial management, and the Senate would appoint former consuls and praetors to govern them in the old way. Octavian was given a new name (*cognomen*) by which he was to be known in future. This was Augustus, meaning 'revered one'. For day-to-day use, more modestly, he was to be called *princeps*, or first citizen.

Of course, the speech was a trick. Augustus had not the slightest intention of handing over any real power. On the face of it, the old Republic as it had been before the civil wars was restored, so there was no despot—and no justification for conspiracy. However, with his vast 'province', Augustus in effect controlled the army, and consequently the state; behind a republican façade lay a military dictatorship. A few years later Augustus was voted the powers of a tribune of the people, so that he didn't even have to go to the bother of standing in annual elections to gain an official post. It meant that he had the right to lay legislation before the Senate and popular assemblies; and—assassins, please note—his person became legally sacrosanct.

The revival of the Republic was an obvious pretence, but it worked. True authority lay with the *princeps*, but he scrupulously observed constitutional appearances. Consuls and all the other officials were no longer in charge of the state, and over time their authority declined as that of the emperors grew. But they did have real, administrative jobs to do—and they knuckled down. The new imperial system of government was a political masterstroke, and it lasted unchallenged for centuries.

11

TOO CLOSE TO THE IMPERIAL FLAME

TINY, pinprick islands are scattered in the seas around Italy. Today they are beautiful spots, perfect for the tourist in search of the picturesque and the peaceful. But some of them have bleak histories. For the system that Augustus set in place had its dark side. If family members did not behave, the emperor could be unforgiving.

Pandateria is a volcanic outcrop 30 miles or so west of Naples.* The emperor Augustus made a point of simple living when he was in Rome, but—away from prying eyes—he built a lavish palace on the island. Perched on a rocky promontory, his holiday home was equipped with all the mod cons of the day. But evidently the emperor tired of the place, for it was here that in 2 BC he exiled his adulterous daughter Julia.† Men, wine and other luxuries were banished; solitude was mitigated only by the

* It is one of the Pontine Islands and today called Ventotene.

† For details of Julia's various shenanigans, see pages 108–9.

presence of her self-sacrificial mother. Julia spent five miserable years here before being moved to the southern provincial town of Rhegium, where she died in AD 14.

Another hapless member of the imperial family, Julia Livilla, who had a weakness for joining conspiracies, was exiled to Pandateria twice—once by her brother Caligula and then by her uncle Claudius, who crossly ordered her execution by starvation. Later in the first century AD Flavia Domitilla, a grand-daughter of Vespasian, was sent to the island by Domitian, probably for converting to Christianity (she is now a saint).*

Then there were the Tremiti Islands in the southern Adriatic. It was to one of these remote specks, Trimerus (now San Nicola), that Julia's daughter, Julia the Younger, was banished by Augustus in AD 8. She resembled her mother in that she too was no better than she should be, although her offence seems to have been as much political as sexual. She gave birth to a child on the island, but the emperor would not let it live—he had it exposed on a mountainside to die. Julia never left her island in the sun, where she expired after twenty years of exile.†

Planasia (today's Pianosa), a low-lying islet south of Elba, was owned in the first century BC by a leading Roman family. It contained a villa, some baths and a tiny open-air theatre; it may have become another of Augustus' luxury bolt-holes. It was to these comfortable surroundings that Augustus despatched Julia the Younger's brother, Marcus Vipsanius Agrippa Postumus. He seems to have had some sort of personality disorder and was judged unfit for public life. On the emperor's death, an assassination team was sent in to make sure Postumus would never return.‡

* Old habits die hard, and the islands have maintained their penal traditions. Between 1939 and 1943 Benito Mussolini imprisoned political opponents on a rock off Pandateria.

† In 1911 more than 1,000 Libyans were confined on the Isole Tremiti (Tremiti Islands) for resisting Italian colonial rule; an epidemic killed off a third of them. In the 1930s one of the islands, San Domino, became a prison for homosexuals, who were persecuted by Mussolini. 'In Italy we only have real men,' Il Duce liked to say. The island was the one place in Italy where it was obligatory to be openly gay. Conditions were harsh, but whatever the intentions of the authorities, for some the experience must have been liberating.

‡ Between 1858 and 1998 Pianosa was the site of a maximum-security prison, which specialized in housing Mafiosi.

iii

A WOMAN SCORNED

THE ROMANS conquered Britannia in AD 43 and established a new province which endured for over 350 years. The Roman presence profoundly altered the character of the island and was certainly not welcomed by all. While some fell in with their new masters, others reacted violently against them.

Boudica, queen of the Iceni, a north Norfolk tribe, raised the standard of revolt, not because she was a patriot or an anti-imperialist, but for personal reasons. Her husband Prasutagus was a client king under Roman patronage, and he made the emperor Nero co-heir with his daughters. But when he died, the will was ignored. Boudica was flogged, the daughters were raped, and Roman financiers called in loans they had made to the late king. Enraged, the queen headed a widespread insurgency in AD 60 or 61, so threatening that at one point the authorities in Rome considered withdrawal from the island. The rebels razed the provincial capital Camulodunum (today's Colchester) to the ground and burned and destroyed Londinium (London), at that time a modest commercial settlement.

The Romans, who had been busy annexing Anglesey and were caught on the hop, marched south and defeated Boudica in a great battle. Order was restored and the queen perished, either from illness or by her own hand.

iv

'THEY CREATE A DESERT AND CALL IT PEACE'

WHILE BOUDICA acted from personal motives, Calgacus, a Caledonian chieftain, opposed the Romans on principle. He faced an invasion of as yet unconquered north Britain in AD 82. In a biography of Agricola, the Roman governor of the day, the great Roman historian Tacitus gives the chieftain a rousing speech, in which he makes the case against imperialism in terms that ring true today:

Robbery, butchery, plunder — the liars say this is empire. They create a desert and call it peace.

Sadly, nothing more is known of Calgacus or his ultimate fate. He may even have been a figment of Tacitus' imagination.

[v]

IF YOU CAN'T BEAT THEM...

PRAGMATIC, rather than heroic, is the figure cut by Tiberius Claudius Togidubnus, king of the Regnenses, a tribe based in what is modern West Sussex. Not to put too fine a point on it, he was a collaborator, a quisling. He seems to have been installed as king of a number of territories, over which he presided at the Roman-style palace excavated in 1960 at Fishbourne near Chichester. This huge building occupied a site larger than Nero's Golden House in Rome, and was modelled on Domitian's new palace on the Palatine hill. If challenged about his complicity with the invaders, Togidubnus would surely have responded by claiming to be a realist. And history bore him out.

Once the new province of Britannia had settled down after the disruptions of the first century AD, peace and an orderly administration created growing prosperity—and consent to Roman rule. A network of roads improved communications (many of their routes are still followed today), allowing pleasant villas to spring up throughout the countryside. Meanwhile, new towns such as Aquae Sulis (today's Bath) introduced the native population to the amenities of urban life. By the third century the British economy was diverse and well established.

Saxons and other foreign invaders had already begun raiding the province by the time the Roman legions were withdrawn about AD 410. Later in the fifth century the Britons sent a final appeal—the so-called 'Groans of the Britons'—to their one-time oppressors for military assistance. The Romans, however, were facing their own crises (see page 296) and could not help. The province was left to its own devices.

[vi]

ROME'S YOUTH OPPORTUNITY SCHEME

IN 1747 some ploughmen working in a field unearthed a large bronze tablet which carried details of an ambitious social welfare scheme. It was called *alimenta* and was funded by the emperor Trajan in the early second century AD (or earlier—it may have been started by his predecessor, Nerva).

We would not usually associate the Romans with such social provision. Ancient historians were not generally interested in this kind of thing, and had it not been for the farm workers we should never have heard of it. But the tantalizing evidence is there to see. Did the Romans really create a welfare state?

The bronze tablet gives details of a child support scheme in which needy free-born children in three local communities were selected for financial support. The boys received 16 sesterces a month, the girls 12 sesterces. In order to cover the cost, the treasury made a capital sum available in the form of cheap five-per-cent loans to local landowners on the security of their farms or estates. The support interest payable on the loans covered the grants to the children. So far as we can tell, the loans never had to be repaid, or at least never were. The scheme appears to have covered all of Italy, and it has been estimated that the total cost was about 311 million sesterces—a huge sum equivalent to three-quarters of the army's annual budget. But what exactly was it designed to achieve?

In the days of the Republic legions were raised from the population of the Italian peninsula, but from the early empire more and more soldiers were recruited from the provinces. The reservoir of Italian peasant manpower on which Rome had depended was drying up. There is evidence, too, that Italy had been suffering from an agricultural crisis.* *Alimenta* must have transformed economic expectations in the countryside. The subsidy for

* Pliny the Younger, for instance, Trajan's contemporary and a substantial landowner, reports that his tenants were finding it hard to pay their rent and were falling into ever greater arrears. He set up his own private scheme, along similar lines to the government's.

selected offspring of citizens (all the free-born inhabitants of the peninsula held Roman citizenship as of right) will have removed the shadow of poverty from a young generation; the boys were presumably expected to grow up into soldiers and farmers, the girls to marry and procreate. The cheap loans themselves encouraged investment in agricultural development. Although this is nowhere spelled out, the mortgagees were surely expected to plough the treasury 'loan' into their farms or at least to redeem previous losses.

Did the injection of so much cash into the Italian countryside have a beneficial impact? It seems so, for the government was moved to issue a series of *alimenta* coins as well as one with the proud slogan *Italia restituta*, 'Italy renewed'.

These policies for youth support and rural development have a familiar ring to them, but they were not the expression of social or economic theory. Trajan was no David Lloyd George, Britain's social reformer at the beginning of the twentieth century. Roman emperors were powerful, but they possessed neither the mindset nor the administrative capacity to establish a welfare state. That said, this was Rome at its best—generous, well-intentioned and intelligent.

Might there have been other such projects for the alleviation of poverty? We await news from today's ploughmen!

vii

HADRIAN'S WALL

ALONGSIDE Stonehenge, Hadrian's Wall is the most famous ancient monument in the British Isles. Extending from Wallsend on the river Tyne in the east to the shore of the Solway Firth in the west, much of it survives in good condition. With a stone facing and a clay and rubble core, the wall was 10 feet broad and 14 feet high with an added battlement; it was finished with plaster and whitewashed. Along its northern side a huge ditch was dug; to the south were two 10-foot-high turf banks separated by a roadway that ran in parallel to the wall.

Every mile there was a guard post, and between each pair of

such posts there were two signalling turrets. At its far western end, the wall became a turfed rampart and curved down the coast to guard against sea raiders. In total, the fortification ran for 73 miles. A ribbon tracing the rise and fall of the rugged green moorland, it could be seen for miles.

What was the point of Hadrian's Wall? Easy: to defend the province of Britannia from the annoying Scots. Apparently not. The Caledonian tribes north of the wall cannot in fact have posed much of a military threat. A loose necklace of forts—the arrangement that preceded the wall—would have held back the barbarians perfectly well. From a practical point of view the wall was unnecessary. So what was the emperor Hadrian's motive for commissioning what must have been an extremely costly project? The clue to the puzzle lies in its appearance.

When he assumed the imperial purple in AD 116, Hadrian made it clear that the empire was now big enough and that there were to be no further conquests. He wanted to show the world that he meant what he said. Great natural boundaries such as the Rhine, the Danube and the Euphrates spoke for themselves. But in Britannia (and in north Africa, where he built another wall) there was no obvious frontier. The shining white ribbon snaking across the barren countryside was an unforgettable visual statement and a symbolic assertion of the greatness—but also the limits—of Rome's power.

[viii]

THE FIVE GOOD EMPERORS

THE EMPERORS were not all psychopaths and serial killers. From the end of the first century AD to late in the second, five intelligent and well-intentioned rulers succeeded one another. These were Nerva, Trajan (his record blotted by a failed invasion of Mesopotamia, today's Iraq), Hadrian, Antoninus Pius and Marcus Aurelius. Each of the first four had the wisdom to adopt his successor with an eye to merit, rather than relying on the erratic qualification of blood.

The eighteenth-century British historian Edward Gibbon,

author of *The Decline and Fall of the Roman Empire* may have overstated it a little when he observed:

> If a man were called to fix the period in the history of the world during which the condition of the human race was most happy and prosperous, he would, without hesitation, name that which elapsed from the death of Domitian to the accession of Commodus. The vast extent of the Roman Empire was governed by absolute power, under the guidance of virtue and wisdom.

But he had a point.*

* For more on Rome's emperors, good, bad and plain ugly, see page 249.

IV

CITY LIFE

I

THE RICH–POOR DIVIDE

For most of its history living in ancient Rome didn't change very much. The everyday experiences of a citizen in the second century BC would not have been unfamiliar to his counterpart more than 500 years later. The thing that made the biggest difference, as ever, was wealth and poverty—whether or not you were rich and a free man (as distinct from being a slave). If you had money, you enjoyed education, health, good housing and many luxuries. The poor, by contrast, had a hard time even feeding themselves, and many relied for food on rations of free grain that the state made available. Their lives were typically short and difficult.

II

A HEAVING HIVE

Rome was a hive of activity and a magnet to outsiders, so it was always full to bursting. The population in the first century BC may have reached between 0.75 and 1 million; by the reign of the emperor Diocletian in the late third century AD it had risen as high as 1.5 million. The city was an overcrowded web of lanes and alleys; there were no wide thoroughfares or avenues. The statesman and orator Cicero wrote that Rome was 'planted in mountains and deep valleys, its garrets hanging above, its roads far from good, merely narrow byways'.

Many of the main streets were lined with shops. Most had a ground-floor room with a counter for selling goods and a space at the back for stock. All kinds of goods were sold: jewellery, clothing and fabrics, pots and pans, books. There were also numerous bars and restaurants that catered for poor working people whose houses did not have properly equipped kitchens.

Epidemics were rife, and death stalked the streets as doctors knew nothing of how bacteria and viruses spread or could be countered. One source of salvation was that large quantities of fresh water were brought to the city by means of aqueducts, and there was a system of sewers to flush out waste, so in Rome's case the water-borne diseases that typically afflict overcrowded cities were less devastating.

iii

ISLANDS OF TERROR, ISLANDS OF REPOSE

HOUSING was a perennial problem in Rome. The solution was to build apartment blocks (*insulae* or 'islands') that were six or seven storeys high. These were badly designed and shoddily made, leading to frequent collapse. Fire, too, was a permanent hazard as there was no fire brigade, and the Tiber flooded regularly. For those without money, urban living was hard indeed.

In stark contrast, the affluent lived in comfort in houses resembling those in Arab cities today. Their homes were havens of peace and quiet, with internal open-air courtyards and no outside windows. The rich also owned villas in the country or in Rome's suburbs, and at seaside resorts such as Puteoli (today's Pozzuoli). Here they could escape from city life and relax.

iv

A CITY OF MARBLE

ROME's political, commercial and legal heart was the Forum, a rectangular piazza, or town square, 200 metres long by 75 metres wide. Here stood the Senate House and a number of important temples. The law courts sat in the open air. From the late Republic onwards, the wealth of empire was invested in grand building developments in the city centre, including new forums, public baths and temples. As the emperor Augustus boasted, Rome had once been a city of brick but was now a city of marble.

[v]

STINK CITY

ROME was a city of horrible smells. Garbage and sewage—occasionally even human corpses—were simply tipped into the street. The sanitary arrangements were basic, to say the least—every now and then a chamber pot would be emptied, with a warning shout, out of a window. Passers-by were so often hit by the contents of these pots that laws were passed regulating the compensation that could be claimed by unlucky victims.

[vi]

MAN ABOUT TOWN (I)

WELL-TO-DO MARCUS

MARCUS Cornelius Lentulus (let us imagine) is a well-off upper-class Roman of the first century AD. He is in his early forties and his wife is Terentia, whom he married when she was only thirteen and he was twenty-five. They live in a fine house on the fashionable Palatine hill and have three children: Marcus, aged fifteen;* a twelve-year-old daughter Cornelia; and Gaius, aged ten.

At first light Marcus rises from his bed in a tiny, barely furnished bedroom (the Romans had no time for lazy lie-ins) and gets dressed. He puts on a loin-cloth and a tunic, over which he drapes his toga. The children have already left the house for school. It is July and in a few days the term ends; the family is looking forward to escaping the stifling city and spending some lazy weeks in their villa at Puteoli.

The couple say a prayer at the little shrine of their household gods, leaving a wheat cake and a bowl of milk on the altar as an offering. Then they grab a quick breakfast consisting of a glass of water and (as Marcus is hungry) some bread dunked in wine and served with cheese, honey and olives.

Terentia goes out shopping with a couple of slaves to buy

* The eldest son was usually named after his father; see page 147.

the ingredients for a dinner party later in the day. Meanwhile, Marcus' clients (dependents; see page 60) gather in the main reception room, or *tablinum*, of his house to wish him good morning. On some days, Marcus does not go out of doors but works in the *tablinum*, which also serves as his study. But today he walks out with his clients to the Forum, where he conducts some political and other business. He has already served as a quaestor (when he was thirty), and then as a praetor (at the minimum age of thirty-nine). He aspires to the top job, the consulship, in a year or so.

When he arrives at the Forum, Marcus notices temporary wooden stands being erected.* It reminds him that tomorrow is a public holiday, and there are to be some gladiatorial games. He decides to attend with his eldest son. It will be the boy's first visit, and Marcus thinks that the sight of real-life fighting will teach the boy about bravery.

Marcus joins his wife for a light lunch of (again) bread, cheese and olives. Sometimes he takes a nap at home in the afternoon, but today he decides to go to the public baths.† There he meets friends and chats about current affairs.

The main meal of the day is served in the mid to late afternoon. Marcus has invited some friends, all of them men, to eat with him. The guests eat lying on couches set out along three sides of the dining room. Terentia and the children are present, as a special treat, but sit on chairs and are on their best behavior.

Wine mixed with water is served after the meal.‡ Once the food has been cleared away, Marcus and friends drink each other's health. They exchange gossip and debate the political events of the day. Some attractive young dancers give a performance. The party ends before sunset—Marcus' guests want to go home while there is still some daylight, for there is no street lighting and muggers prowl. And so early to bed.

* The imaginary events recounted here take place a century before the great amphitheatre, the Colosseum, was built at Rome.

† There were many public baths at Rome, though as a rich man Marcus would also have a bath-house at home.

‡ Such a mixture of wine and water would have had roughly the alcoholic strength of beer.

[vii]

MAN ABOUT TOWN (II):
HARD-UP SEXTUS

Sextus Scutarius is a young man in his mid-twenties. He lives with his parents and a brood of brothers and sisters in two sparsely furnished rooms on the top floor of a cheap apartment block (*insula*) in the working-class district called Subura. Sextus earns a bit of money doing odd jobs. He will probably not find a wife until he is over thirty and has managed to put aside a few sesterces. Without regular employment he will not be able to afford the cost of raising a family.

His mother Fulvia does her best to feed her family, but none of them has a full-time job and money is short. Like the other menfolk, Sextus gives her his monthly ration of free wheat, which is provided by the state. She cooks it into bread, scones or a kind of porridge mixed with herbs and vegetables. Sometimes a piece of cheese is on the table, or some dried fish—and very rarely a wedge of tough pork. The only heating in the apartment is a smoky brazier,* while water has to be fetched from a public fountain two streets away and lugged up six flights of stairs.

Sextus sleeps badly at night. Only a couple of weeks earlier a nearby *insula* crumbled into a mound of dust and rubble without warning; twenty people were killed, and five times that number made homeless. He is terrified of the same thing happening where he lives, and keeps an ear cocked for the tell-tale cracking sound of imminent collapse.

He spends most of his days outside in the open air. The streets are noisy and crowded, but at least there is no traffic blocking the narrow lanes.† Amongst the numerous shops, bars and restaurants that litter the streets Sextus finds a fast-food stall, where he buys a bowl of greasy stew for his dinner. Then he goes down to the docks near Tiber Island, not far from the Forum, to see if he can find some light work. There is none available today, however, so he decides to fill his time by spending a few lazy hours in the public baths.

* A metal pan on a stand, which held burning coals or charcoal.

† In 45 BC Julius Caesar passed a law banning wheeled traffic (carts and carriages) in the city during daylight hours.

Sextus pays an entry fee of one *quadrans* (the lowest-value Roman coin). The baths are the one place in Rome where wealth and poverty do not matter—nakedness hides social class. Everyone can afford to go, and everyone does. Sextus leaves his clothes in the dressing room, picks up a towel and goes into the hot-room (*calidarium*) to have a good sweat. He sits next to a man some years older than he and politely exchanges the time of day. The man is Marcus Cornelius Lentulus, who soon gets up and joins some well-heeled friends around the splash pool.

Marcus and Sextus are from very different walks of life and they have very different prospects. In the street or the Forum, the rich man and the unemployed docker would not recognize one another—and would not admit to it if they did. They share the same city, but live in separate worlds. In the baths, at least, the paths of these two Romans briefly cross.

[*viii*]

PATRON AND CLIENT

THE CLIENT system was a crucial feature of Roman life and politics. A powerful Roman was a patron, or protector, of many hundreds or even thousands of clients, not just in Rome and Italy but also across the Mediterranean. These networks of mutual aid cut across social classes and linked Romans to people in the provinces. A patron might give his clients food, money or small parcels of land, and would stand up for them if they got into trouble with the law. In return, they supported him in any way they could, voting as he wished at popular assemblies and campaigning for him when he ran for office.

ROME AT WAR

I

THE WINNING FORMULA

IN ROME's main square, the Forum, there stood a tiny temple of Janus, the god of beginnings and endings. Its doors were only closed during a time of peace. This was a very rare occurrence: only twice, it seems, during the many centuries of the Republic. The Romans were nearly always at war, and practice made perfect: in the course of time they developed an unrivalled military expertise.

One of the main reasons for Rome's success in the field was its reservoir of human capital. In return for military service alongside the legions, the Romans offered generous alliances and full or partial Roman citizenship to the peoples they conquered in Italy. In this way they acquired an almost inexhaustible supply of soldiers. Rome's enemies would win major victories only to find themselves facing another brand-new army a few months or even weeks later.

II

THE ROMAN LEGION

ROME'S ARMY was based on the *legio*, the legion or regiment, which—in theory if not always in practice—consisted of about 4,500 men (in an emergency this could rise to 5,000). In Hannibal's day, the core of the legion was a body of about 3,000 heavily armed foot-soldiers. These were grouped into tactical units of between 60 and 120 men called maniples, which were arranged in a chequer-board pattern and commanded by regimental officers called centurions.

The infantrymen were ordered in three lines: the ones nearest the enemy were the *hastati*, young and inexperienced troops; the second line were the *principes*, mature men in their late twenties or early thirties; and in the rear were hardened veterans, the *triarii*. Things were going very badly if the *triarii* were called on to fight. This formation allowed for flexibility and was more practical on rough ground than the Greek phalanx, a single, compact body which tended to break up if not deployed on a flat plain that was clear of obstacles. In front of a drawn-up legion were 1,200 lightly armed skirmishers, who withdrew behind the infantry lines when the battle was fully under way. Each legion also had a small force of 300 cavalry.

During the first century BC the maniple gave way to a larger tactical unit, the 480-strong cohort. A legion commander found communicating with ten cohorts an easier process than dealing with thirty maniples. The legions in a Roman army were matched by the same number of troops recruited from the Italian allies and organized on the same principles.

111

MARIUS' MULES

GAIUS MARIUS (157–86 BC), one of Rome's greatest generals (see also page 29), saw that a major weakness of the Roman army was its large, slow and undisciplined baggage train. This carried soldiers' equipment and was crowded with slaves, prostitutes and other unnecessary hangers-on. He slashed the size of the train and chased away the camp-followers. This meant that the individual soldier was obliged to become more self-sufficient, carrying with him everything he needed for life and war.

Legionaries wore metal helmets and body armour and protected themselves with a shield; they carried a short sword (*gladius*), mainly used for stabbing but also for slashing; and the first two lines were equipped with two javelins or throwing spears (*pila*). The *triarii* wielded a thrusting pike. In addition to all this, the legionary had a pole on his shoulder on which he carried three days' emergency rations; a cooking pot and pan; engineer's tools for making camp or building roads (two stakes for the camp defences and one or more of the following: pickaxe, spade, scythe, saw and turf-cutter); a blanket; a cloak and cloak bag; a leather bottle for a mix of drinking water and vinegar; a satchel for spare clothes; and—not so onerous—a sewing kit.

With all this on their backs the men looked like beasts of burden—and soon gained the nickname 'Marius' mules'. We don't know exactly what weight they were carrying, but the best estimate is about 66 pounds.*

⟨iv⟩

THE NAP RAP

SOLDIERS on guard duty at night had a natural tendency to drop off—with potentially disastrous consequences when in enemy territory. To prevent this occurring, each guard post was allocated a marked tablet. At an appointed time an officer, accompanied by some of his friends as witnesses, did the rounds of the guard posts. If he found the guards awake, he collected their tablet. But if a guard was asleep, he called on his companions to witness the fact and went on his way.

At the end of his round the officer handed over his tablets to a superior (a military tribune), and if one was missing, marks on the tablets made it easy to establish which post it belonged to. The sleepy guard was confronted by the officer and his witnesses, and if the evidence was clear, a court martial was convened. The penalty for anyone found guilty was *fustuarium*, a beating. The military tribune touched the man with a cudgel and the soldiers present then fell on him with clubs and stones. The convicted man seldom survived, but if he did manage to escape from the camp, he was little better off. He was not allowed to return home and his family would not dare help him. In effect, he was an outlaw. No surprise, then, that, as a contemporary observer noted, 'the night watches of the Roman army are faultlessly kept'.

The same penalty was inflicted on those who stole from the camp, perjured themselves, committed homosexual offences or had been convicted three times for the same crime. It was also an offence carrying the death penalty to run away in battle or throw down one's weapons.

* Surprisingly, this happens to be more or less the same, on average, as today's yomper lugs about on the march. In fact, in today's inhospitable Afghanistan, our contemporary soldiers have done better than the Romans. On extended foot patrols, weights of up to 120 pounds have been recorded. Despite the efforts of technologists to make equipment as light as possible, today's soldiers have a way of simply adding new stuff to their rucksack or pockets. Perhaps it has always been so.

[v]

A BLOODY LOT

A BEATING was effective when an individual was at fault, but if a large body of men were all guilty of a capital offence—fleeing the battlefield, say, or just deserting their posts—a different penalty was used: *decimatio*, or decimation.* It was impractical to beat to death or execute everyone who was guilty, so Roman officers adopted a neat but terrifying solution. A military tribune called his legion on parade and selected by lot one-tenth (or thereabouts) of the total—hence decimation, from Latin *decem*, 'ten'. These men were then beaten to death by their own comrades.

Decimation did not always work. Mark Antony, usually a popular commander, tried it once on an army in 44 BC. After the soldiers had openly criticised him and refused to applaud when he addressed them, Antony lost his temper. 'You will learn to obey orders,' he growled, and launched a decimation. As the executions began, the men's mood became angrier still. He halted the process and instead tried conciliation, but it was too late. He left the camp disconcerted and disheartened. As soon as he had gone, most of the legionaries revolted and abandoned his service for that of his rival, the young Octavian.

[vi]

DIGGING FOR VICTORY

JULIUS CAESAR had spent nearly ten years conquering Gaul. Then, in the blink of an eye, all that had been achieved was placed at risk, when, in 52 BC, a young tribal chieftain called Vercingetorix raised the standard of revolt. To begin with, the Gallic leader won a great victory over the Romans, but when his cavalry was unexpectedly routed, he withdrew to the

* Today, the word 'decimation' is mostly used to indicate a radical reduction in number—far more than one-tenth—and sometimes means a virtual annihilation. The whole point of the Roman punishment, however, was to deter others, forcefully and effectively, in a way that did not radically reduce the number of fighting men.

impregnable hill fortress of Alesia (near modern Dijon).

Caesar, commanding an army of perhaps 40,000 men, encircled Alesia with siegeworks; these consisted of a ditch and a rampart that connected twenty-three forts. Then, learning that a relief force was being organized, he had his men build an outer ring of fortifications that linked the surrounding hills. Sharpened stakes were hidden in pits to impale unwary Gallic attackers. To accomplish this astounding feat of engineering, the remains of which have been revealed by archaeologists, Caesar's legions were required to dig 24 miles of trenches and palisades in little more than one month.

Vercingetorix and his army in Alesia were beginning to starve, but at last a huge force of 250,000 infantry and 8,000 cavalry—or so Caesar claims in his book on the Gallic wars—arrived and began to besiege the besiegers. The relieving force fell on the outer defences, while Vercingetorix and his men poured down the hill from Alesia. The newly arrived army concentrated its attack on a Roman hill camp but was caught in the rear by Caesar's cavalry. A bloodbath ensued. The following day the Gauls surrendered unconditionally.

Hoping for clemency, the defeated chieftain handed himself over. He put on his most beautiful armour and came out of Alesia proudly on horseback. He rode around the dais where Caesar was seated, stripped off his armour, and fell on his knees as a suppliant. But his conqueror showed no mercy. Vercingetorix spent the next six years a prisoner, while Caesar went off to fight and win a civil war. In 46 BC he was paraded in Caesar's triumphal procession and then strangled in the damp little execution chamber just off Rome's Forum.

[*vii*]

FOLLOW THE CODE

SECRECY has always been a vital part of military strategy—and a general can never be too careful. During the Second Punic War, towards the end of the third century BC, letters between Hannibal and his brother Hasdrubal were captured by the

Romans. They revealed the Carthaginians' plans and quickly led to Hasdrubal's defeat and death.

A couple of centuries later, Julius Caesar, ever the innovator, was the first commander known to have used a cipher—in this case, a substitution cipher in which the required letter was replaced by the one three places further along the Latin alphabet. This is a very simple code, as there are only twenty-five possibilities, but it is easy to complicate matters by choosing an alternative, non-alphabetical permutation of letters. We don't know if Caesar took the trouble to do this, but if so, he could have created an astronomically large number of substitution ciphers, which would challenge even a modern computer.

[viii]

WHO SOUGHT OCTAVIAN'S ARSE?

IN 41 BC Mark Antony's wife Fulvia and his brother Lucius were conducting an unsuccessful war against Octavian, Antony's partner in government. Lucius and his army were holed up in the hill town of Perusia (today's Perugia in Umbria), and Octavian had the place under siege. Both sides hurled stone and lead slingshot at each other.

About eighty of these lead balls have since been discovered by archaeologists. Many have brief, extremely rude comments scratched on them by Roman legionaries, who were famous for their caustic sense of humour. One soldier inscribed the message 'I seek Octavian's arse', and it wasn't only his backside that attracted attention. Others balls read 'Octavian can't get it up', 'Hi, Octavius, you suck dick' and 'Slack Octavius, sit on this'. Other insults include 'I seek Fulvia's clitoris' and—rather feebly—'Lucius is bald'.

ix

PRISING AWAY THE ENEMY GODS

In their early centuries the Romans controlled only a tiny territory in central Italy surrounded by fiercely hostile tribes. In 395 BC a long war between Rome and one such enemy—the Etruscan city of Veii—was drawing to a close. The city occupied a plateau on top of a steep-cliffed rocky outcrop and was almost impregnable; the Roman commander Camillus feared that Veii would never fall, however long he besieged it. A superstitious man like most of his fellow citizens, he was terrified of Veii's tutelary goddess Juno, wife of Jupiter and queen of the gods. According to legend, she had always loathed the Romans and done her best throughout their history to place obstacles in their way.

A good general like Camillus realized that he had to win Juno's favour and that he would have to offer her something tempting if she were to turn coat. At an army parade, he called on Juno to 'leave this town where you now dwell and follow our victorious arms into our city of Rome, your future home, which will receive you in a temple worthy of your greatness'. The trick worked, and Veii fell. Camillus kept his word and a splendid new shrine was built in Rome for the delighted goddess.

Camillus' was an early example of *evocatio*, literally a 'calling out' or 'calling forth' (from which we have our word 'evocation'): a ritual to persuade the tutelary gods protecting the enemy to switch sides. Such ritual observances were second nature to the Romans, a highly superstitious people who had a ceremony for practically every occasion.

x

A SHAKESPEAREAN EVOCATION

Towards the end of Shakespeare's great romantic tragedy *Antony and Cleopatra*, there is a mysterious scene. It is night-time in Alexandria. On the following day Mark Antony will fight and lose his last battle against Octavian.

As four bored soldiers stand on guard outside the royal palace, a strange music is heard from beneath the earth. One of the men optimistically sees it as a good omen for the coming encounter. 'No,' says a pessimist. 'What should this mean?' asks another. ''Tis the god Hercules, whom Antony loved, now leaves him,' responds the pessimist.

This was a real historical episode—although the Bard makes a mistake; he should have said Dionysus, the god of wine, not Hercules.* Mark Antony fancied himself as a latter-day Dionysus and believed that the god was his ancestor. What must have happened is that Octavian, who was a devout young man, had held an evocatio to detach the deity from his loyal servant. We may surmise that somebody in Octavian's PR department made up the story of the spooky music. History, sadly, does not record the nature of the bribe that persuaded Dionysus to turn coat.

[*xi*]

QUINCTILIUS VARUS, GIVE ME BACK MY LEGIONS!

IN SPITE of its billing, the battle of the Teutoburg Forest in AD 9 was in fact little more than an ambush—there was much slaughter but little real fighting. The repercussions were immense, however, dramatically shifting the course of Roman history.

The general Publius Quinctilius Varus was well connected, but he was a lawyer and had no real military experience. His task was to settle half-conquered Germanic lands to the east of the river Rhine. On the advice of ostensibly loyal Germans, he led his army of up to 15,000 men through unmapped forest. They were marching into a carefully laid trap.

* The great twentieth-century Greek poet C. P. Cavafy revisits the moment in his *The God Abandons Antony*:

> At midnight, when suddenly you hear
> an invisible procession going by
> with exquisite music, voices,
> don't mourn your luck that's failing now,
> work gone wrong, your plans
> all proving deceptive…

(C. P. Cavafy, *Collected Poems*. Translated by Edmund Keeley and Philip Sherrard. Edited by George Savidis. Revised Edition. Princeton University Press, 1992)

For 2,000 years nobody knew exactly where the disaster had taken place or exactly what had happened. But then in the 1990s the detritus of a deadly encounter was unearthed near Kalkriese in Lower Saxony: this was where Varus and his legions had met their doom.

A pathway led through woods, running between the steep Kalkriese Hill and a bog. At its narrowest it was about 200 metres wide. Along the hillside the Germans built a long camouflaged turf rampart with a wooden fence on top and fortified in part with limestone. Here the ambushers lay in wait. Through the rain the legions approached along the pathway. Once they had entered the narrows the Germans launched volleys of spears from behind the turf rampart and then charged, cutting the Roman army in two. They achieved total surprise.

A substantial number of legionaries and most of the officer corps managed to emerge from the ambush zone and made camp not far away. For two days the Romans pushed on, under constant attack, passing through open country and then plunging into woods again. On the third day, the situation became hopeless and Varus and his staff realized that the end was near. They felt it was their duty not to be captured and slaughtered by the enemy, so they ran themselves through with their swords. It was now every man for himself. Some soldiers followed Varus' example, others simply lost heart, dropped their weapons and allowed themselves to be slaughtered.

Of Varus' three legions few men survived to tell the tale. The Germans took about 1,500 prisoners, of whom two-thirds were sold into slavery (some eventually won their freedom and made their way back to Italy). The remainder were sacrificed as religious offerings. The German gods clearly appreciated variety, and the captives were put to death in different ways: some had their throats cut, others were hanged from trees, crucified or buried alive. Victims' heads were nailed to trees in the forest as a ghastly warning to any intending to invade in the future. Once they had exacted their punishments and removed their dead, the Germans left the scenes of battle as they were, for time and nature slowly to restore the mutilated landscape.

The news eventually reached Rome and the aged emperor

Augustus. He was so upset that, as a sign of mourning, he tore his clothes and would not shave for months. He used to beat his head against a door, crying out: 'Quinctilius Varus, give me back my legions!'

All hope of conquering Germany, as Julius Caesar had Gaul, was given up. The Rhine remained the empire's frontier for good.

[xii]

FRONTIER GOSSIP

THE VOICES we hear from ancient Rome are those of the ruling class, the generals and the politicians. The voices of ordinary people are always muffled or silent. Or *almost* always...

There is one remarkable exception. In northern England, along a frontier that followed the route later taken by Hadrian's Wall (see page 49), there was a strong point called Vindolanda. Here were high ramparts topped by a palisade—the regular ingredients of a Roman camp; inside stood tidy rows of barracks, storehouses, a hospital and the commander's residence. The amenities of urban life were also available nearby in the shape of a stone bath-house and a temple.

The early forts at Vindolanda were made of wood and replaced every seven or eight years. Rather than clear a site, the Romans simply demolished the old building and overlaid the wreckage with a clay or turf layer. To ward off the pervasive damp, dried bracken and straw were laid on the floor. All kinds of object were dropped and lost. The wet conditions ensured an oxygen-free environment and preserved everything the legionaries had discarded. Since the early 1970s archaeologists have investigated this material and dug up priceless and well-preserved evidence of life as it was lived in an outpost of empire 2,000 years ago. Shoes, belts, textiles, wooden tools, bronze and iron utensils have been found.

Astonishingly, so has correspondence, including personal letters, accounts, requests for leave, even drawings. Most of these documents were penned in ink on slivers of local oak or alder, some were scratched into wax-layered tablets; usually they are the size and shape of a modern postcard or half a postcard. They re-animate the long-forgotten dead—among them Flavius Cerealis, prefect of the ninth cohort (the Batavians), and his wife Sulpicia Lepidina, who were posted to Vindolanda around the end of the first century AD.

A colleague apologizes to the commander for not having turned up at his wife's birthday party, and a woman friend dictates a note to Lepidina inviting her to *her* birthday celebrations. She has added in her own slightly wobbly hand: 'I shall expect you, sister. Farewell, sister, as I hope to prosper, and hail.' The same woman gets her husband's permission for Lepidina to visit her at her home in another fort, for she has 'certain personal matters' she wants to discuss. Lonely in Vindolanda one winter and in need of company, Cerealis asks an influential correspondent to 'furnish me with lots and lots of friends that, thanks to you, I may enjoy a pleasant period of military service'.

The officers appear to have been Germanic noblemen, and the Vindolanda documents show that they and their families willingly Romanized themselves. Education of the young was a key tool: a couple of tablets reveal the efforts of a little boy, doubtless Cerealis and Lepidina's son, to learn lines from Rome's national epic, Virgil's *Aeneid*. He wrote down from memory a famous quotation: *interea pavidum volitans pinnata p' ubem*: 'Meanwhile, the winged creature [Rumour] flying through the trembling city.' The boy abbreviated *per* with *p'* and accidentally left out the *r* of *urbem*. Here we have a tantalizing glimpse of a young German learning to grow up into a proper Roman.

In their remote outpost people are thirsty for news. Solemnis writes to his 'brother' Paris (their names suggest they are slaves, not soldiers): 'Many hellos. You should know that I am well, and I hope you are too. You are a most disloyal man, for you haven't sent me a single letter. I think I am being much nicer by writing to you.' Another correspondent, the thoroughly Germanic Chrauttius, complains to an old mess-mate who is now the governor's groom: 'I am surprised you haven't written anything back to us for such a long time.'

VI

HANNIBAL AND CARTHAGE

I

THE REPUBLIC'S EXISTENTIAL THREAT

THE DEFINING encounter in republican Rome's history was the titanic struggle with its rival Carthage, a north African port with a maritime empire stretching from Spain to Sicily. In the First Punic War (264–241 BC), Rome challenged Carthage for control of Sicily, and after a conflict that lasted more than twenty years, she finally prevailed.

A generation later, the masterly Carthaginian general Hannibal, bent on revenge, launched a second struggle, striking at Rome's heartland of Italy. This protracted and bloody conflict—the Second Punic War (218–201 BC)—presented the most grievous threat to Rome's survival, but it ended in the complete defeat of Carthage and left the Romans as the undisputed masters of the Mediterranean.

II

THE TANK WITH TUSKS AND TRUNK

THE ELEPHANT was the not-so-secret secret weapon of ancient warfare. Like a First World War tank, it was large, lumbering and terrifying. In a group, the animals could turn the outcome of a battle. Their main advantage was that they scared the enemy, and horses would not face them, especially if they had not come across them before.

The trouble with elephants was that they would not necessarily go in the right direction. They could do serious damage to their own side if they were maddened by wounds or for some reason panicked and ran amok. Another problem was capturing and training them in the first place. Rearing elephants in captivity was a wearisome process and it took years before they were mature enough to fight in a battle. Female elephants could only be used for transport, for they tended to run away from males.

The Greeks first came across elephants on the battlefield when

Darius III, the Persian King of Kings, fielded them, unsuccessfully, against Alexander the Great at the battle of Gaugamela in 331 BC. They were imported from India and were large enough to carry a howdah with a mahout and a few soldiers armed with missiles.

Alexander never used elephants himself. They were too unreliable, as he discovered when an Indian king marshalled some against him. They blundered about, wheeling and shoving this way and that, and trampled to death as many friends as foes.

III

ELEPHANTS OVER THE ALPS

IN THE THIRD century BC, the great Carthaginian general Hannibal had high hopes of the elephant, which by this time had become a favourite 'weapon' of Alexander's successors, the Hellenistic monarchs of the Middle East. He must have come to regret his optimism.

In 218 BC, seeking revenge for Carthage's defeat at the hands of Rome a generation earlier, Hannibal marched into Italy through the south of France. He crossed the Pyrenees and advanced into Gaul with a force of 50,000 infantry, 9,000 cavalry and—his secret weapon—37 war elephants. He then forced a crossing of the river Rhône, with difficulty persuading these nervous beasts to be drawn across the water on large earth-surfaced rafts.

The Alps proved to be a more serious obstacle. Hannibal and his army encountered aggressive mountain tribesmen and unseasonable snow. Both men and animals made heavy going of it. At last, however, they found themselves in sunny pastures with woods, flowing streams and friendly locals. All Italy lay before them.

The feat was a public relations triumph, but the price was high. Since leaving Spain five months previously, Hannibal had lost more than half his army. Only 20,000 infantry and 6,000 cavalry, plus a handful of elephants, made it across the mountains. The greater part of Hannibal's supplies had been lost along with many pack animals.

Hannibal recruited more troops among the Gauls in north Italy. He spent the next sixteen years in Italy winning battle after battle, but never the war. He could not replace his elephants and they played hardly any part in his campaigns. Recalled home to save Carthage, he deployed eighty of the beasts in a final battle at Zama in 202 BC against the young Roman general Publius Cornelius Scipio (see also page 148). They were a disaster. The Roman legions opened up 'lanes' or gaps in their line, down which the elephants hurtled, to be despatched at leisure in the rear. Others stampeded back into their own forces. The Carthaginians were routed. The triumphant Scipio was rewarded with the *cognomen* Africanus or 'of Africa'.

Rome had learned how to cope with elephants when facing them, but never troubled to make use of them herself. Rome's generals took the same view as Alexander.

[iv]

CATASTROPHE AT CANNAE

IN THE EARLY stages of the Second Punic War Hannibal had already smashed two armies, but the Romans managed to assemble a huge new force of 87,000 men—eight Roman legions plus roughly the same number of Italian allied troops. This gave them a numerical advantage over Hannibal, who had only about 50,000 soldiers. Two consuls shared the command: one of them, Lucius Aemilius Paullus, was against a battle and believed Hannibal should be slowly starved out of his winter quarters in southern Italy; but the other, Gaius Terentius Varro, argued that Rome should make the most of its advantage and provoke a full-scale battle as soon as possible.

The consuls tracked Hannibal down to a dusty plain near Cannae, a small town in Apulia in southern Italy. As was the convention, they alternated command daily. Paullus was in charge when Hannibal led his army out and offered battle; he declined the invitation. The next day—2 August 216 BC—Varro accepted the challenge. He formed up his army with cavalry on the wings and a mass of infantry in the centre; the right wing abutted against a river, the left wing against rising ground.

Hannibal looked carefully at the enemy. He noticed that the Roman foot-soldiers were short of space, and as a result were in deep formation and rather squashed together: they would find it hard to manoeuvre. The Carthaginian general formed his troops in a way that would exploit the potential weakness. He placed his Celtic and Spanish infantry in a convex curve opposite the Roman centre. Behind them, at either end and out of sight, he placed two substantial detachments of his best troops—Libyan infantry, well trained and reliable. On his wings, his cavalry faced the Roman horse.

When the fighting started, the Roman centre pushed back the Celts and Spaniards so that their line changed from convex to concave. Pleased to find more space to fight in, the Romans unwisely continued to press forward until the Libyans suddenly came into view on either side and turned inwards to attack them on their flanks.

Meanwhile Hannibal's cavalry on his left wing routed its Roman counterpart. With great self-discipline, the victorious horsemen then disengaged and crossed along the back of the Roman army to attack from behind the enemy cavalry on the far wing, which fled in panic. For a second time, they pulled away and proceeded to charge the rear of the Roman infantry, which now found itself boxed in on all four sides.

The rest of the battle consisted merely of exhausting hours of blood-slippery butchery. Gradually the packed mass of legionaries and allied troops, caught like netted tuna, was cut down. Paullus, felled by a sling-stone, fought bravely to his last breath, but Varro escaped with a troop of horsemen. At the end of the day, an estimated 70,000 Romans lay dead on the battlefield, including twenty-nine senior commanders and eighty senators.

It was Rome's greatest military catastrophe, and the name of Cannae would reverberate as a source of horror for future generations of Romans.*

* The brilliance of Hannibal's tactics and his masterly execution of his battle plan have ensured that what took place near Cannae on that terrible day is still studied at military colleges today.

[v]

HANNIBAL AT THE GATES

CHILDREN, both Roman and Carthaginian, were indoctrinated to fear and hate. When Rome's nemesis Hannibal was a boy of nine, his father, Hamilcar Barca, took him to a temple and made him swear never to be a friend of Rome. He kept his word.

On campaign years later, Hannibal marched his army to the walls of Rome and flung a javelin over them. He became a bogeyman for Roman children. If they misbehaved, their parents would frighten them by saying *Hannibal ad portas*, 'Hannibal's at the city gates'.

[vi]

AN ELDERLY BIRD THAT CANNOT FLY

THE ROMANS were still too frightened of Hannibal to leave him alone after his crushing defeat at Zama in 202 BC. They chased him out of Carthage and all over the Middle East. After twenty years on the run, Hannibal was cornered and killed himself. He left a letter behind, in which he wrote: 'Let us relieve the Romans from their long-standing anxiety.' Some senators even felt a touch of compassion for him, for it was obvious that he was no longer a danger. The once fearsome general was said to be like 'an elderly bird that has lost its tail and can't fly'.

[vii]

DELENDA EST CARTHAGO

IN 202 BC, after two long wars, Rome's legions finally and comprehensively defeated the last Carthaginian army at the battle of Zama (see page 79). The seafaring Carthaginians lost their fleet (bar a few token vessels), were made to pay a huge indemnity, and were no longer allowed to run their own foreign policy or to declare war without permission. Otherwise, though, they were left alone to manage their own affairs.

This they did with conspicuous success and were soon enjoying an economic boom. They concentrated less on international trade than in the past, for Rome now ruled the waves. Instead they developed their agriculture, and they exported foodstuffs to Italy in large quantities. Nearly fifty blameless years passed, but Roman hatred remained undimmed.

A visiting senatorial delegation was horrified to notice the revival in their old enemy's fortunes, but it was hard to know what could be done about this, for Carthage had clearly given up its ambition to be a great power and was keeping strictly to the terms of the peace treaty. The Carthaginians went out of their way to be helpful to Rome, sending free grain when the Republic was engaged in wars in the Balkans and the Middle East.

An aged patriot, Marcus Porcius Cato the Elder,* launched an anti-Carthaginian hate campaign. He ended every speech he gave in the Senate, whatever the topic, with the same sentence: 'And in my considered opinion, Carthage must be destroyed'—*delenda est Carthago*.

Carthage was a ripe fruit ready for the plucking. Leading senators privately decided on war and waited for a convenient pretext. This soon came along when the Carthaginians foolishly allowed themselves to be provoked by an aggressive local African king and fought a brief and unsuccessful campaign against him. Rome showed its displeasure and began raising troops, just 'in case of an emergency'. The Carthaginians were not deceived, and at once submitted their unconditional surrender.

This did not stop the Senate from sending out in 149 BC a large army to northern Africa with secret instructions to destroy the city. Inconveniently, the Carthaginians agreed to every Roman demand, until they were given a final ultimatum: 'Abandon your city, and rebuild another one nine miles inland.'

This was too much for a proud nation with a history of seafaring, and the desperate but enraged Carthaginians decided to

* So called because he had a later namesake—Cato the Younger—who fought against Julius Caesar and lost.

resist. It was a hopeless struggle, and they knew it. It took four years, but the city finally fell in 146 BC. All survivors were sold into slavery. What remained of buildings and temples was razed to the ground, and the victorious Roman commander, Publius Cornelius Scipio Aemilianus, Africanus' adopted grandson, uttered a solemn curse that where Carthage once stood should forever be pasture for sheep.

[viii]

ROME'S GREATEST ATROCITY?

THE ROMANS made a great deal of noise about their honesty and good faith. In theory, they only fought defensive wars and were never the aggressors. It was always their opponents who were underhand, and they complained bitterly in wartime when the enemy laid ambushes. They kept their special scorn for the cheating Carthaginians and their fundamental untrustworthiness. *Punica fides*, literally 'Carthaginian good faith', was a phrase that signified the exact opposite.

In reality the Romans were by no means averse to using underhand tactics themselves. And perhaps no act in Roman history was more cynical and calculated than the utter destruction of the great sea-port of Carthage in 146 BC—at that time an ally who had done nothing wrong. There was not one jot of justification for this murderous vandalism, the only motive for which was greed for Carthaginian wealth. What price *Romana fides*?

THE GODS

i

THE SQUEAK OF A RAT

THE ROMANS were deeply religious, but their religion was a complex web of superstitions. It had little or nothing to do with individual spirituality or with theological doctrine. In fact, the life of the spirit was regarded with deep suspicion; all that was required were ceremonial formulas for ascertaining the will of the gods and averting their displeasure.

Every aspect of life, from large to small, was governed by ritual, whether it was the repair and maintenance of a bridge or the business of making a treaty. The crucial point was that religious ceremonies had to be conducted with absolute accuracy. If a mistake was made, or there was some interruption—for example, if a rat squeaked or a priest's hat fell off—the entire procedure had to be repeated. On one occasion a sacrifice had to be conducted thirty times before the priest got it right.

ii

AN UNPREDICTABLE PANTHEON

THE GODS were incalculable powers who had to be placated at every turn. And across the Mediterranean, or *mare nostrum*, 'our sea', there was a multitude of them. Few objected to this and there was little sense of competition. This was because people tended to see the gods of others as being the same as their own, but worshipped under different names. The Romans had a list of deities who looked and behaved like human beings and had counterparts among the gods and goddesses of ancient Greece. So the king of the gods was called Jupiter in Italy and Zeus in Greece; Venus, the Roman goddess of love, corresponded to the Greek Aphrodite; and Rome's god of war Mars had his counterpart in the deity known to the Greeks as Ares.

Gods were everywhere. Minor divinities or spirits populated the Roman landscape and the home. Rivers and woods had their individual tutelary gods and celebratory festivals marked the agricultural year. These various deities were not examples of moral perfection, although mortals were expected to acknowledge a moral code. Rather, they represented human passions and unmanageable external forces writ large. Their judgements and interventions were almost impossible to predict, and the purpose of religion was to work out what the gods had in mind and to get them on one's side.

[III]

KILLING THE FATTED CALF

IT IS HARD to exaggerate the centrality of the ceremonial killing of animals to Roman religious activity. It was an everyday event—it was how one could give thanks to the gods, ask them for a favour or find out what their wishes were.

Specialist priests from Etruria (Tuscany), the *haruspices*, examined and interpreted the intestines of sacrificed animals for anything irregular or unusual. Domestic animals—a lamb, a goat or a young ox, or more modestly a chicken—were slaughtered in vast numbers. Their throats were slit with a special knife and their blood was gathered in a shallow dish for pouring on the altar. The meat was cooked, formally offered to the relevant god, and then eaten by the worshippers. Altars swam in the detritus of death.*

Even the minor divinities of the field and farmyard received their sacrificial dues. The poet Horace illustrates the point in a famous ode he wrote in honour of a spring on his farm in the Alban Hills, the 'fountain of Bandusia'. He plans to sacrifice a young goat in its honour, pouring its blood into the water as a libation:

> Spring of Bandusia, whose crystalline
> Glitter deserves our garlands and best wine
> You shall be given a kid
> Tomorrow. Horns half-hid
> In a bulging forehead forecast love and war –
> A fine destiny, but not the one in store.†

* As well as examining the entrails of sacrificed animals, *haruspices* explained prodigies and portents, especially when lightning struck in public places. Emperors and consuls were often assisted by a personal *haruspex*.

† Translation by James Michie; see Further Reading for bibliographical details. For more on Horace and other poets of ancient Rome, see pages 160–62.

[iv]

AUGUSTUS IN LILLIPUT

ROMAN RELIGION pinned down public officials like Gulliver in Lilliput: its rules and regulations limited their freedom of action and took up an inordinate amount of their time. The emperor Augustus was no fool: when establishing his regime in 27 BC, he made his life significantly easier and streamlined his workload by arranging to have state power conferred on him without actually having to hold high office.*

[v]

A YEAR OF FESTIVALS

THE ROMAN year was liberally sprinkled with public festivals. It has been calculated that in the first century AD Rome enjoyed one day of holiday for every work day. At first sight this looks like an almost suicidal approach to agricultural and industrial productivity. But in practice workers did not down tools for every festival—and the idea of a weekend had not yet been invented.

Rome had a system of market days which were held after every eight days (the so-called *nundinum*, or ninth day). Under the emperors this was reduced to a seven-day week (inspired by the seven planets of the solar system, as then understood). But there was as yet no 'Lord's Day' for rest, relaxation and religious observance.

Some festivals were moveable feasts. The *pontifices*—priests who were members of the College of Pontiffs and had supreme control of the state religion—decided the dates of these celebrations. They also kept a record of the major events of every year, the Annals. Some days were believed to be lucky (*fasti*) and others accursed (*nefasti*). Public business could only be conducted on a lucky day, and the *pontifices* decided which days fell into which category.

* For further details of Augustus' dispensation in 27 BC, see page 43.

[vi]

LORDS OF MISRULE

A FAVOURITE festival was the Saturnalia, a pagan version of Christmas. It was named after Saturn, who had been the chief god before his son Jupiter supplanted him. He was supposed to have presided over a Golden Age, a time when all people were equal.

The fun and games usually lasted between 17 and 23 December and were a time of general disorder and anarchy. Ordinary social rules were turned on their head. Among families a Lord of Misrule was appointed; everyone had to obey his instructions—to dance, sing or commit any kind of absurdity. Slaves were treated as equals, ate in the family dining room and were served by their owners. People kept their front doors open and exchanged presents—symbolic candles and clay dolls. Respectable men went out into the street and sang—usually taken to be a sure sign of madness. Buskers, snake-charmers and jugglers filled the Roman Forum.

Those without a sense of humour complained. 'It is December and yet the whole city is in a sweat,' Seneca, Nero's tutor, moaned. 'It takes courage to remain dry and sober when everyone else is pissed and puking.'*

[vii]

READING THE BIRD SIGNS

A SECOND priestly college, after the *pontifices*, was that of the augurs. These religious officials, too, were elected for life. On major public occasions and at moments of crisis, an augur's task was to take the auspices, or 'bird signs'. He did not foretell the future, but searched for signs of divine approval—in the song, behaviour or flight of birds, in thunder and lightning, or in the movement of animals—which he would then interpret.

* The Christian connotations of Christmas seem to be fading fast, and we are apparently regressing to the simple joyfulness of the Saturnalia.

Augurs observed the heavens, indicating with a wand the part of the sky he would watch for birds to fly through. This sacred space was called the *templum*, from which comes our word 'temple'.

[viii]

NEVER SNUB THE CHICKENS

ON ONE FAMOUS occasion during the First Punic War, in the third century BC, a Roman admiral, Publius Claudius Pulcher, took the auspices before sailing into battle against the Carthaginians. Unfortunately the sacred chickens refused their food. This was a bad sign, and Claudius would have been wise to cancel his plans to sail that day. Instead, he lost his temper and threw the fowls into the sea, with the words 'If they won't eat, let them drink.' He went on to fight his battle—and lost convincingly.

[ix]

A VESTAL SNUFFED OUT

FOR THE ROMANS their country, the Republic, was a very large household. And at the heart of every household was the hearth; with its warmth-imparting fire it embodied the comfort and security of the home.

In Rome's central square, the Forum, there stands to this day the ruin of a small circular pillared structure. This was the temple of the goddess of the hearth, Vesta, and inside flickered an eternal flame. It was tended by six priestesses, the Vestal Virgins, who lived in a special convent next door.

The Vestals were selected by lot from six- to ten-year-old girls of good family and were appointed for a term of thirty years, after which they were allowed to retire. As priestesses, they could expect a life of luxury and prestige; they were highly respected and enjoyed important privileges—unlike other women, they were free to own property, to write their wills and even to vote. If one of them touched a condemned man, he was immediately pardoned.

But a Vestal had to be careful. If the fire died on her watch, she would be stripped and whipped by the Vestals' guardian, the high priest or *pontifex maximus*.* To preserve the proprieties, this was done in the dark and (belt and braces) with a screen interposed. There was one more serious downside. A Vestal Virgin was obliged, not unreasonably, to be a virgin. If she was found to have slept with a man, a terrible fate awaited her: she would be buried alive. Early in the reign of the emperor Domitian, three Vestals—half the complement—were found guilty of lewdness, but Domitian was in a forgiving mood and allowed them to choose their own form of death.

Some years later the senior Vestal, Cornelia, who had already been acquitted of the same charge, was again arraigned. Domitian seems to have decided to make an example of her. He tried her in her absence and no witnesses were called. Cornelia vigorously asserted her chastity, and a political insider and contemporary, Pliny the Younger, observed: 'Whether she was innocent or not, she certainly appeared to be so.' Nevertheless, Domitian convicted her and, in his capacity as *pontifex maximus*, accompanied her to a stretch of rising ground just inside the city walls called the Campus Sceleratus, the 'Field of Crime'.

Here there was a small underground chamber, containing a couch, a lamp and a table with a little food on it (this was so that the state could not be accused of directly bringing about her death). Cornelia's dress caught on something as she climbed down a ladder into the tiny vault, and Domitian, who was standing beside her, offered her his hand. She drew back in disgust and pushed his arm away. She took care to lower herself onto the couch without offence to her modesty. The ladder was pulled up and the access hole filled with earth. Cornelia was left alone to meet her end, whether through eventual asphyxiation or, perhaps, by means of a more immediate suicide with poison or knife.

The affair left a very bad impression, and a senator was persuaded to make a tardy confession of having had sex with the Vestal. Nobody believed him.

* Curiously, in light of its pagan origin, the title *pontifex maximus* is still used in the Vatican.

[x]

HONOURING THE FAMILY GODS

FAMILIES all had shrines to the *lares*, guardians of the hearth who protected the home, and the *penates*, who were spirits of the larder and the store cupboard, who looked after the family's food, wine, olive oil and other supplies. These shrines were cupboards which stood in the corner of the *atrium*, or entrance hall, of a Roman house or hung on the wall and contained small statuettes of the household divinities (or painted images of them). To honour them, a portion of the family meal would be set aside and thrown on the flames of their hearth.

[xi]

MIGHTY MICE

DEVOTION to duty is expected of public servants, especially soldiers, but the Romans took the idea to an extraordinary and bloody extreme. In a dire emergency, a consul, one of the state's two chief executives and commanders-in-chief (see page 24), was empowered to consecrate himself to death and the Underworld in a bizarre ritual called *devotio* (from which we derive our word 'devotion'). The sacrifice of *his* life would bring the same *devotio* onto the heads of his enemies—in other words, it would destroy them too.

In 340 BC it so happened that both of the year's consuls, Titus Manlius Imperiosus Torquatus and his colleague Publius Decius Mus, were commanding a Roman army during a war with the Samnites, fierce hill tribesmen who lived in the Apennine mountains. A soothsayer scrutinized the livers of some sacrificial animals for any abnormality that might reveal the displeasure of the gods; in that case hostilities would have to be called off. He gave Manlius a clean bill of health; however, he pointed out that the head of Decius' liver had been cut in the wrong place. That apart, the victim was acceptable to the gods. Decius replied coolly: 'If my colleague's sacrifice went well, then that should be good enough.'

The army advanced with Manlius on the right wing and Decius on the left. The lines clashed and the Romans were pushed back. It looked as if the day was lost. In this moment of crisis, Decius called to a priest from the college of *pontifices*, who presided over the army's religious rituals: 'We need the gods' help. Come on now, you are a state pontiff of the Roman people. Dictate to me the form of words by which I may "devote" myself.'

The priest told him to put on his purple-edged toga, to veil his head, and with one hand protruding from the toga to touch his chin, stand on a spear laid on the ground and repeat the following words:

> Janus, Jupiter, father Mars, Quirinus, Bellona, Lares,* New Gods, Native Gods, divinities who have power over us and our enemies, and gods of the Underworld: I supplicate and revere you, I seek your favour and beseech you, that you prosper the might and victory of the Roman people, the Quirites, and afflict the enemies of the Roman people, the Quirites, with terror, dread and death. As I have pronounced the words, on behalf of the Republic of the Roman nation of Quirites, and of the army, legions and auxiliaries of the Roman nation of the Quirites, so I devote myself and with me the legions and auxiliaries of our enemies to the gods of the Underworld and to Earth.

Decius then sent a message to his colleague to tell him what he had done. He reorganized his toga so that his arms were free, leapt on a horse and rode directly into the enemy's ranks. He fell under a hail of missiles. In due course the battle was won and the Samnites fled. Decius was found beneath a pile of corpses and given a hero's funeral.

Nearly fifty years later his grandson, also called Publius Decius Mus, is reported to have done the same thing in another battle with the Samnites. Both events seem to have been historical. Each of these acts of divinely approved suicide, followed in short order by the rout of the enemy, proved to be a powerful spell.

The word *mus* is Latin for 'mouse', an implausibly pusillanimous name for such a heroic pair. They more than made up for it by their courage in the field.

* Quirinus was a name for Rome's founder Romulus; Bellona was a goddess of war; the Lares were household gods.

[xii]

THE CULT OF THE GREAT MOTHER

THE ROMAN state religion, with its obsessive rituals and lack of concern for personal religious experience, was dry and unsatisfying for those with more emotional needs. Exotic foreign cults, which offered spiritual gratification and release, were very popular. They kept opening up shop in Rome and, under the Republic, kept being closed down. The Senate was nervous of excitable gatherings which often met in secret or at least unsupervised. But sometimes it had no choice but to let cults in.

In 206 BC a prophecy was discovered which stated that if ever a foreign enemy were to invade Italy, he would only be driven out if Cybele, the 'Great Mother', was brought to Rome (in the shape of a holy black stone). Cybele was a goddess of fertility and wild nature, the centre of whose cult was in Phrygia. Desperate to magic Hannibal and his army away from Italy, the Senate welcomed her into the city and built a new temple for her on the Palatine.

Cybele and her youthful consort Attis expressed the annual cycle of life, death and rebirth in a manner that a Roman traditionalist would find distinctly unappealing. At her spring festivities, self-castrated eunuchs danced to cymbals and drums. These were her *galli*, or cockerels (so called from their ravings); they wore women's clothes and heavy make-up, and whipped themselves till they bled. The goddess's partner Attis had set the precedent. As the poet Catullus of the first century BC writes, he

> moved by madness, bemused in his mind,
> lopped off the load of his loins with a sharp flint.
> Woman now, and aware of her wasted manhood,
> still bleeding, the blood bedaubing the ground still,
> with feminine fingers she fetched the light drum
> that makes the music, Great Mother, at your mysteries.

The arrival of Cybele and her disreputable acolytes did the trick, for it was not long before Hannibal left Italy for a last stand near Carthage in northern Africa (see page 81).

Respectable opinion found Cybele and her disciples to be most un-Roman. However, it would be *lèse-majesté* to get rid of her now that she had done her bit. She stayed, but great care was taken to control the impact of the new cult. The goddess's priests were and remained foreigners, and their numbers and activities were strictly limited.

xiii

GODS, MORTALS AND IN-BETWEENERS

'I THINK I AM becoming a god,' the emperor Vespasian remarked in AD 79 when he recognized he was on the point of death. This was a typical dry joke of his. He was referring to the fact that most rulers of the Roman world were awarded a posthumous honour—a vote by the Senate to deify them.

As far as we can tell from the surviving record, of the fifty-four emperors in the period between Augustus' death in AD 14 and AD 337, thirty-six were deified, together with twenty-seven members of their families. Each received a cult and had his (or occasionally her) own priests and festival. Altars and temples were consecrated to them.

To the modern mind, making a man or a woman a god seems mystifying and absurd, but the ancient Greeks and Romans did not draw such a clear distinction between the mortal and the immortal. Their gods—the likes of Mercury, Bacchus and Apollo—looked and acted like human beings, although they were of course much more powerful. Then there were the in-betweeners. A mythical hero like Rome's founder Romulus wasn't quite a god, but he was more than an ordinary man. Religious ceremonies were held in his honour.

In exceptional cases a bridge could be built between the human and the divine. In Asia Minor there was a tradition of worshipping great men and according divine status to rulers. People there were happy to worship the emperor Augustus, although he was careful to forbid his cult in Italy where republican sentiment was still strong. With the Senate's approval he was deified after his death, though, and this became a tradition for many of his successors.*

[xiv]

A SHRINE FOR TULLIOLA

It wasn't only kings or emperors who qualified for divinity. In the first century BC, the Roman statesman Cicero was overwhelmed with grief when his daughter Tullia—his beloved Tulliola—died a month after giving birth to a son. He planned a permanent shrine to her memory. If the heroes of Greek mythology could be raised to heaven, he told himself, then she deserved the same honour—'and I shall give it to her'. In the event he gave up the idea, but nobody would have objected if he had built the shrine.

[xv]

THE DIVINE PUMPKIN

Did the Romans truly believe that their rulers became gods? It is hard to be sure, but we do know that some rationalists found the whole business deeply silly. Seneca, writer and politician in the first century AD, was one of them. He was so irritated by the deification of the emperor Claudius, with whom he had been on bad terms, that he wrote a skit about it.

He called it the *Apocolocyntosis*, or 'Pumpkinification', of the Deified Claudius—a play on words with apotheosis, the process of deification. He has Claudius arrive on Olympus, the home of the gods, where he is tried for various crimes and sent down to hell. Claudius was an inveterate gambler and his punishment was to roll dice in a box without a bottom—for eternity.

* The exceptions were despots such as the emperor Domitian, whose memory was cursed.

[xvi]

BOY GOD VERSUS SON OF GOD

It was a close call, but for a time the cult of a Bithynian boy called Antinous promised to outstrip in popularity that of a Judaean called Jesus. Had things turned out differently, we might be talking today of our Antinoan rather than our Christian civilization.

Antinous was in his teens when he caught the eye of the emperor Hadrian, who fancied male adolescents. Their affair seems to have been happy, but in AD 130 the imperial favourite drowned in the Nile. The official verdict was misadventure. But Hadrian was ailing, and some said that Antinous had sacrificed himself in a magical rite for his lover's recovery.

Whatever the truth, the emperor was devastated. He had the dead boy officially deified. Respectable opinion was shocked, but the cult of Antinous spread like a forest blaze throughout the empire. Temples and shrines were built in his honour and cities everywhere commissioned numberless statues of the dead boy; 115 survive of an estimated 2,000 carved in antiquity. In Egypt a new city, Antinopolis, was founded in his memory.*

The worship of the reborn Bithynian was genuinely popular, so much so that Christian worthies were seriously rattled. St Athanasius fumed at the 'new god Antinous', a creature who had been the 'sordid and loathsome instrument of his master's lust'. In fact, Antinous and Christ had more in common than appears at first sight. They shared a Unique Selling Point, in that both of them were young men who died before their time and returned to life as gods.

* Two thousand years later, this ageless youth still has his followers. He is the only personality from the ancient world known to the author to have websites dedicated to his cult—three at the last count; they tend towards the homoerotic.

[xvii]

ROMAN CANDLES

CHRISTIANS—or Galileans, as they were initially called—made their first appearance in Rome during the reign of the emperor Claudius, who, probably in 49 BC, expelled them for causing riots. The authorities were a little vague about the Christians at this early stage and regarded them as no more than a Jewish sect. They were wrongly blamed for the great fire of Rome that caused widespread devastation to the city in AD 64. The historian Tacitus described their gruesome fate:

> Nero fabricated scapegoats—and punished with every refinement the notoriously depraved Christians (as they were popularly called) … Their deaths were made farcical. Dressed in wild animals' skins, they were torn to pieces by dogs, or crucified, or made into torches to be ignited after dark as substitutes for daylight.

[xviii]

A THREAT TO PROPER ORDER

ORDINARY Romans under the empire had no objection to novel cults provided that they did not practise cruel or outlandish rituals. In fact, they saw them as a supplement to the state religion. At the beginning of the second century AD Christianity was still very much a minority sect. It apparently presented no threat to the political status quo, and many of its believers were pacifists.*

Yet from time to time the authorities launched persecutions in an attempt to suppress the religion. Non-citizens who admitted their Christianity faced execution, and citizens (like St Paul) would be deported to stand trial in Rome, where they could be condemned to death.

So what made Christianity so unpopular with the Roman authorities? One simple reason: they refused to take part in

* There was a popular slander that Christians practised cannibalism behind closed doors, but there was no proof of this: it was an obvious misunderstanding of the Eucharist.

religious ceremonies venerating the emperor. This was counter to the natural and proper order of things, it was felt, and might persuade the gods to withdraw their blessing from the Roman empire.

[*xix*]

THE ENLIGHTENED GOVERNOR

IN AD 111 Pliny the Younger, a civilized and compassionate man, took up his new post as governor of Bithynia, a province in north-west Asia Minor (in what is now Turkey). He was baffled by the high incidence of complaints against Christians in the province. An anonymous pamphlet outing a number of Christians was being circulated and an informer had come up with yet more names. Knowing little about the sect, he made some enquiries. He found that Christians met for church services and sang hymns, after which they ate a meal with harmless ingredients. All quite innocent.

The line Pliny took at first was to question suspects. If they insisted on confessing to be Christian, he applied the usual penalties. But what should he do in the case of those who denied being Christian? Or those who had renounced their belief and been perfectly willing to take the usual test and make offerings of wine and incense to a statue of the emperor? Perhaps they should be pardoned. And what was the real crime—simply being a Christian or committing the kind of offence associated with being Christian?

The governor was uneasy. He was not sure how far to take his investigation and whether or not to press charges, so he wrote to the emperor Trajan seeking advice 'about this wretched cult'. In his response the emperor complimented Pliny on his thoughtful approach. Trajan was quite clear that there should be no persecution:

> These people must not be hunted out; if they are brought before you and the charge against them is proved, they must be punished, but in the case of anyone who denies he is a Christian, and proves it by praying to our gods, he should be pardoned as a result of his repentance, however suspect his past conduct. But pamphlets circulated

anonymously must play no part in any accusation. They create the worst sort of precedent and are quite out of keeping with the spirit of our age.

Now here, one might think, was an emperor worth venerating.

[xx]

A HIGHER DUTY

MANY CHRISTIANS, when arrested, recanted or denied their beliefs. But a few sought martyrdom with an intensity of will that to modern eyes seems suicidal. In AD 203 Perpetua, a 22-year-old Carthaginian woman, left some notes written during her last days before being thrown to the wild beasts for professing Christianity. In them she rejects the ties of duty and affection towards her family:*

> While we were still under arrest, my father, out of love for me, was trying to persuade me to turn away and to cast me down from the faith.
>
> 'Father,' I said, 'do you see this vase, for instance, lying here, or waterpot or whatever it is?'
>
> 'Yes, I do,' he said.
>
> And I told him, 'Could it be called by any other name than what it is?'
>
> And he said, 'No.'
>
> 'So neither can I be called anything other than what I am, a Christian.'
>
> At this word, my father was so furious that he moved towards me as if to pluck my eyes out. But he only upset me, and then he left. He was, in fact, beaten, he and his Devil's arguments.
>
> For a few days afterwards, I gave thanks to the Lord that I was separated from my father, and I was refreshed by his absence.

In spite of her unmoveable determination, father and daughter were reconciled before she was sent to the arena, where she was gored to death by a wild bull.

* It was the kind of attitude of mind shown by Perpetua that led Pliny the Younger to call Christianity a 'degenerate sort of cult carried to extravagant lengths'. The kind of mutual incomprehension seen here is reminiscent of relations between today's secular West and the more extreme forms of political Islam.

[xxi]

A MARTYR TO THE FAITH

THE PROPAGANDISTS of Christ needed plenty of strong stuff to stir the admiration and the fears of the faithful. The imaginative accounts we have of the martyrdom of St Eulalia in Spain in the early fourth century more than fitted the bill.

At Barcino (today's Barcelona),* Eulalia was asked to recant. When she refused, she was subjected to thirteen tortures. Among other things, her breasts were cut off, she was rolled down a city street inside a barrel studded with broken glass, she was locked naked in a stable full of fleas and had boiling lead poured over her, she was crucified on an X-shaped cross, and finally she had her head chopped off. According to tradition, a dove flew out of the severed neck.

Eulalia died on 12 February AD 303,† during the first year of the Great Persecution launched by the emperor Diocletian. This lasted for nearly a decade and 20,000 people are reported to have lost their lives. Diocletian's persecution was Rome's final attack on the Christians. The year after it ended the emperor Constantine converted to the faith, and before the century was out Christianity had become the official religion of the state.

* So named after Hannibal's father, Hamilcar Barca.

† The Catalans remember Eulalia to this day and an annual festival in her name is held across Spain. The poet Federico Garcia Lorca, whose imagination was stirred by the exotic terrors of Spanish Catholicism, wrote a memorable poem about her fate, from which these lines are taken:

> For the breasts of Eulalia
> The Consul demands a platter
> ...
> Her sex trembles, disarrayed
> Like a bird in a thicket.
> On the ground, unruly
> Her severed hands writhe,
> still crossed in a feeble
> decapitated prayer.

(From *The Selected Poems of Federico Garcia Lorca*, New Directions Publishing Corporation, New York, 1955 and 2005)

SEX AND MARRIAGE

i

A MIXED AND BALANCED DIET

For the Romans, sexual desire was an appetite to be satisfied, like hunger or thirst. It had little or nothing to do with love, and it was not expected to play a role in the formation of relationships. The shame that Christianity came to associate with love-making—and which is still a mark of Western civilization—was missing from the ancient world.

Nor did the Romans have any idea of sexual status, of being gay or straight. Sex was what one did, not what one was; in Rome it didn't matter much whom you fancied—man or woman, boy or girl. Homosexual behaviour was widespread and generally acceptable. However, taking pleasure exclusively in one object of desire or in one kind of sexual practice *was* suspect. There was nothing wrong with sodomy, but you shouldn't specialize in it (or anything else): a varied diet was best.

And having too much sex was another sign of effeminacy. Excessive ejaculation was considered to be weakening. Once the elder Cato, a stickler for morality, came across a young nobleman leaving a brothel and told him: 'Keep up the good work!' When he came across him again in similar circumstances, he snapped: 'When I complimented you on good work, I didn't mean you should make the place your home.'

ii

NICOMEDES' BITCH

Julius Caesar's soldiers, marching in a triumphal procession to celebrate his victories in Gaul, sang rude songs about their leader:

Home we bring our bald whoremonger;
  Romans, lock your wives away!
All the bags of gold you lent him
  Went his Gallic tarts to pay.

Sexual virility in a man was something to be proud of. Caesar had a reputation as a sexual omnivore, and both sexes were on the menu. When it was quipped that he was 'the husband of all women and the wife of all husbands', there was as much envy as criticism in the remark.

But an alleged incident when Caesar was a youth was something different. Apparently he had let himself be buggered by a randy king of Bithynia, Nicomedes IV. It was not good for a Roman's reputation to be charged with effeminacy, with playing the passive role in bed: upstanding men should penetrate, not be penetrated. The legions sang about that too, and Caesar had to smile and put up with it.

iii

NO EXTRAMARITAL SEX, PLEASE —WE'RE ROMANS!

IN ROME there was one immutable rule that limited sexual activity—if only in theory. Outside marriage, a Roman was not meant to have sex with another free-born citizen, of whatever gender. It was fine for a chap to satisfy his urges with a prostitute, provided that such an arrangement prevented him from bothering his friends' wives. Marriage in the upper class was seldom an affair of the heart.* Generally it was a business or political alliance, and romance wasn't allowed to get in the way.

One result of these constraints was that good-looking slaves were in great demand. They were obliged to have sex with their masters if required, and in the absence of reliable contraception, this was likely to result in slave women giving birth to the illegitimate sons of their owners (or for that matter of their owners' legitimate sons). Blood lines inside a household could become exceedingly complicated.

* Turia and the poet Sulpicia were rare exceptions; see pages 230 and 223 for their stories.

iv

A POET'S TIPS ON PULLING

THE POET OVID was a man who not only fancied women, he *liked* them. He wrote many erotic poems, and they express what it was like to be a sexually active and straight young Roman about town two thousand years ago.*

Ovid's usual subject matter was the pursuit of pretty girls. He enjoyed hunting down married women or respectable young girls. He didn't believe in paying for sex (and some of his poems may in fact be about his wife), though at a pinch a hooker would suffice. In practice, this meant going cruising.

'Here's what to do,' he says. 'Stroll down some shady colonnade. But the theatre's curving tiers should form your favourite hunting ground, whether you are looking for a lover or a playmate, a one-night stand or a long-term affair.' The theatre was 'always dangerous for pretty girls'. Women of fashion swarmed there like ants or bees. 'They come to look, they come to be looked at. Chastity doesn't stand a chance.'

Then there was the racecourse, the Circus Maximus:

> You'll sit right beside your mistress, be sure to press against her whenever you can. Keep an eye on whoever may be sitting behind you, don't let him rub his knee against her smooth back.

And Ovid advises young men to look smart if they want to score:

> Keep pleasantly clean. Do your exercises and get a good tan. Make sure your toga fits and is spotless. Don't lace your shoes too tightly, check your buckles are rust-free, and avoid loose-fitting shoes. Don't let your looks be ruined by a hopeless barber... keep your nails short and clean. Get rid of nose hairs and freshen your smelly breath.

* His *Amores* ('My Love Affairs') first appeared in 16 BC and the *Ars Amatoria* ('The Art of Love') about 2 BC.

v

EVERYONE HAS HIS OFF DAYS

OVID RECALLS lying in bed with an attractive pick-up—but nothing happened. 'I was limp, disgusting, dead.' The young woman tried every trick, but 'my member hung slack, as though numbed by hemlock'. Eventually she lost her temper. 'You're sick,' she said. 'Stop wasting my time. Either some witch has hexed you or you've just been making love to another girl.' She jumped out of bed, nightdress flying, and ran off.

Being a writer, Ovid felt impelled to pen a poem about his predicament. As he described the fiasco, something stirred, too late:

Yet now – what terrible timing! – just look at it, stiff and urgent
 Eager to go campaigning, get on with the job.
Oh why can't you lie down? I'm ashamed of you, you bastard –
 I've been caught out by your promises before.
You let me down, it was *your* fault I landed weaponless
 In this embarrassing and expensive fix.

vi

A BAD, SAD END

OVID'S WRITINGS infuriated the emperor Augustus, who wanted to revive Rome's traditional virtues and did not appreciate a sex guidebook, however poetical it was. However, they were right up the street of the emperor's daughter Julia, who knew how to have a good time.* We are told that she took part in drinking parties in the Forum, walked the streets looking for excitement, and committed adultery with various leading Romans. But Julia was very careful. She is said to have restricted full intercourse to times when she was pregnant: 'Passengers are never allowed on board,' she remarked, 'till the hold is full.' Eventually someone told Augustus of his daughter's activities and

* She had something in common, in this respect, with the House of Windsor's Princess Margaret.

she was banished to a small island in the Mediterranean.

Ovid was a friend of Julia's equally flighty daughter, Julia the Younger, who also got into trouble with Augustus.* The poet was somehow involved in the scandal, and in AD 8 he was dismissed to a dreary town on the Black Sea. Here, he lived out his days writing an interminable poem about his miserable fate, called *Tristia*, or 'Sad Things'.

vii

A BREACH OF FAITH

EARLY in the second century BC the consul and general Lucius Quinctius Flamininus was conducting an affair with a notorious rent boy from Carthage called Philippus. He persuaded the boy to join him on campaign in Cisalpine Gaul (today's Po Valley). Philippus complained at having to leave Rome just before the gladiatorial games, which he had had to miss. One evening they were having a dinner party and were flushed with wine when a senior Gallic deserter arrived in the camp and requested the consul's protection. He asked for an audience.

The man was brought into the tent and began to address Flamininus through an interpreter. While he was speaking, the consul turned to his lover and said: 'Since you missed the gladiatorial show, would you like to see this Gaul die?' The boy nodded, not taking the offer seriously. Flamininus then drew his sword, which was hanging above his couch, struck the Gaul on the head, and then ran him through as he tried to escape. This breach of good faith towards someone seeking Rome's friendship was shocking enough, but what was really dreadful even to a hardened Roman mind was the casual ending of a life at a boozy party.

* For more on the fates of the younger Julia and her mother, see pages 44 and 45.

viii

A GNARLED OLD GLADIATOR

Like boxers and footballers today, gladiators were sex objects. They were virility in armour, their glamour much enhanced by the risk of an early death in the arena. In Pompeii an anonymous graffito has been found scrawled on a wall: 'Celadus the Thracian gladiator is the delight of all the girls.' And not only girls, the writer might have added, for gladiators won male admirers too.

The Roman satirist Juvenal wrote some scalding verses about an ageing heart-throb who attracted the attention of a middle-aged millionairess. He may have had a real person in mind:

> What were the youthful good looks that set Eppia ablaze?
> What did she see in him to put up with
> Being called a fighter's groupie? For her sweetheart, her Sergius
> Was no chicken, forty at least, with one gashed arm that gave
> Prospect of retirement. Deformities disfigured his face –
> A scar where his helmet chafed, a great wen on his nose, a nasty
> Discharge continually trickling from one eye. So what?
> *He was a gladiator.* That makes anyone a pretty boy;
> And this was what she chose over her sons, her country, her sister,
> And her husband.

ix

'WHERE YOU ARE GAIUS, I AM GAIA'

All that was legally necessary for a Roman marriage to take place was for a man and woman to live together with the intention of establishing a lasting union. When that intention ceased, so did the marriage.

By the first century BC old forms of marriage which placed the wife in her husband's power had given way to an arrangement which allowed her to control her own property and either remain under her father's authority or act as an independent person. She brought a dowry with her, repayable in the event of a divorce. The happy couple had to be Roman citizens (or should possess a right of *conubium*, intermarriage). As a rule, a woman married young, as early as thirteen or fourteen years, but men were often much older.

Weddings often took place in June. The bride wore a white tunic of flannel or muslin with a brilliant orange veil. As with a modern wedding dress, she never wore it again. Her hair was parted into six locks fastened by woollen ribbons into a cone. The partings were made by a bent spearhead, preferably one with which a gladiator had been killed (this may have been to ward off evil spirits).

The young woman (or girl) presented herself to the groom and declared herself his wife by repeating an old formula: *ubi tu Gaius, ego Gaia*, 'where you are Gaius, I am Gaia'. After a banquet, the groom pretended to abduct her and she was escorted from her old home to her new one in a rowdy procession. She decorated the front door with strands of wool and smeared it with lard and oil. She was lifted over the threshold (as if she had never entered the house for the first time and had always been a member of her new family). A sacrifice was made, usually of a pig, and a marriage contract was signed.

The happy couple retired to the bedroom to obscene comments from the guests. Of course happiness was not the point, and certainly not the invariable outcome. A bachelor once dreamed that he was being crucified. An interpreter of dreams predicted marriage: 'a bond but not an easy one.'

[*x*]

A GRIM TRADE

NONE OF the forms of contraception available to Romans was particularly reliable. The only sure method of birth control was infanticide.

For much of Rome's history, fathers had the power of life and death over their family members, and even when this was forbidden by law, they regularly got rid of a newborn baby because it was another girl or disabled or illegitimate, or just because it was one too many. In its first days of life the infant would be taken and abandoned somewhere in the open, where it died of cold or starved or was eaten by dogs. In towns, babies would often be left beside a public latrine or cesspit.

If a child's luck was in, it might be found and cared for by a childless couple, but it was more likely to fall victim to the dismal trade in exposed children. Some were snatched by slave traffickers and brought up for sale, while others were taken by men of almost unbelievable cruelty, who would cripple their victims and, when they were old enough, force them to go out and beg. A disgusted commentator writes in the first century AD:

> Finding a different barbarity for each child, this bone-breaker cuts off the arms of one of them, slices the sinews of another. He deforms, and he castrates. With another child, he stunts its shoulder-blades, beating them into an ugly hump, looking for a laugh from his barbarity.

The frequency of female infanticide led to the population of the Roman empire being heavily skewed towards boys. We don't know the exact figures, but it has been estimated that of its 60 million inhabitants, only about 24 million were women. Perhaps a third of infants died in their first year, whether from exposure or disease.

xi

A LIFE-OR-DEATH DECISION

At about the time of the birth of Christ, a certain father, Hilarion, was away from home on business. To his much loved and pregnant wife he sent a letter which was later unearthed in an ancient rubbish tip in the sands of Egypt. In it he wrote:

> Should you have the baby before I come back, if it's a boy, keep it. If it's a girl, throw it away.

[xii]

DESPERATE MEASURES

Contraception was a woman's responsibility and apparently Roman males did not know of condoms. Natural techniques such as coitus interruptus were available and there was always the option of chastity, but these called for willpower. Some women chose to smear the opening of the uterus with old olive oil, honey or cedar resin, sometimes mixed with white lead. Moist alum was also used. This last option had the advantage of being spermicidal, but few methods could truly be relied on.

Many had recourse to amulets and charms. One absurd remedy was to cut open a type of hairy spider with a large head. Inside, two little worms would be found which were tied in deerskin to a woman before sunrise. It was claimed that this acted as an infallible contraceptive for twelve months and was 'especially useful for women who had a lot of sex'.

Doctors were not meant to help with abortion, but they often did, one risky technique being to pierce the amniotic membrane around the foetus with a metal probe. Alternatively, they prescribed concoctions of drugs that were sometimes dangerous, sometimes innocuous. Less expensive techniques included jumping up and squatting down, making oneself sneeze and heavy massage; or, according to one doctor, a woman 'might drink something cold'.

[xiii]

THE AFRICAN WONDERDRUG

A method that seems to have worked, for both contraception and abortion, was for a woman to drink a small amount of the juice of silphium—a kind of giant fennel that was native to Cyrene in north Africa—mixed with water once a month. According to an ancient expert, this 'does not just prevent conception but destroys anything existing'.

Rome's greatest love poet, Catullus (see pages 159 and 225), swore by silphium. He wrote to his lover Lesbia:*

> How many kisses satisfy,
> How many are enough and more?
> You ask me, Lesbia. I reply
> As many as the Libyan sands
> Sprinkling the Cyrenaic shore
> Where silphium grows...

This was a polite and poetic way of saying 'I'll shag you as often as possible so long as you're taking silphium and won't get pregnant.'

Silphium was so popular in ancient times that it appears to have died out as a consequence of over-harvesting. It was replaced by asafoetida, a member of the same plant family. This has been tested by modern researchers and found to inhibit implantation of fertilized eggs in rats.†

[xiv]

THE WANDERING WOMB

MANY IN the ancient world believed that the uterus was an independent animal living inside a woman's body. This misogynistic theory meant that mothers could not claim credit for the achievement of giving birth to a new human being.

The Greek philosopher Plato wrote that the uterus wanted to produce children, but that it grew impatient if unable to do so: 'When it remains unfruitful long beyond its correct time, it gets discontented and angry and roams in every direction through

* Lesbia—who, for the avoidance of doubt, was very much not a lesbian—was the poet's nickname for Clodia, sister of Publius Clodius Pulcher, rabble-rousing politician and nemesis of Cicero (for more on Clodia, see page 224). Although Catullus wrote some long poems, it is on his short personal verses about his life and loves, especially the highs and lows of his passionate affair with Lesbia, that his reputation today depends.

† Asafoetida is also an ingredient of Worcestershire Sauce, so in case of need it might be worth gulping down a cupful.

the body.' The consequences were shortness of breath, seizures and pains in the groin. These were treated by the application of 'strong smells', which would entice the uterus back to its proper place.

Logically enough, widows and virgins were the main victims of the wandering womb.

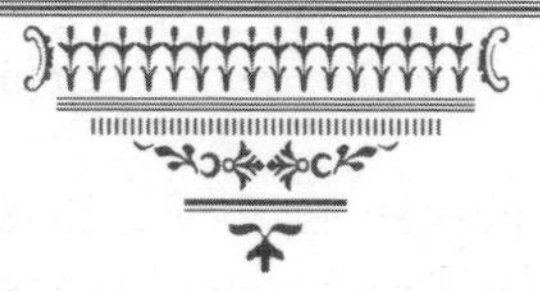

DEATH

1

A TALENT FOR SELF-SLAUGHTER

THE ROMANS did not see self-killing as a distinct category or offence. They had no single term for it, but used general phrases and euphemisms—for instance, 'to bring death upon oneself', 'to withdraw from human affairs', 'to strive after death', 'to emit oneself', 'to take refuge in death', 'to seek death' and 'to rage against oneself'.*

Faced with an impossible situation, ancient Romans were likely to kill themselves, and nobody would blame them in the slightest. They held a very different attitude to suicide from that insisted on in Christian cultures.†

People put an end to their lives in many different ways and for many different reasons, as they do today. Someone concerned with his reputation and self-respect would choose a method of dying that damaged the visual appearance of his body as little as possible, so using a sword or dagger was preferable to hanging or jumping from a height.

For many, to have had enough of life was a good enough reason for leaving it. This might be caused by mental suffering—grief for a dead husband, say—or by physical pain. Pliny the Elder lists diseases known to lead to suicide because of the unbearable agony they brought: stones in the bladder, bad stomach pains and headaches (often in reality, one supposes, cancers or tumours of one kind or another).

Among the upper classes and in military circles, there was what could be called a culture of suicide. In some circumstances it was the honourable thing to do and had about it a certain gloomy glamour. The two main justifications for a 'noble' suicide were *desperata salus* ('no hope of rescue or deliverance') and *pudor* ('shame'), or a mixture of the two.

* There is a Latin word *suicidium*, 'suicide', but it does not come from the classical period; it was coined in the seventeenth century by a Christian theologian.

† Until 1961 suicide was a criminal offence in Britain and those who failed in the attempt were prosecuted for attempted murder. In today's increasingly secular society we are becoming rather more Roman in our attitude.

In his account of the wars he fought in Gaul Julius Caesar gives a spectacular example of *desperata salus*. An army of nearly two legions was ambushed and defeated by Gallic insurgents. One of their commanders was treacherously killed during a parley. Caesar wrote that the survivors 'had hard work to withstand the enemy's onslaught till nightfall; in the night, seeing that all hope was gone, every single man committed suicide'.

By *pudor*, a Roman meditating self-destruction did not mean a sense of guilt for some bad thing he had done (although this could be the case) so much as the prospect of a terminal loss of face, of a catastrophic collapse in social or political standing. Such reversals of fortune happened from time to time, and for a senior politician suicide was a recognized professional hazard.

11

AN INELEGANT DEATH

THE STOIC PHILOSOPHER, poet and rhetorician Lucius Annaeus Seneca, who believed that suicide was a noble act, was much impressed by the action of a reluctant German gladiator who specialized in fighting wild beasts.

At his training school the German was getting ready for the morning show. He went to the lavatory to relieve himself. This was the only thing he was allowed to do in private and without the presence of a guard. Once he was alone, he picked up the stick of wood, tipped with a wet sponge, that was used for wiping one's bottom,* and stuffed it, just as it was, down his throat. In this way, he blocked his windpipe and choked the breath from his body.

'That was truly to insult death!' noted Seneca, approvingly.

* For more on public toilets, see page 190.

AN ELEGANT DEATH

Under the emperors a man guilty of a serious political offence might be put to death, but sometimes he would be instructed to kill himself. This was intended as a sign of mercy, of special favour. The historian Tacitus writes here of the death of Petronius, one of Nero's favourites and author of *The Satyricon*, a prototype of the European novel:*

> Gaius Petronius spent his days sleeping, his nights working and enjoying himself. That success which most men achieve by energy, he won by laziness. Yet unlike other wastrels, he was not regarded as either a spendthrift or a debauchee, but rather as a refined pleasure-seeker. Indeed, his behaviour had a casualness and unconventional freshness that people found charming... He was admitted as arbiter of taste into the small circle of Nero's intimates. No imperial pastime or entertainment which lacked his approval could be regarded as either elegant or luxurious.
>
> [Petronius was accused] of friendship with Scaevinus, a conspirator against the emperor. A slave was bribed to incriminate him; no defence was heard and most of his household were taken into custody... Delay with its attendant hopes and fears was not to be endured. So he severed his veins and then bandaged them as the whim took him, meanwhile conversing with his friends, not seriously or sadly or with ostentatious courage. And he listened while they talked and recited, not disquisitions on the immortality of the soul or philosophical questions, but light and frivolous verses. Some slaves were rewarded, others beaten. He dined and then dozed so that his death, even though compulsory, might still look natural.
>
> Nor did he adopt the conventional deathbed routine of flattering Nero. Instead, he wrote out a list of the emperor's debaucheries, citing by name each of his sexual partners, male and female, with a catalogue of his sexual experiments, and sent it off to Nero under seal. Petronius then broke his signet ring so that it could not be used later for the purpose of incriminating others.

* For more on Petronius' *Satyricon*, see pages 132–33.

iv

WHEN WE DEAD AWAKEN

THE FORUM, Rome's main public square, and the Capitol were crammed with the dead—with commemorative statues of the great men of old, going back centuries to the days of the kings.* There were so many of them that it was as if some Gorgon, the mythical monster whose gaze turned people into stone, had passed that way on a busy shopping day. Living citizens might be forgiven for feeling outnumbered by myriads of the departed.

So, when an ancient Roman of the ruling class went about his business, he was constantly reminded of his glorious predecessors, and at his death these ancestors, almost literally, came back to life. Every leading family had highly realistic masks made of its former members, generation by generation, which they displayed in their houses. When the time came for a funeral, these masks were handed out to relatives or others to wear. They were chosen for their similar body shape to the particular forebear.

The substitutes arrived in the Forum in high style in chariots, dressed in the formal costume of the highest public office which the dead men had reached in life: a toga with a purple border for a consul or a praetor; one embroidered with gold for a victorious general who had celebrated a triumph, a military procession through the heart of the city. A mask of the dead man was also made and worn by a substitute, so he was a guest at his own funeral.

Funerals were held at night, illuminated by torchlight. The body was carried into the Forum, which was crowded with people who had come to watch. When the time came for the eulogy, all the 'ancestors' sat on a row of ivory chairs at the front of the congregation and listened to what was said. The speaker was usually the son of the deceased, who recounted his father's virtues and successes during his lifetime.

What a spectacle this must have provided! The dead had

* The forest of statues was almost exclusively male—only a few women received the honour of a graven image.

reawakened—perhaps they had only ever fallen asleep—and were now hearing the life story of their descendant. The current generation of Romans could see, with all the sharpened focus of a waking dream, that they themselves were on trial and their forefathers were the jury.

v

ENDGAME

MANY EPITAPHS inscribed on Roman gravestones offer no hint of salvation. Poets like Virgil (see page 159) speak of a legendary underworld where the dead congregated, but ordinary people knew better. They convey the gloomy acceptance of a final end.

One typical epitaph reads: *non fui, fui, non sum, non curo* ('I did not exist, I did exist, I don't exist, I couldn't care less'). This verbal formula was so popular that it often appears in abbreviated form: *nffnsnc*.

Another epitaph gives much the same message: *in nihil ab nihilo quam cito recidimus* ('Into nothing from nothing how quickly we pass!').

But there were some who left a rather more cheerful reminder that they had lived life to the full: *es, bibe, lude, veni* ('Eat, drink, play, follow me').

EATING AND DRINKING

1

THE ART OF ROMAN DINING

DINNER PARTIES were as important a form of hospitality in ancient Rome as they are today in Notting Hill or Islington. They combined pleasure and relaxation with the opportunity for a little confidential business on the side and political networking.

A well-to-do Roman's house contained a dining room, or *triclinium*. Diners ate lying down and there would usually be three couches, arranged in the shape of a horseshoe and each with enough room for three guests. Most business was done in the morning, after which it was time for a visit to the baths. Then came dinner, the *cena*, which was usually served in the early to mid-afternoon. Women might be invited, but according to convention they sat on chairs.*

There were usually three courses: hors d'oeuvres, a main course and a dessert, featuring fruit and seafood such as molluscs and shrimps. A range of different dishes would be served in a single course.† Diners used their hands to help themselves from tables and two kinds of spoon, one of them with a prong for use with shellfish, but larger pieces of food had to be cut up for them. Bones, shells and other leftovers were thrown onto the floor to be swept up by slaves.

Once the meal was over, dancers, musicians, tumblers and even poets might perform. Wine flowed (usually mixed with water) and so did conversation. As a rule guests would take their leave before sunset, for there was no street-lighting in Rome and the city was dangerous after dark. At less respectable households, drinking might go on till late into the night, and tireless revellers would stagger home in the cold light of dawn.

* In Cicero's day, the first century BC, women were sometimes allowed to recline on a couch, but he for one felt this to be a bit racy.

† Common ingredients in modern, and especially Mediterranean, cooking, were missing from the ancient world. Spinach, potatoes, pasta, aubergine, tomatoes, peppers and oranges were yet to make their appearance in the kitchen or on the dinner table. Lemons, however, were available.

ii

THE ART OF ROMAN VOMITING

NEXT TO the *triclinium*, or dining room, in a rich man's house was the *vomitorium*. Here diners could tickle their throats with a feather and vomit up their food. In this insalubrious way they could return to their meal and go on eating without filling up.

Or so everyone thinks—everyone, that is, who studied classics under Cecil B. de Mille. In fact, it is all nonsense. It is true that a Roman dinner party could be a fairly disgusting affair, marked by drunkenness and gluttony. Julius Caesar once warned his host that, to help him maintain his intellectual energy, he would need to vomit after dinner, and the emperor Nero's tutor, Seneca, speaks of a man who ate more than he could hold and 'expends greater effort in vomiting everything up than he did in forcing it down'. Slave attendants, he goes on, have a terrible time: 'From the moment we take our places at dinner, one of them mops up the spittle and another on all fours gathers the "leavings" of the drunken diners.'

However, there was never a special room for being sick in.*

iii

DON'T HURRY BACK...

AMUSING and gossipy, the statesman and orator Cicero was in his element at the dinner table. He was much in demand by hosts and could never resist an invitation, even if it was to eat with political opponents. Sometimes his lack of discrimination brought him to grief; on one outing, a fashionable vegetarian style of *nouvelle cuisine* resulted in a three-day bout of diarrhoea.

On one occasion Julius Caesar invited himself to dinner at one of Cicero's country retreats, and the great man, then at the height of his power and sole ruler of Rome, turned up with a bodyguard

* There was such a thing as a *vomitorium*, but it wasn't a room to vomit in—it was the entrance way to an amphitheatre; for more on this see note to page 167.

of 2,000 soldiers and a large entourage. Conversation flowed and the occasion was a success, albeit a massive inconvenience. Cicero heaved a sigh of relief when his illustrious guest had left. 'He is not the kind of person to whom one says, "Do drop by when you are next in the neighbourhood." Once is enough.'

IV

THE EMPRESS'S DINING ROOM

By a stroke of great good fortune, the summer dining room of Livia, wife of the emperor Augustus, has survived amid the ruins of her palatial villa at Prima Porta, a few miles outside Rome. Dating to the late first century BC, the murals that adorn this room express a delight in the natural world as intense as that of the French Impressionists two millennia later.*

The frescoes, which have been restored, cover the four walls of a large chamber from floor to barrel-vaulted ceiling, depicting a luxuriant garden. For Livia's guests the experience of entering this cool, half-subterranean space must have been very much like that of walking into a real garden. The Circlorama effect has been matched only by Claude Monet's *Nymphéas* suite of murals at the Orangerie in Paris. In fact, the anonymous artist (for his name is lost) whom Livia commissioned could have given the French painter a run for his money.† As we look around, we enjoy an almost *trompe-l'oeil* illusion of natural abundance. There are tall trees—spruce, cypress, pines and oaks; ornamental trees—oleander,

* The frescoes have been transferred from the ruins of the villa at Prima Porta to the Museo Romano Nazionale near the city's Termini railway station, where they are now on display.

† These magical murals pre-echo that greatest of garden poets, Andrew Marvell, who flourished in the seventeenth century. In *The Garden*, he writes as if he had attended one of the empress's dinner parties:

> Ripe Apples drop about my head;
> The Luscious Clusters of the Vine
> Upon my Mouth do crush their Wine;
> The Nectaren, and curious Peach,
> Into my hands themselves do reach
> Stumbling on Melons, as I pass,
> Insnared with Flow'rs, I fall on Grass.

myrtle, boxwood and laurel; fruit trees—apple, pomegranate and quince, on one of whose branches a swallow is landing. The grass beneath the trees is carpeted with flowers, among them roses, poppies, chrysanthemums and camomile. Everything is in bloom at once, as though the seasons have been rolled into one. It seems that the Golden Age has returned.

v

THE HOUSE OF THE GOLDEN BRACELET

YOU DID NOT need to be a ruler of the world to own a garden room—they were popular features of well-to-do households. Nor were they a substitute for real gardens, as they are found in homes that were finely endowed in this respect. Rather, it is as if the Romans wanted to bring nature indoors.

A particularly fine example is to be seen at the so-called House of the Golden Bracelet in Pompeii (see also page 274), which was discovered in the 1960s. This building extended over three levels, on the lowest of which are two neighbouring rooms. One of them—perhaps the man of the house's study—is a horticultural riot. On the complete north wall is a wild garden, crowded with plants and birds. A scalloped fountain and herms (busts of the god Hermes on stone columns) are the only signs of human intervention. Otherwise we have nature untamed, painted with the decorative formality of a prototypical Douanier Rousseau.

vi

A MOUNTAIN OF JARS

ROMANS consumed copious quantities of olive oil and wine, as can be seen in one of the wonders of their city. This is not a temple of Artemis or a statue of Jupiter, breathtaking though these creations were. It was, as we can still see today, a rubbish dump.

A short distance from the east bank of the Tiber a hill about a kilometre in circumference rises some 30 or so metres from the ground (it was probably higher in antiquity). This is the Monte Testaccio. It is not a natural feature but an artificial mound made from the remains of more than 50 million amphorae.

Amphorae—large two-handled earthenware jars—were ideal containers for wine and olive oil, two of the staples of life in the Roman world. With a typical capacity of about 70 litres, they were very cheap to make and not worth returning to sender, so they were broken up after use and discarded. Hence the Monte Testaccio.

Trade throughout the Mediterranean was busy, even though cargo vessels were fragile and liable to sink in storms. As well as luxury goods, grain and thousands of gallons of wine and olive oil were transported long distances by sea.* By the first century BC Rome was too large for its hinterland to supply its needs; it depended for survival on imports from across the Mediterranean.

Most of the amphorae in the hill were used for carrying olive oil, much of which came from southern Spain. As well as forming part of everyone's diet, olive oil was used for indoor lighting, in cosmetics and medicines, and as a substitute for soap. Demand from a large city such as Rome was huge and perhaps as many as 200,000 hectolitres a year were consumed.

Today the hill provides rich pickings for archaeologists who analyse trade routes and densities from the exporters' marks painted or stamped on the broken pottery.†

* Poor roads and the absence of the internal-combustion engine or rail locomotion made transport by land slow and prohibitively expensive.

† The hill has had an exciting history. On Good Friday it used to stand in for Golgotha; the pope led a procession there and three crosses represented those of Jesus and the two thieves. In the Middle Ages pigs were put into carts and unkindly rolled down the steep slopes. In the nineteenth century an October festival on the Monte Testaccio with wine and refreshments attracted Roman crowds. And in 1849 Garibaldi, Italy's liberator, placed a gun battery on its summit when he was defending Rome against the French.

[vii]

TRIMALCHIO'S BANQUET

TRIMALCHIO is one of the great fat men of literature, alongside Falstaff, Friar Tuck and the Fat Controller. Former slave and multimillionaire, he is the star turn of a bawdy novel, *The Satyricon*, written by Gaius Petronius, a favourite of the emperor Nero in the first century AD.* A man without taste who aspires to taste, Trimalchio holds a sumptuous banquet attended by hangers-on, down-at-heel intellectuals and hustlers. The fictional menu reflects the real-life meals of the very rich.

Hors d'oeuvres are served on a tray on which stands a bronze donkey with two panniers, one of them holding green olives and the other black olives. In dishes made to resemble small bridges lie dormice dipped in honey and rolled in poppy seeds. Then a peahen, carved from wood and sitting on her eggs, is brought in. The eggs turn out to made of hard-baked pastry and contain small cooked birds seasoned with pepper, a favourite delicacy.

The next tray displays the twelve signs of a culinary zodiac. The chef has chosen appropriate items of food for each sign: a pair of testicles and kidneys over Gemini, for example, and a virgin sow's belly over Virgo. Underneath, in still another tray, lie capons, sow's bellies and a hare tricked out with wings like Pegasus. Petronius adds:

> At the corners of the tray are four little gravy boats, all shaped like the satyr Marsyas [a follower of the wine god Bacchus], with phalluses for spouts and a spicy hot gravy dripping down over several large fish swimming about in the lagoon of the tray.

Two *pièces de résistance* follow. An enormous roasted wild sow is carried in; a carver gives its side a savage slash, the wound opens and out fly dozens of thrushes. Bird-catchers with limed twigs are standing by and soon all the terrified birds are snared. Wine is now served and grapes taken round by a pretty little boy.

Finally a live hog is selected by the guests for immediate cooking. It soon reappears, apparently having been cooked whole.

* A film, loosely based on Petronius' work, was made by the Italian director Federico Fellini in 1969.

Trimalchio pretends to lose his temper and summons the chef. 'You forgot to gut the pig,' he said. 'Well, gut it now.' When the chef opens the animal, out pours not the bowels and guts but an avalanche of sausages and black puddings.

Now comes the time for serious drinking. An unfunny clown holds up a ladder and tells a slave boy to climb up it. The boy then jumps through flaming hoops. Unfortunately he lets the ladder fall on Trimalchio, and the future looks bleak for him. But the host unexpectedly gives him his freedom. 'Let no one say the great Trimalchio has been hurt by a mere slave.'

Games, riddles and presents follow, and still more food is served, including pastry thrushes with raisin-and-nut stuffing, and quinces impaled with thorns to resemble sea urchins. The final course appears to be a fat goose surrounded by fish and little birds of every kind; in fact, it is a *trompe-l'oeil* masterpiece of misdirection, for the whole confection is made out of roast pork.

viii

SIMPLE FARE AND GOOD COMPANY

NOT EVERYONE had the means or the no-holds-barred vulgarity of a Trimalchio. The poet Martial, who lived in the first century AD, recalls a bailiff's wife on a country farm bringing him the ingredients of a green salad—lettuce, leeks, mint and kale—to accompany a plain but tasty and filling meal:

> My simple dinner will be served in one main course –
> A kid rescued from the jaws of a savage wolf;
> Meatballs that need no carving; the workman's staple, beans
> And early sprouts. To these, we'll add a chicken and
> A ham that has already survived three dinners.

When Martial and his guests have eaten their fill, there are apples for dessert and a nine-year-old wine. In addition, he promises

> Laughter without malice and free speaking
> You won't regret the morning after,
> Nothing that had better been left unsaid.

[ix]

HOW TO ROAST A TESTICLE

THE ESCOFFIER of the classical world was Apicius, the famous gourmet who reportedly lived in the first century AD. Many apocryphal tales are told about him. He observed that flamingo's tongue was delicious and that red mullet was tastiest if, before cooking, the live fish was drowned in a mullet sauce.

Apicius probably did not write the encyclopedia of recipes that is given his name. The book contains a recipe for one of the delicacies served at Trimalchio's banquet:

> You make roasted testicles and kidneys in this way: they are opened up in two parts and stretched out, and ground pepper, pine nuts, finely chopped coriander and pounded fennel seed are sprinkled on them. Then the testicles and kidneys are closed up again, sewn together and wrapped in animal intestine, and in this state they are fried in oil and *garum* (fermented fish sauce), and then roasted in a small oven or grilled on a gridiron.

After spending 100 million sesterces on food (a fortune), he found he only had 10 million left (still a fortune) and committed suicide.

[x]

A POMPOUS POMPEIAN

POLITENESS was at a premium, if we may judge from the precaution taken by a citizen of Pompeii. He painted instructions on the walls of his *triclinium* telling his guests how they should behave at his dinner parties:

> Let a slave wash your feet with water and dry them;
> He should lay a coverlet on your couch—don't make it dirty.
> Spare that other man's wife your lecherous glances and melting eyes,
> and keep your conversation clean.
> Be nice and avoid unpleasant arguments if you possibly can. If not,
> go back to your own home.

But who would want an invitation from this moralizing martinet?

[xi]

FISH MANIA

FISH, such as lamprey and barbed mullet, were highly prized and fetched absurdly inflated prices. Roman noblemen farmed them in fishponds on their country estates, sometimes on a lavish scale. After his death, the ponds of the fabulously rich Lucullus were sold for the astonishing sum of 12 million sesterces.

A celebrated lawyer, Hortensius, wept over the death of a favourite fish and refused ever to eat from his own collection, shopping instead at a local market. A friend of his observed: 'He is as upset over a sick fish as over an ailing slave.' Another contemporary, the multimillionaire Crassus, went into mourning when a prized lamprey passed away. When criticized for his ridiculous behaviour, he was unrepentant. What he had done, he insisted, had been entirely fitting.

A notorious gourmet and friend of the emperor Augustus, Vedius Pollio, kept a pond of lampreys and fed them slaves who had displeased him. This made for an unpleasant death, for lampreys bore into the flesh and suck blood. Once when the emperor was his guest at dinner, a slave accidentally dropped and broke a valuable crystal glass. The slave fell to his knees and begged Augustus to intervene and win for him a less painful demise.

No slouch when it came to political violence, Augustus was disgusted by domestic cruelty. He ordered the entire set of glasses to be smashed and the fishpond filled in. A classical commentator remarked that Pollio was unable to punish the slave for an offence the emperor himself had committed. It seems the man was given his freedom.

[xii]

YUM-YUM

GARUM was a favourite sauce of the Romans, and they used it indiscriminately. It was made from the intestines of small fish, which were macerated with salt and left to rot in sunlight for between one and three months. Clear liquid formed on the surface of the decayed matter. This was strained off and bottled.

[xiii]

THE RECIPE FOR SPARKLING REPARTEE

BEFORE attending an ancient Greek or Roman dinner party, a nervous guest could prepare himself by consulting a book called *Table Talk* by the essayist and biographer Plutarch, who lived in second half of the first century AD. He lists a whole series of handy topics guaranteed to make the table talk flow, among them:

> Which came first, the bird or the egg?
> Why do old men get drunk easily, and women only with difficulty?
> Why are mushrooms believed to be produced by thunder?
> What is the best time of day for a man to have sex with his wife?
> Why do Jews abstain from pork?
> Why are sleeping men never hit by lightning?
> Should one make decisions when drunk?
> Is there an odd or an even number of stars?

XI

POISON

I

WHEN POISON'S TO BLAME, THE KILLER'S A DAME...

IN 331 BC an epidemic raged at Rome. When a serving maid reported to the authorities that many of the deaths were actually due to poisoning, she was believed. Large numbers of upper-class women were arrested. Two were found to be preparing suspicious potions; they were made to drink them and, apparently, dropped down dead. In total 170 women were tried, found guilty of murder by poison and executed.

These women must surely have been innocent. In all likelihood the potions were, as those accused claimed, medicines they were preparing for their sick menfolk. Doctors in the ancient world had little understanding of hygiene, and both they and the general public often mistook infection for murder.

Nevertheless, it is true that the Romans did know about a range of plant and animal poisons, including mushrooms, mandrake, deadly nightshade, opium, spiders, vipers and some kinds of marine creature. It must be supposed that on occasion these were put to malevolent use.

In any case rumours of such nefarious behaviour helped to reinforce two of the Romans' abiding phobias—of femmes fatales and of poison.

II

ULYSSES IN A FROCK?

IN THE PANTHEON of poisoners, history has been especially unkind, indeed positively brutal, to Livia, wife of Rome's first emperor, Augustus. Writers of the imperial age, such as the historian Tacitus and the biographer Suetonius, dropped hints of her apparently murderous nature. She was called 'that feminine bully', and her great-grandson, the emperor Caligula (see page 251), referred to her as 'Ulysses in a frock' (*Ulixes stolatus*), the Homeric hero being a byword for deception and guile. Livia was variously credited with eliminating some or all of the numerous male relatives who stood between Tiberius, her son by a first marriage, and his succession to the imperial throne of Augustus.*

The homicide charge sheet includes Augustus' promising young nephew Marcellus, his two grandsons Gaius and Lucius, and—her crowning achievement—Augustus himself, when he incautiously showed signs of preferring another heir to Tiberius. The emperor enjoyed fresh figs, which he liked to pick for himself from a tree. The story goes that Livia smeared a number of the fruits with poison; eating some that had not been smeared herself, she recommended the tainted ones to her husband.

Most, if not all, of these are tall tales. In fact, so far as we can see, Livia steered clear of politics and murdered nobody. She knew better than to interfere openly in a man's world, although she understood very well the power of influence. She behaved like the typical virtuous Roman housewife, weaving her husband's clothes and managing the comparatively modest family home in Rome with ostentatious thriftiness. She was fond of making up her own medicines (see page 193), a habit that could well have contributed to her reputation as a poisoner.

Behind the scenes, Livia was a successful businesswoman. She owned a copper mine in France, palm groves in Judaea and estates in Egypt, including papyrus marshes, arable farms, commercial vegetable gardens, granaries and olive and wine presses.

After her husband's death, the widowed empress fell out with the son on behalf of whom she had supposedly schemed for a lifetime. Tiberius wanted to be his own master, and all her efforts—and crimes, if there were any—had gone for nothing. She was reduced to keeping the new emperor under her thumb by threatening to publish unflattering letters about his character which Augustus had written to her.

When she finally died at a great age in AD 29, her son was beside himself with joy. Getting his own back at last, he refused to attend her funeral and vetoed plans to award her divine honours. She had to wait another thirteen years until her grandson Claudius became emperor and gave her an entry ticket to Mount Olympus, home of the gods.

* The *coup de grâce* was delivered in the twentieth century by the author and poet Robert Graves, whose historical novel *I, Claudius*, subsequently televised, portrays Livia as the embodiment of the evil stepmother and a scheming serial killer.

MARTINA AND LOCUSTA

In the early empire professional poisoners were able to enjoy successful careers in Rome, and they often moved in the highest circles. A certain Martina was credited with the death in Antioch in Syria, in AD 19, of Germanicus, a glamorous young commander and member of the imperial family. He himself was sure he was being poisoned, and so was public opinion. But if he was on his guard, it is hard to see how Martina could have succeeded.

Nevertheless, she was sent to Rome for investigation, but died en route in mysterious circumstances at the Italian port of Brundisium (today's Brindisi). Her body showed no signs of suicide, but some poison was found hidden in a knot of her hair. Conspiracy theorists enjoyed themselves, but historians have no idea what really happened.

Then there was the more famous Locusta. The story went that the emperor Claudius' wife Agrippina, Nero's mother, commissioned her to prepare poisoned, or perhaps poisonous, mushrooms, which were served to the emperor at dinner. The difficulty here is that, while most contemporaries accepted that Claudius was poisoned, nobody could quite agree when, where and by whom.

Locusta continued on her murderous career, according to the historian Tacitus. In AD 55 Nero commissioned her to poison his half-brother Brittanicus, who was Claudius' son and so had a better claim to the imperial throne than he did (Nero was Agrippina's son by a previous husband). A first attempt failed and Locusta was put to torture. She did better the second time around with a stronger potion. The boy's drink was tampered with and he died in convulsions at a supper party.

When he learned of the revolt of the legions against his rule in AD 68, Nero fled, taking with him in a golden box some of Locusta's poison; in the event, though, he stabbed himself to death with a dagger.* Locusta was executed by Nero's successor, Galba, who reigned only for a few months but found time to arrange her punishment.

* There is more on Nero's nefarious career on pages 253–54.

For all the circumstantial detail, it remains uncertain whether the fearsome reputation of such women as Martina and Locusta rested more on gossip than achievement.

iv

MITHRIDATES AND THE SECRET OF LONG LIFE

MITHRIDATES, king of Pontus, succeeded in removing most of the Middle East from Roman control for some years in the first century BC. Brought up in an oriental court, he was used to palace intrigues and was careful to protect himself against threats to his life. He regularly took a special antidote before consuming small amounts of poison, in the hope of building up a resistance.

A leading doctor in the age of Augustus published the king's antidote, called Mithridatium. It contained:

Costmary	1.66 grams
Sweet flag	20 grams
Hypericum, gum, sagapenum, acacia juice, Illyrian iris, cardamom	8 grams each
Anise	12 grams
Gallic nard, gentian root and dried rose leaves	16 grams each
Poppy tears and parsley	17 grams each
Casia, saxifrage, darnel, long pepper	20.66 grams each
Storax	21 grams
Castoreum, frankincense, hypocistis juice, myrrh and opopanax	24 grams each
Malabathrum leaves	24 grams
Flower of round rush, turpentine resin, galbanum, Cretan carrot seeds	24.66 grams each
Nard and opobalsam	25 grams each

Shepherd's purse .... 25 grams
Rhubarb root....................... 28 grams
Saffron, ginger, cinnamon.......... 29 grams each

These ingredients were pounded and mixed with honey. Against poisoning, a helping the size of an almond was dissolved in wine.

Doctors made money by marketing the antidote, whether or not the recipe they sold really was the one Mithridates took. We do not know if anyone has used it in modern times, nor if it was efficacious.

According to another account, after Pompey the Great defeated Mithridates, he found a notebook of the king's in which he had written a simpler recipe. It consisted of two dried walnuts, two figs and twenty leaves of rue, pounded together with salt. Anyone taking this on an empty stomach would be immune to all poison for a day.*

In 63 BC, after years on the run, the king was tracked down by the Romans to a remote castle. He decided to commit suicide by poison. Unfortunately, thanks to his precautions, the toxin, whatever it was, had no effect. He had to ask one of his bodyguard to run him through with a sword.

v

DEATH BY ASP

THE DEATH of Cleopatra, beautiful siren queen of Egypt, features history's most famous snakebite. Caught up in the final struggle of the Roman Republic, she had sided with Mark Antony against Octavian, the future emperor Augustus; facing defeat and humiliation in 30 BC, when all else had failed, she decided to take her own life. A prisoner of Rome, she had two poisonous asps smuggled to her in a basket of figs, let them bite her on her breasts and died almost at once.

Or so the story goes. Like much else that we think we know about Cleopatra, this is largely fabrication.† The queen may or

* A trial of these concoctions is not recommended. Most of the ingredients appear innocuous enough, but if the antidote doesn't work, the poison of course will.

† For other aspects of the Cleopatra legend, see pages 228–29.

may not have killed herself, but we can forget about asps. The asp, aka the hooded Egyptian cobra, is typically 2.5 metres long—rather large for a basket of figs and awkward to press to one's bosom. As for the venom, it can take as long as two hours for an asp bite to kill.

Perhaps the story of the asp was the work of Roman spin doctors anxious to cover up the fact that, triumphant or not, Octavian had found Egypt's last pharaoh dangerous even in misfortune. The logic was to have her put down. We shall never know if he followed it.

NAMES

1

A RECIPE FOR CONFUSION...

ANY SENSIBLE system of naming should make it easy to distinguish one person from another. The Romans' system failed this test absolutely and was both complicated and confusing—even to themselves. Rome's history is littered with different people bearing the same name, and historians both then and now have had difficulty recognizing who was who.

Men usually had three or more names. The first was the *praenomen*, or given name. Annoyingly, there were only a few of these. They included Decius, Gaius, Gnaeus, Lucius, Marcus, Publius, Quintus ('fifth'), Septimus ('seventh'), Sextus ('sixth') and Titus. The very grand Claudian clan boasted an exclusive *praenomen* of its own—Appius. Fathers would almost invariably pass their own given names down to their eldest son. Younger sons were often called after grandfathers or uncles.

The *praenomen* was followed by the *nomen*, the name of the *gentes* or clans—the rough equivalent of our surname. Many clans were supposed to have had their origin in the family groups that founded Rome. Among these were the *gens* Aemilia, Claudia, Cornelia, Domitia, Julia, Junia, Metella, Pompeia, Antonia and Valeria.

After the *nomen* came the *cognomen*. This denoted the particular family within the *gens* a man belonged to. It often originated as a humorous nickname to distinguish people of the same clan. Hence Cicero, meaning 'chickpea', was added to Marcus Tullius, and Lentulus, meaning 'lentil', to Gaius Cornelius.*

Men were often adopted by parents without a male child. When Gaius Octavius was adopted posthumously by Julius Caesar, he became known as Gaius Julius Caesar Octavianus (whom we know as Octavian); the 'Octavianus', being a further *cognomen*, or *agnomen*, was a reminder that he had been born into the *gens Octavia*. Once he became Rome's first emperor, he

* The Roman system of names can make life something of a trial for users of modern indexes. Scholarly books usually list an individual by his *nomen*, even if it feels more natural to look up his *cognomen*. Thus Gaius Julius Caesar, for instance, will be found under Julius, not Caesar. This book too follows the practice.

broke all the rules and was officially known as Imperator Caesar Divi Filius Augustus—that is, in translation, 'Emperor [or Commander-in-chief] Caesar son of the deified [Julius Caesar] Revered One'.

Generals were sometimes allowed an extra name, *agnomen*, to signal a great military achievement. So Publius Cornelius Scipio, the youthful victor over the Carthaginian general Hannibal at the crucial battle of Zama in northern Africa in 202 BC (see page 79), was awarded the honorific title of 'Africanus'.

In its complete bureaucratic form, a Roman's name would also include a reference to his father and his membership of one of Rome's tribes or administrative divisions. So the historical personage we know simply as Marcus Cicero was listed in full as Marcus Tullius Marci filius Cornelia tribu Cicero.

11

... AND YET MORE CONFUSION

IF THE ROMAN system for naming males was bad, the system for women was even worse. Absurdly, they were not allowed a *praenomen* and were called by the feminine version of their *nomen*. So Julius Caesar's much loved daughter was called Julia. So would her sisters have been, had she had any. In fact, every woman of the Julian *gens* was called by the same name.

So how did people cope at a family reunion? The answer is that when there was a real risk of confusion, another name could be added. For example, Tertia ('third') might be used to distinguish one daughter from another.

A woman kept her family *nomen* when she married, but her husband's *nomen* or *cognomen* could be added. Hence Caesar's daughter Julia became Julia Pompeii, literally 'Julia [wife] of Pompey', when she married Pompey the Great.

111

WHAT'S IN A NAME?

COMMODUS, a generally barmy emperor who reigned in the latter half of the second century AD, had a thing about names.* He added and took away his own names at will. He changed his *praenomen* from Lucius to Marcus and then back again. His full style ended up, absurdly, as Lucius Aelius Aurelius Commodus Augustus Herculeus Romanus Exsuperatorius Amazonius Invictus Felix Pius. The word *exsuperatorius* means 'supreme' and was applied to the king of the gods, Jupiter; Amazonius refers to Hercules' victory over the Queen of the Amazons (Commodus saw himself as a reincarnation of the demi-god); *invictus* means 'unconquered', *felix* 'fortunate' and *pius* 'respectful'.

Commodus did not stop there. Following a great fire, he renamed the city of Rome 'Colonia Lucia Annia Commodiana'. The months of the year were restyled to reflect each of his own twelve names, and the legions had to be referred to as Commodianae. After his widely welcomed assassination in AD 192, the Senate cancelled all these innovations, and Rome became Rome once more.

* More on Commodus' inglorious imperial career can be found on pages 261–62.

XIII

EDUCATION

I

FIRST STEPS

THE MOTHER gave birth to her son, but it was the father, the *paterfamilias*, who after seven days made the decision whether or not to accept him as a family member. If he rejected him for any reason, the infant was exposed in a public place to die.*

Literacy was a crucial skill which boys from well-off Roman families needed to acquire, so at the appropriate time an educated slave tutor (*paedogogus*) would be appointed to teach a boy to read and acquire the basics of practical mathematics. Alternatively, he would be sent to a primary school. While many fathers were content that their offspring's education amounted to no more than having the three Rs dinned into their heads, the more conscientious among them would keep a close eye on his upbringing. Cato the Elder, for instance, not only made a point of always being present at his son's bath-time but took over his literacy classes as well, as he did not like the idea of him being disciplined by a slave. He also taught the child the principles of law, athletics, swimming, riding, boxing and throwing the javelin.

II

A SCHOOL OF HARD KNOCKS

AN AMBITIOUS family sent its sons to a secondary school, run by a *grammaticus*, a teacher of literature and language. This was a perilous step into the world of grown-ups, a fact that well-to-do parents understood very well. The duties of the *paedogogus*, or slave tutor, included supervising children at home and guiding them from home to the classroom. He was all the more necessary as his charges approached puberty and attracted the attentions of lecherous men in the street (not to mention teachers). Boys were more at risk than girls because the latter went out in public less frequently and were usually educated at

* For more on this grisly topic, see page 111.

home. The risk of sexual abuse was accompanied by the certainty of physical abuse. Teaching methods were both brutal and boring, being based on the use of memory rather than intelligence. Masters routinely flogged idle or rebellious students, or just lively ones. So central was the experience of corporal punishment to the learning process that the juvenile expression for being too old for school was *manum subducere ferulae*—to 'snatch one's hand from under the cane'.

There were, in essence, only two related subjects of study—literature and oratory; and two languages—Latin and Greek. Students were introduced to the great classics of both languages, foremost of which were the two epics of Homer, the *Iliad* and the *Odyssey*, the Athenian dramatists and the great orators. The teacher specialized in textual analysis, examining syntax and the rules of poetic scansion and explaining obscure or idiomatic phrases. He also introduced the student to rhetoric, or the art of public speaking (on which more below).

The Roman form of schooling had a long life: it survived into the Dark Ages and was reinvigorated in the Renaissance. In certain respects there was little real difference in the teaching of Latin and Greek between the classrooms of imperial Rome and the nineteenth-century English public school.*

iii

A TRENDY LIBERAL

LIKE A GOOD DEED in a naughty world, one Roman stood out from a legion of school disciplinarians and sadists. He was Quintilian, who lived during the first century AD. He promoted the shocking idea that children learned more if they had a good time, anticipating today's educational thinking by some two millennia. 'I disapprove of flogging,' he wrote. 'We must take care that the child, who is not yet old enough to love his studies, does not come to hate them. His studies must be made a pleasure.'

* The classics—ancient Latin and Greek—were at the heart of British education, especially in grammar and public schools, until halfway through the twentieth century. The sciences barely got a look-in. For this we have the Romans to thank.

Quintilian founded his own school and was a popular teacher. The cruel emperor Domitian made him tutor to two young cousins, whom he named as his heirs. We do not know how they turned out, for they soon vanished from the historical record. Perhaps Quintilian did too good a job, producing well-balanced and civilized young men who found themselves out of place in a paranoid and murderous imperial court. If that is what happened, they will not have long survived.

iv

THE ART OF PERSUASION

ROMANS placed great weight on public speaking. Adolescents were taught rhetoric, which was an essential skill for a politician or a lawyer, and eloquence was reduced to a method that could be learned. Speakers could choose from different styles—in particular, the Asiatic, which was florid, elaborate and copious, and the Attic, which was plain, dry and unemotional.*

Boys were trained to compose and deliver speeches, and they would declaim them before their class and sometimes invited guests. They were set exercises, or scenarios, by their schoolmaster or, a year or two later in Rome's version of higher education, by an expert tutor; many would go to Athens or other Hellenic cities for 'finishing' at the hands of a famous rhetorician. These exercises would confront the pupil with tricky choices or dilemmas. For instance:

> Hannibal after Cannae debates the rights and wrongs of marching on Rome.
>
> The law states that, if a woman has been raped, her assailant shall be executed or forced to marry her without a dowry, according to her choice. On one and the same night a man raped two women. One demanded his execution, the other that he marry her. So what is to be done?

* Shakespeare captures the essence of these two styles in the speeches he gives to Mark Antony (Asiatic) and to Marcus Brutus (Attic) in his play *Julius Caesar*.

Orators like Cicero in the first century BC wrote learned tomes on public speaking, and a hundred years later Quintilian set out complicated rules and procedures in his book *The Principles of Oratory* (*Institutio oratoria*). He identified five broad categories of study: *inventio*, the process of developing and refining an argument; *dispositio*, how to arrange an argument to the greatest effect; *elocutio* (style) and *pronuntiatio* (presentation); *memoria*, the importance of memory during the delivery of a speech; and *actio*, delivery of a speech in a charming and agreeable manner.

Some were impatient with too academic an approach. Cato the Elder, for instance, remarked dismissively: 'Just concentrate on the meaning and the words will follow.' But everyone agreed on the importance of verbal articulacy.

Was rhetoric associated in any way with morality? Here there were two opposing opinions. For Cicero, whom Quintilian dubbed 'that supreme manipulator of hearts', a good speaker must inevitably be a good man, knowledgeable about all areas of human life and culture, and a moral guide to the state. Speaking well meant speaking justly. For others, however, rhetoric simply taught people how to mislead and, as the ancient Greeks put it, make the worse seem the better cause.*

* Rhetoric may no longer be taught in schools as a discrete subject, but it is certainly alive and well today: in university communications departments, in marketing and public-relations companies, in town halls and parliaments. Politicians still use rhetorical devices to shape opinion. Whether anyone now thinks that *virtue* is a necessary ingredient of the art of persuasion is a different matter.

POETS

I

A PRETTY PAIR!

THE YOUNG poet Catullus was an excellent hater and often thoroughly disgruntled. In 57 BC he had gone out to the province of Bithynia on the governor's staff, hoping to enrich himself (as many Roman officials did) at the expense of the locals. He failed to do so and, on his return home, found that—by infuriating contrast—people he knew who had attached themselves to Julius Caesar were becoming fabulously rich.

The poet was particularly bitter about a notorious playboy called Mamurra, who was on Caesar's payroll and lording it with his ill-gotten gains. Catullus composed various heated poems about him and his patron which he would have been wiser to drop into the wastepaper basket:

> They make a pretty pair of debauchees,
> Sex-sick Mamurra and his bedroom-brother
> Caesar...
> Companions of one sofa-bed, they fuck
> The girls in friendly rivalry and share
> The same unholy itch. A pretty pair!

Catallus' lampoons made an impact and Caesar was not at all amused. He was perfectly happy to hire the services of disreputable men such as Mamurra, but not to be publicly painted with their vices. He made his displeasure felt, and Catullus was forced to say sorry.

Caesar could lose his temper, but he never bore a grudge. For him the apology was the end of the matter. On the very same day he received it, he invited the angry young man to dinner.

II

POETRY AND PROPAGANDA

THE POET Virgil was, and still is, regarded as Rome's national poet. His masterpiece the *Aeneid*, published after 19 BC and modelled on the Greek epics of Homer, tells the story of the journeys of Aeneas, Trojan prince and originator of the Roman state. It is an exciting narrative told in majestic verse.*

The phrase 'national poet', however, ought to arouse our suspicions. For all its literary beauties, the *Aeneid* is, at one level, a work of propaganda. Rome's first emperor Augustus was an aggressive imperialist and Virgil had the task of spelling out Rome's duty to go out and rule the world. This he did, in no uncertain terms. 'I have awarded them empire without end,' he has Jupiter, king of the gods, say of the Romans, while the ghost of Aeneas' father claims: 'You, Roman, must remember that you have to guide the nations by your authority.'

iii

IMPERIAL ROME'S MINISTER OF CULTURE

THE EMPEROR Augustus had his own unofficial minister of culture: Gaius Maecenas, an old school friend and a generous patron of the arts. Maecenas enjoyed his comforts: he could almost 'outdo a woman in giving himself up to indolence and soft luxury'. He loved silks and jewels and was said to have been the first person to build a heated swimming pool in the capital.

Voluptuary he may have been, but Maecenas gathered around himself the rising poets of the day, including Virgil and Horace. They saluted the end of the endless civil wars and the arrival of peace in works that still speak vividly of their relief and joy. They could also recognize reality when they saw it, and one-time opponents quickly made their peace with the regime. In those days before print, each copy of a book had to be laboriously and expensively handwritten by a scribe. Writers had no large middle-class market to buy their books. They needed rich backers like Maecenas (and Augustus) for the wherewithal on which to live.

Maecenas was far too civilized to behave like an ancient version of Dr Goebbels, but he did expect his little circle to produce the political goods from time to time. Even Horace, the chubby laureate of the pleasures of private life, kept a straight face once

* For more on Aeneas as the founder of the Roman state, see pages 3–4.

in a while and produced something solemn and grand if the occasion demanded it. While Virgil writes of a Caesar 'whose empire/ shall reach to the Ocean's limits, whose fame shall end in the stars', Horace begs the goddess of luck to 'guard our young swarm of warriors on the wing now/ to spread the fear of Rome/ into Arabia and the Red Sea coasts'.

These great poets did their bit—and the expected rewards followed.

iv

A RURAL IDYLL

AS A GIFT from his patron Maecenas, Horace received a delightful villa in the countryside beyond Tivoli. Its ruins still stand on a hillside around which a river flows.* The poet was inordinately proud of his country idyll and his finest lyrics celebrate its simplicities. While his verse is hard to render into English (as Robert Frost said, 'poetry is what gets lost in translation'), many have tried, including the British prime minister William Ewart Gladstone and Gerard Manley Hopkins. Here is a fine version, by the eighteenth-century poet William Cowper, of one of Horace's mini-masterpieces, *Persicos odi apparatus*:

Boy, I hate their empty shows,
Persian garlands I detest,
Bring not me the late-blown rose,
Lingering after all the rest.

Plainer myrtle pleases me,
Thus outstretch'd beneath my vine;
Myrtle more becoming thee,
Waiting with thy master's wine.

Did Horace pay too much for his rural retreat? Did he deserve John Dryden's jibe that he was 'a well-mannered court slave'? We can imagine Horace side-stepping this slap in the face with a wry smile and saying that everything has its price, including the peace of Caesar Augustus.

* The remains of Horace's villa have been excavated, and can be visited.

[v]

LIVING FOR THE MOMENT

IT IS HARD to imagine an odder pairing than the Roman poet Horace and the English poet Rudyard Kipling. True, they both wrote of empires, but while Kipling is a whole-hearted celebrant of nineteenth- and early twentieth-century imperialism, Horace's heart isn't really in promoting the *pax Romana*.

In the face of death and eternity Horace spoke up for the irresponsible moment. He invented the phrase *carpe diem*, or 'pluck the day [as if it were a flower]'. What he liked (among other things) was sex—lots of it, with boys as well as girls. He fastened mirrors to his bedroom ceiling to add to the pleasure of lovemaking. He versified a wet dream. He explored with elegant and concise bravura the seamy side of lust.

None of this was Kipling's bag, one might think. But he knew his Horace really well and loved him. Horace wrote only four books of odes; Kipling imagined a fictional fifth, for which he conjured some fine pastiches in English. He penned an abbreviated translation of an ode which catches the Roman amoralist's tone of voice better than any other English imitator or translator:

> Lucy, do not look ahead: We shall be a long time dead.
> Take whatever you can see: and, incidentally, take me.

Perhaps there was more to the private Kipling than meets the eye, but he took care that his personal life was erased from the record. By contrast the Roman poet was candid about his amours, and indeed about both his person and his personality. Thus he describes himself:

> As for me, when you want a laugh, you will find me
> In good condition, fat and sleek, a porker.

And:

> Of small build, grey before my time, fond of the sun,
> Hot-tempered, but very easily appeased.

If a time machine could be found, who would resist a weekend with Horace at his country retreat?

[vi]

THE POETRY OF INDIGNATION

THE SATIRIST Juvenal was a man with a temper, and that was the quality which made him one of Rome's greatest poets. 'Even if I have no talent,' he wrote, 'indignation will power my poetry.'

He lived through the terrible times of the emperor Domitian in the first century AD, and it is apt that he was master of the savage caricature. The world he conjures into being in thirteen satires mingles every kind of sexual deviance with images of the corruption of power and the squalor of city life. His gallery of grotesques, rather like those of Dickens, was grounded in reality and infused with outrage.

After Domitian's assassination in AD 96 Juvenal's indignation cooled a little. He had spent much of his life in what he called 'pretentious poverty', but under the benevolent gaze of the emperor Hadrian he had less to complain about. He received a pension and a small house in the country (not far from Horace's old rural retreat). And, like Horace before him, Juvenal learned not to bite the hand that fed him. It seems out of character, but he appears to have mellowed with good fortune.

[vii]

A MEMORABLE WAY WITH WORDS

JUVENAL may not be as much read today as he deserves,* but he lives on nevertheless. He had a talent for the memorable phrase, some of which we still use, mostly unknowingly, to this day.

quis custodiet ipsos custodes?

'Who will guard the guardians themselves?' The expression and its

* Though his satires were much admired by seventeenth- and eighteenth-century English poets from John Donne to Samuel Johnson. Many of them produced 'imitations' that brought Juvenal up to date—and allowed them to smooth over indecent passages in the Latin.

underlying question—who can really be trusted with power?—tend to crop up in serious political discussions. The saying is a favourite of newspaper leader-writers (does the *Guardian* owe its title to Juvenal?). When Juvenal coined the phrase, though, he was thinking of something rather more pornographic: how to keep a wife from having sex with an unexpectedly virile eunuch. Answer: lock the woman up and have her watched. Yes, says Juvenal, that's one way of doing it, but who will keep an eye on the guards and what *they* are getting up to?

mens sana in corpore sano

'A sound mind in a sound body.' This pithily encapsulates what really matters in life—what people should really strive for, rather than all the things they usually ask for and which are bad for them.

panem et circenses

'Bread and circuses.' Most famously of all, Juvenal argued that the mass of people paid little thought to serious issues such as their liberty; all they cared about was their own immediate needs and pleasures. Juvenal was referring to the grain dole for poor citizens—'bread'; and to chariot-racing (not the gladiatorial shows)—'circuses'. Today the phrase has a wider meaning encompassing welfare benefits and popular culture.

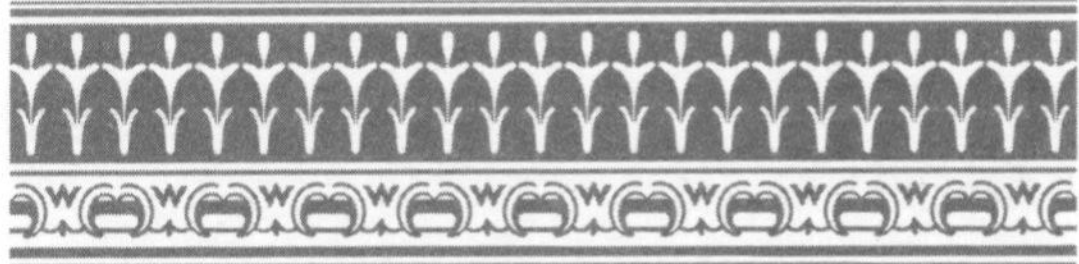

XV

ENTERTAINMENT

1

THEATRE OF DREAMS...

ROME's most impressive ruin and the largest amphitheatre in the world—a record it still holds today—is the Colosseum. The outer wall is a little under 160 feet high and the central arena is an oval measuring 287 feet by 180. The building could seat between 50,000 and 80,000 people. There were eighty entry/exit ways, known as *vomitoria*, and it is estimated that the building could be emptied in fifteen minutes.*

The official opening of the Colosseum in AD 80 was an elaborate affair. Shows took place on 123 days; 11,000 animals, tame and wild, were killed and 10,000 gladiators fought contests. The Colosseum was known officially as the Flavian Amphitheatre (after the ruling family of the day, the Flavian emperors) but informally as the Amphitheatre or Hunting Theatre.

The opening celebrations apparently included a battle between elephants. Gladiators fought in single combat or groups, and there were also infantry and naval battles. For the latter, we are told, the arena was filled with water. One of the sea-fights was inspired by a famous historical event: the struggle in 413 BC between the Athenians and the Syracusans, first in the grand harbour of Syracuse and then on land. In this Roman restaging, 3,000 men took part, but we do not know how many died; and on this occasion the judgement of history was reversed and the 'Athenians' defeated the 'Syracusans'.

* The abrupt disgorging of spectators from these exits must have suggested an analogy with throwing-up, hence the name *vomitorium* (from the Latin *vomere*, 'to vomit'). For the old chestnut that a *vomitorium* was a special room in which diners vomited, see page 128.

ii

… AND NIGHTMARES

THE ROMANS greatly enjoyed watching criminals relive—or more accurately, perhaps, re-die—the bloodier stories of Greek and Roman mythology. According to legend, Prometheus was punished for giving humankind the secret of fire; he was chained to a mountain crag and an eagle consumed his ever-renewing liver. In a re-enactment at the Colosseum a wild boar replaced the bird and gored a man to death. As the contemporary poet Martial complacently remarked:* 'What had been a play became an execution.'

In another colourful legend, Pasiphae, queen of Crete, fell in love with a handsome white bull and gave birth to the Minotaur, the famous monster, half man and half beast, who lived in the labyrinth at Knossos. In an imaginative revival, a woman was mated with a bull. We are not told exactly how this was engineered, nor whether she survived the ordeal.

iii

A DEAD-END JOB

MOST GLADIATORS were forced labour, slaves who had no choice in their own fate. They were often prisoners of war or condemned criminals. But for some, fighting in the arena was a freely chosen career. One emperor issued a decree forbidding well-to-do, respectable citizens from taking up the trade. But Commodus, who reigned in the second century AD, had no hesitation in getting involved himself.†

Gladiators were first hired, or so it is said, in the third century BC as part of a Roman aristocrat's funeral ceremony, and they probably originated in Campania, south of Rome. Over time they became glamorous popular entertainers, and the best of them were highly trained at special colleges.

* To Martial's poetry Lord Byron applied the apt adjective 'nauseous'.

† As we see in the film *Gladiator*. For more on Commodus' eccentricities, see pages 261–62.

Some people sensed that there was something disreputable about taking pleasure in death and injury and justified the arena by saying that it taught spectators how to be brave in battle. The Christian Church disapproved of gladiatorial combats; they were first officially banned in AD 325, but only finally disappeared in the seventh century.

iv

A NOT SO BLOODY BLOODFEST

THE POPULAR picture is that a gladiatorial show was awash with blood and guts, but most fights were not in fact to the death. Far from it. Such shows were phenomenally expensive and the entrepreneurs who staged them would not have stayed in business for long if their highly trained and expensive-to-keep human livestock was wiped out at every display. We know of one gladiator, Publius Ostorius of Pompeii, who survived fifty-one fights. The gravestone of another, a certain Flamma, sets out his record:

> Flamma lived 30 years, fought 34 times, won 21 times, fought to a draw 9 times, was defeated 4 times, a Syrian by nationality. Delicatus made this for his deserving comrade-in-arms.

In their heyday it has been estimated that there may have been 16,000 gladiators at any given time throughout the Roman empire and that there was a 'wastage' of about 13 per cent for every show.

Still, the publicity promised blood, and gladiators are reported to have chanted: 'Hail Caesar, greetings from men about to die.' 'Or not, as the case may be!' shouted back the eccentric emperor Claudius, unwilling to be taken in by a false prospectus.

v

THUMBS UP OR THUMBS DOWN?

ROMAN EMPERORS, from Peter Ustinov's Nero in the Hollywood blockbuster *Quo Vadis?* to Joaquin Phoenix's Commodus in *Gladiator*, have hosted gladiatorial combats in the arena. When the moment arrives to pardon or condemn a defeated fighter, they raise a thumb up for the former and point it down for the latter.

As ever, what really happened appears to have been rather different.* A fallen fighter would point a finger of his left hand upwards as a plea for mercy. The provider of the games (in the city of Rome usually the emperor) decided whether or not to spare his life, but often took account of the audience's noisily expressed wishes. If he chose death, he would raise his thumb, imitating the fatal weapon; or if he showed mercy, he would turn his thumb down, signifying that the weapon should be dropped.

vi

A CARNIVAL OF ANIMAL CARNAGE

THE ROMAN was like the upper-class Edwardian Englishman: he loved animals so much that he couldn't stop killing them. Admittedly, he did enjoy looking at them too, especially when they performed tricks. And there were plenty to look at, as just about every imaginable kind of wild beast was exhibited in public in Rome.

Elephants first appeared in Rome in the third century BC in a general's triumphal procession. After the wars with Carthage, the next creatures to arrive were ostriches, leopards, panthers and lions from northern Africa, and in 58 BC the first hippopotamus and crocodiles were put on display. Cleopatra, queen of Egypt, donated a giraffe for Julius Caesar's Victory Games of 46 BC. Tigers turned up during the reign of the emperor Augustus, and

* We cannot be absolutely certain, but the interpretation given here is the most natural reading of the Latin terms describing the gestures.

in Nero's day polar bears were exhibited in pools chasing seals. Elephants were trained to walk tight-ropes, lions to play with hares, and performing bears climbed poles.

All of this was, relatively speaking, good clean fun. But what the public really enjoyed were the holocausts of the arena, and for shows where animals were killed people would queue all night to get good seats. Over the years many thousands died and their natural habitats were substantially depopulated.

There were three different kinds of spectacle: armed men fighting or hunting animals; animals set against other animals; and unarmed men or women thrown to animals. The last category was a form of execution. As a rule, victims were tied to a stake or sewn up in animal skins and then exposed to starved beasts which ripped them to pieces.

Even the apparently virtuous Christian emperor Constantine threw a multitude of German prisoners of war to the beasts—'for the entertainment of us all', as a flattering orator put it. The speaker added, sociopathically, that the men suffered more from 'the fun we had with them' than from their actual deaths.

[vii]

A SYMPATHETIC VOICE

THE CATALOGUE of animal slaughter did not go entirely unopposed. Cicero, the orator and statesman, wrote a gossipy letter to a friend about Pompey the Great's games of 55 BC, which were about halfway through at the time:

> That leaves the wild-beast hunts, two a day for five days, marvellous of course—nobody disagrees—and yet, what pleasure can a civilized man get out of seeing a weak human being torn apart by an extremely powerful animal, or a splendid animal being shot through by a hunting spear?

Cicero stayed away and missed an event that nearly wrecked the celebrations. Eighteen elephants were hunted by men with javelins, specially brought over from Africa. One was hit below the eye and died. Another, wounded and crawling on its knees, seized its attackers' shields and threw them up in the air like a juggler with plates. The remainder stampeded and tried to break out through the iron railing that enclosed them. They raised their trunks and trumpeted, as if begging for mercy.

For once, the spectators were touched by the spectacle and wept. They booed and cursed Pompey. In only a few years he would be put to death in Africa, where the elephants had come from. Public opinion was gratified.

[*viii*]

THE HUMANITY OF ELEPHANTS

ELEPHANTS may have been exploited in circus acts and massacred in animal hunts, but the Romans nevertheless endowed them with an almost human intelligence. According to Pliny the Elder, they had 'qualities rarely apparent in man, namely, honesty, good sense [and] justice'.

Among the more or less plausible beliefs that the Romans held about elephants was the idea that they understood the spoken language of their country of origin; that, like human beings, they made love in private; that they knew that they were hunted for their ivory tusks and, when cornered, knocked them off and offered them to hunters as a ransom; that they refused to fight each other even when ordered to do so; and that they were affectionate and had good memories (one beast in old age was reported to have recognized the mahout it had had when it was young).

Even the less bright animals showed their native wit. 'It is a known fact,' claimed Pliny, 'that one elephant, somewhat slow in understanding orders, was often beaten with a lash and was discovered at night practising what he had to do.'

A DAY AT THE RACES

CHARIOT-RACING was a hugely popular sport among all social classes. It was as expensive and dangerous as Formula One racing is today and generated as much on-course betting as a meeting at Aintree or Epsom.

Drivers and chariots belonged to two teams or factions (the Reds and the Whites), later changed to four and then back to two again. In Rome these were massive organizations which employed buyers, trainers, doctors, vets, grooms and stablemen and were controlled by a team manager (*dominus*). The factions attracted fierce, sometimes violent, loyalty among their fans.

There were two main racecourses in Rome: the Circus Maximus beneath the Palatine hill and the smaller Circus Flaminius. Chariots were usually drawn by four horses, but on occasion up to ten, while novices drove two-horse chariots. They waited in twelve starting boxes, charged down a long straight, manoeuvred sharply and dangerously around a cluster of three turning posts, galloped back, turned again, and so on for seven laps. A race at the Circus Maximus, which was more than 350 metres long and had a capacity of 250,000 spectators (now it is only a scrappy stretch of grass), lasted about a quarter of an hour.

Racing was extremely dangerous, and there were frequent spectacular and lethal pile-ups, especially at the turns; charioteers always carried a knife with them to cut themselves free in the event of a crash. Great tactical skill was required. It was important not to take a turn too wide, for it could allow space for a competitor to overtake. A favourite trick was to crowd opposing chariots and cause a collision.

[x]

LORDS OF THE TRACK

CHARIOT-RACING was reserved for professionals, and young men from the upper classes were excluded from entering and driving their own chariots. The more raffish emperors might encourage an exception. Predictably, the emperor Nero allowed elite men and women to compete as charioteers.

Charioteers were hugely popular. Many of them began their careers as slaves, but bought their freedom with their prize money. They could earn giddyingly large sums. One of the most successful, in the second century AD, was a Spaniard called Appuleius Diocles, who styled himself the 'greatest of charioteers'. Driving teams of horses for twenty-four years, he took part in more than 4,000 races and came first nearly 1,500 times. He won a staggering total of almost 36 million sesterces (though presumably some of this was payable to his faction or management team) and earned himself a place among the super-rich of ancient Rome.

Not every charioteer was as successful as Diocles. The owners of a dead slave, a 22-year-old called Eutyches, paid for his gravestone. The epitaph shows their fondness for him—despite the fact that he was obviously not much good at his job. It imagines the dead man, who died from an illness and not on the racecourse, speaking with touching modesty about his brief career:

> In this grave rest the bones of an inexperienced charioteer…
> I had the guts to drive the four-horsed chariots,
> But never won promotion from the two-horse teams…
> Please, traveller, place some flowers on my grave.
> – Were you perhaps a fan of mine when I was alive?

xi

BLIND FANATICS

Some educated Romans were mystified by the popularity of the races and looked down their noses at them. For instance, Pliny the Younger complained:

> Once seen is enough. So it astonishes me all the more that so many grown men should have such a childish passion for watching horses galloping and men standing up in chariots, again and again and again. If they were attracted by the speed of the horses or the drivers' skill, one could account for their fanaticism, but in fact it's the racing colours they love, that captivate them. If the drivers swapped colours mid-race, the fans would change sides and desert the famous drivers and teams of horses they had been cheering to the echo a little before.

THE UNIVERSE

i

A SMALL WORLD, FUZZY AT THE EDGES

THE ROMAN world was very different from ours. It was small and fuzzy at the edges. This was because most explorers—usually traders—did not travel far from the Mediterranean, and in any case accurate measuring equipment had not been invented.

The Romans accepted that they lived on a globe. The known world's land mass, they believed, was a roughly circular disk that consisted only of Europe and the Middle East (with the island of Britannia perched on its north-western edge) and was surrounded by an expanse of sea, Oceanus. Some geographers supposed that there might be undiscovered countries a long way away, but had no idea that the American and Australasian continents existed, nor even that there was land beyond India.

The Roman empire took up a large part of the world as it was believed to be, and it was tempting for ambitious rulers to dream that Rome might one day conquer it all.

ii

PICTURING THE WORLD

IN ROMAN times maps were rare. The first known world map was commissioned by Julius Caesar in 44 BC, not long before his assassination, probably as part of a triumphal monument on the Capitoline hill in Rome, which showed him in a chariot with the world, in the form of a globe, at his feet. It was a major project and called for much detailed research. It took at least twenty years to be completed.

Augustus commissioned his deputy, Marcus Vipsanius Agrippa, to work on a more detailed world map, called the *orbis terrarum* ('globe of the earth'). This showed hundreds of cities linked by Rome's road network and was based on reports sent in by Roman generals and governors and by travellers. While a broadly recognizable picture was drawn, distances and shapes became less and less accurate as the mileage from Rome increased.

The main purpose of Agrippa's map was as a practical aid for imperial administrators. As a visual representation of the empire, it was also a powerful metaphor of Roman power. The map was painted or engraved on the wall of the Porticus Vipsania, a colonnade built by Agrippa's sister, and was on permanent public display. Agrippa also provided copious notes which gave details not easily shown on the map itself, as when he claimed that high cliffs along the coastline of the Caspian Sea prevented ships from making landfall for 400 miles.

We don't know exactly what the *orbis terrarum* looked like, but a medieval copy of a Roman world map has survived that may give a clue. It is more of an itinerary than a geographical representation. Distances, facilities and relevant geographical features along the thousands of miles of Roman roads are marked up in a schematic fashion. The design was based on much the same principle as the map of the London Underground railway system, in that its aim was to guide travellers to their destinations rather than to give a picture of what the world looked like from some imaginary position in space.

111

VOYAGE TO THE MOON

IF THE GREEKS and Romans had an incomplete idea of the nature of the earth, they knew even less of the moon, planets and stars. This gave a comic writer, Lucian of Samosata, who lived in the second century AD, just the opening he needed. His skit on travellers' tall tales, *A True History*, is the first known example of science fiction.

Lucian embarks on a voyage of exploration and is sailing westwards across the Atlantic when his ship is struck by a violent whirlwind. After seven days being blown through the air, it lands on the moon. Here Lucian and his friends meet the Moon People and help them wage an interplanetary war with the armies of the Sun. They fight alongside the Vulture Cavalry, the Flea Archers and the Garlic Fighters.

The Moon People are strikingly odd. There are no women and men marry men; when pregnant, they carry their babies in the calves of their legs. Lucian continues:

> I'll tell you something even more peculiar. There is a race of people among them called Tree-men. They are born as follows. They cut off a man's right testicle and plant it in the ground. From this grows a very tall tree, made of flesh and looking like a large erect penis, with foliage and fruit in the form of acorns about two feet long. When these are ripe, they pick them and shell out the men. These are given artificial genitals made of ivory (or wood for the poor). In sexual intercourse, they work remarkably well.

[iv]

SPACE TRAVEL

In his study of politics and philosophy, *The Republic*, written between 54 and 51 BC, Cicero imagines what it must be like to leave earth and move around among the stars. His vision of the universe is as unscientific as Lucian's, but it evokes the grandeur of infinite space.

The book is an imaginary dialogue *à la* Plato. One of the speakers is Scipio Aemilianus, the man who captured and razed to the ground the city of Carthage.* He reports that he had a dream one night. The ghost of his adoptive grandfather, Scipio Africanus, the general who defeated Hannibal (see page 148), transported him to a transcendently high point among the constellations. This was where those who led good, patriotic lives went after death. 'They live in that bright circle of light which you see over there,' the old man says, pointing at the Milky Way. Scipio's grandson was astounded and humbled:

> When I looked all around me from that point, everything appeared extraordinarily beautiful. There were stars invisible from earth, all larger than we have ever imagined. The smallest was the most distant and the one closest to the earth [the moon] shone with a reflected light.

* For more on the destruction of Carthage, see pages 81–3.

> The starry globes were much larger than the earth. In fact, the earth itself seemed so small that I felt scornful of our Roman empire, which is only a kind of dot.
>
> Beneath the moon there is nothing that is not mortal and doomed to decay, except for the souls which, by the grace of the gods, have been conferred on human beings. But above the moon everything is eternal.

Aemilianus couldn't stop looking at the distant earth. His grandfather told him that only a few places were inhabited, with vast deserts in between. 'The distances are so great that no communication is possible. The whole territory which you Romans hold is really only a small island surrounded by the sea which you on earth call the Atlantic, the Great Sea and the Ocean.'

Unusual to come across a Roman willing to be modest about his empire.

XVII

HEALTH AND MEDICINE

i

BREAK A LEG

Much of classical medicine was a hit-or-miss affair, often based on philosophical theory rather than observation. One exception was bone surgeons—especially those serving in the army—who were given plenty of practice. Procedures such as trepanning the skull, treating broken bones and amputations were conducted with techniques that changed little before the nineteenth century, when proper anaesthetics and antisepsis were discovered.

Evidence of a successful leg amputation dating to the second century AD has been found at Rome's port, Ostia. The end of a femur of a tall man was found to have saw-marks. He seems to have made a recovery from the operation, for the bone shows traces of wear attributed to an artificial leg, perhaps a wooden peg.

An artificial limb dating to about 200 BC has been unearthed near Capua, south of Rome. It was made to resemble a real limb, consisting of a wooden core covered by a bronze sheet shaped to look like a shin and calf.

ii

CLEAR THE THROAT

When a fishbone sticks in your throat, explains Pliny the Elder, it will go down immediately if you plunge your feet into cold water. If such an accident occurs with any other kind of bone, the proper remedy is to apply to the head some fragments of bone taken from the same dish. In cases where bread has stuck in the throat, the best idea is to take some of the same bread—and insert it in both ears.

[111]

THE HYPOCHONDRIAC

Intelligent, rich and well-born, Aelius Aristides believed himself to be chronically ill and spent much of his life flitting about the Mediterranean on the lookout for anything that might restore his health. Born in AD 118 to wealthy Anatolian landowners, he travelled to Rome at the age of twenty-six to launch a career as an orator, but was taken ill.* On and off for the rest of his days he was beset by a multitude of maladies. His symptoms included respiratory problems, a distended stomach, fevers, chest ailments, deafness and toothache. As far as we can judge, some at least of his ailments were psychosomatic in origin.

Miserable and desperate, Aristides consulted the best doctors, without success. And then he discovered Aesculapius, the Greco-Roman god of healing.† At a fashionable resort near Smyrna, he had a dream in which he met the god, who told him to walk barefoot. A trivial exchange, but it changed his life. He became a devotee.

Aristides believed he had a direct line to Aesculapius. He never lost faith, although his health never seems to have improved permanently. Tellingly, though, whenever he had something important to do (write a major speech, for example), he got better. He wrote five orations in which he narrates the ups and downs of his condition. Called *The Sacred Stories*, they are the nearest thing to a personal memoir to have come down to us from the ancient world.

He recalls that in AD 148, when he was thirty-one, a tumour grew in his groin for no apparent reason. 'Everything was swollen and terrible pains ensued.' Aesculapius told Aristides to do nothing and to foster the tumour's growth. Friends accused him of being cowardly for refusing surgery or cauterizing drugs. In fact, in the absence of real anaesthetics and adequate anatomical knowledge, surgery was painful and often killed. The god was a softer alternative to the rigours of secular medicine.

* Public speaking was a much admired art; see page 155.

† Or Asklepios, as he was known in his Greek persona.

Eventually Aesculapius prescribed a drug, the contents of which Aristides curiously forgets: when rubbed on, the growth rapidly disappeared.

[iv]

IN SEARCH OF THE DREAM CURE

ACROSS the Roman empire, especially in the East, there were centres dedicated to Aesculapius, god of healing, where the well-off unwell were looked after.

The centre at Epidaurus, a small city-state in southern Greece, was particularly grand. In its heyday the city featured not only a stone theatre (which seats up to 15,000 people and still survives), but also a stadium, temples, colonnades and, most important of all, the Abaton, or dormitory. Here Aesculapius' worshippers slept and were said to 'see' dreams, in which they received guidance, generally from the god himself. Patients would either be cured at once or receive instructions, often bizarre, of what to do to effect a cure. Priests would help to interpret patients' dreams and then issue prescriptions—frequently medication or physical exercises.

The Aesculapian centres catered for all sorts, including hypochondriacs and valetudinarians, rather in the manner of today's health spas, private nursing homes and rehab clinics, nestling deep in the costly countryside. The treatment, with its emphasis on the interpretation of dreams, anticipates Freud and the inventions of psychoanalysis. The nature of the cures echoes the miraculous certainties of faith healing.

[v]

COUNTRY MATTERS

TREE MOSS from Gaul, advises the author and naturalist Pliny the Elder, is useful in the bath for infections of the female private parts.

[vi]

THE LICK OF A DOG OR A SNAKE

At the great Aesculapian centre in Epidaurus, archaeologists have discovered stone columns on which thankful accounts of miraculous cures have been inscribed. Some of them feature animals that were especially associated with Aesculapius: dogs and snakes. These were believed to have healing powers and to restore a diseased or failing body part to health, usually by licking. First, a snake or serpent:

> A man had his toe healed by a serpent. He was suffering dreadfully from a malignant sore on his toe. During the daytime servants took him outside the temple and placed him on a seat. When sleep overtook him, a snake emerged from the Dormitory and healed the toe with its tongue, and afterwards went back again to the Dormitory. The patient woke up and was healed. He said that he had seen a vision; it seemed to him that a beautiful young man had put a drug on his toe.

And then there was a dog:

> A dog cured a boy from the Greek island of Aegina. He had a growth on his neck. When he came to the god, one of the sacred dogs healed him—while he was awake—with its tongue and made him well.

What are we to make of such events? Charlatanry is unlikely to have been a major factor. Autosuggestion, the placebo effect, simultaneous routine medical treatment and something as simple as rest and good food could all have played a part. It is not inconceivable that some form of hypnotism was involved.

[vii]

SEX, SNAKES AND REFERRED PAIN

A man, Pliny reports, who has been stung by a serpent or scorpion is said to gain relief by having sex. Unfortunately, the pain then passes to the woman.

[viii]

ROMAN EXHIBITIONISM (I)

THE BATHS

Bathing, for us, is generally a solitary activity. Not so for the Romans: they liked to do it in public. It was, in fact, the social high point of their day.

Bath-houses became widespread in the first century BC, and by the time of Augustus there were as many as 170 of them in Rome. In the heyday of empire huge establishments were constructed. The most sumptuous and elaborately decorated were the Baths of Diocletian, which opened around AD 306 and covered 32 acres. Approximately 3,000 people could use them at one time.

At the centre of the bathing complex were hot rooms, steam rooms, cool rooms and swimming pools. There were also gardens, open-air gymnasiums, libraries and reading rooms, perfume shops and fast-food counters, and lecture halls. Everywhere there were statues around which fountains played. The price of entry was very cheap and Romans of all classes rubbed shoulders, chatted, did deals and watched the world go by. Women usually bathed separately, although sometimes the sexes were allowed to mix. Even emperors could be found at the baths.*

One might have thought health and hygiene were what made bathing so popular. In fact, medical experts knew there were dangers to the practice. Water was seldom changed and residues of oil, grime and even urine or excrement built up and were kept riskily warm: bacteria were in heaven. One famous doctor warned: 'Going to the baths, while a wound is still open, is one of the worst things to do; for... there is a tendency for gangrene to occur.'

In truth, it was the pursuit of pleasure that drew the crowds, as the epitaph of a certain Tiberius Claudius Secundus makes clear:

> Baths, wine and women ruin our bodies, but baths, wine and women make life worth living.

* The British flirted briefly with the Roman idea of bathing. In the mid-nineteenth century Turkish baths, similar in design to their Roman predecessors, became fashionable, and about 600 of them opened throughout the country. But after the Second World War their popularity faded and (at the last count) only fourteen remain.

[ix]

ROMAN EXHIBITIONISM (II)

THE TOILETS

PUBLIC CONVENIENCES in Rome were public in the full sense of the word. Dotted around the city there stood splendid establishments for the evacuation of human waste. One of the grandest has survived the centuries and can be seen today. It features twenty marble seats arranged around a large rectangular room; each seat was framed by sculptured brackets in the shape of dolphins, under which water flowed (often second-hand from nearby public baths). As marble was chilly in winter, the most luxurious *foricae*, as they were known, were centrally heated.

No concessions were made to the shy. The fact is that these toilets had a secondary function which modesty screens would only have inhibited. They were places where the fashionable met for conversation, for gossip and to exchange invitations to dinner; they were where the upper crust liked to congregate and chatter. Sometimes officials continued negotiations there with visiting foreign dignitaries.

[x]

THE JOYS OF THE SECOND-HAND SPONGE STICK

LAVATORY PAPER had not yet been invented, and bottoms were wiped with sponges on sticks. At the user's feet ran a narrow channel with running water, and this was where dirty sponges were doused (sometimes a water-filled jar was used instead). If you were lucky, a servant boy would soak your sponge in vinegar—a minimal concession to hygiene. Was the sponge attached to a stick or reed moistened with vinegar that was given to Christ on the cross borrowed from a *forica*, one wonders? If so, it was one more humiliation for the dying man.

[xi]

TAXING THE PISS

THERE WAS MONEY in urine. In addition to public toilets, piss-pots stood at street corners and their contents were collected for use in the tanning industry and for bleaching togas and other clothes. Some private houses boasted a latrine, whose contents were channelled into a cesspit periodically emptied by manure merchants, but most people made do with chamber pots.

None of this was lost on the wise old emperor Vespasian, who reigned in the first century AD. In response to his son Titus, who was prudishly disgusted by a new tax on the sale of urine, the emperor held up a gold coin and said: '*pecunia non olet*'—'Money doesn't smell.'* Cash is cash wherever it comes from.

[xii]

REMEDY FOR WARTS

TO GET RID of warts, Pliny the Elder notes, some people lie on a footpath with their face upwards when the moon is at least twenty days old. They then fix their gaze on the moon, stretch their arms beyond their head, and rub themselves with anything they find within their reach.

* Vespasian is still remembered for his interest in public conveniences. His name is associated with them in France, where pissoirs were called *vespasiennes* and were a common sight until the 1990s. In Italy, likewise, they were called *vespasiani*, and in Romania *vespasiene*.

[xiii]

CABBAGE, QUEEN OF VEGETABLES

FOR US the cabbage is a worthy but dull vegetable—hardly something to get worked up about. How wrong we are. The Romans knew better, believing it was pretty much a panacea for every ailment.*

If you are planning a pub crawl or a boozy banquet, you should eat as much cabbage as possible, seasoned with vinegar, before going out and a few leaves after the meal. A Roman farming expert, Cato the Elder, explains: 'It will make you feel as if you had not dined, and you can drink as much you please.'

If you want to clean out the digestive tract, squeeze boiled cabbage in a cloth and mix the juice with salt and some crushed cumin. Before taking a dose of this, you should drink honey-water and go to bed having fasted. Early next morning drink the juice and take a long walk. You will feel nauseous and 'evacuate such a quantity of bile and mucus you will wonder where it all came from'.

If you are feeling out of sorts, an infallible remedy is to bathe in the urine of someone who regularly drinks cabbage water. Babies washed in this urine will be strengthened and poor sight will be relieved if the eyes are bathed in it.

Cabbage is also a sovereign cure for colic and effective as a poultice for suppurating wounds and for dislocations.

[xiv]

ONE IN THE EYE

ONIONS are an alternative to urine as a cure for poor vision. They work by making you cry, writes Pliny. 'Even more effective is to apply onion juice directly to the eye.'

* A notable Roman cabbage-fancier was the emperor Diocletian; see page 265.

[xv]

AN EMPRESS'S PRESCRIPTION

LIVIA, wife of Rome's first emperor, Augustus, lived to the age of eighty and was a great believer in a healthy lifestyle and 'natural' remedies.* Here is her prescription for a sore throat and tonsillitis. The empress always had this ready to hand, stored in a glass vessel:

8 grams of each of the following:
costus,† opium, anis, aromatic rush, red cassia, seed of hazelwort
4 grams of coriander
3.5 grams of cardamom
4 grams of split alum
5 grains the size of chickpeas from the centre of oak apple
7 grams of saffron
3.5 grams of saffron residue
3.5 grams of myrrh
15.5 grams of Greek birthwort
11.5 grams of cinnamon
19.5 grams of the ash of baked chicks of wild swallows
3.5 grams of a grain of nard

All these ingredients, thoroughly ground up, are mixed with skimmed Attic honey.‡

[xvi]

IF YOU SIT ON YOUR ARSE ALL DAY...

TO PREVENT chafing when you set out on a journey on horseback, Cato says, place a sprig of wormwood under your anus, and all will be well.

* For more on the extraordinary life of Livia, see pages 140–41.

† An oriental aromatic plant.

‡ You should avoid trying Livia's recipe. Not only are some of the ingredients hard to find—how does one readily obtain the chicks of wild swallows?—but birthwort contains aristolochic acid, which can cause kidney damage or even failure.

ARCHITECTURE AND ENGINEERING

i

'A WONDERFUL ACHIEVEMENT BEYOND ALL DESCRIPTION'

AMONG THEIR MANY remarkable feats of engineering, the Romans developed the dome, the arch, the vault and the apse. They were also the first to make extensive use of *opus caementicum*—cement which was made from crushed rock with lime as a binder and which would set hard under water. Many of their works have survived to the present day. Hadrian's Pantheon, which for 1,700 years was the largest dome in the world, is still in use as a place of worship nearly two millennia after it was built. The Colosseum; the massive Tabularium, ancient Rome's records office overlooking the Forum; Domitian's grand palace on the Palatine hill: all are hardy reminders that Roman architects built to last.

Indeed, one of their admirers, the intellectual and antiquarian Dionysius of Halicarnassus, writing in the first century BC, praised Roman engineering as 'a wonderful achievement beyond all description. In fact, in my opinion the three most magnificent works of Rome, in which you can best see the greatness of its empire, are the aqueducts, the paved roads and the construction of her sewers.'

ii

THE WALLS OF ROME

THE ROMANS didn't have to be told twice. In 390 BC a host of marauding Gauls marched down Italy and had little difficulty capturing Rome: the city's early defences were clearly inadequate (see pages 22–3).

Once the invaders had gone, work started on a set of massive new fortifications, the so-called Servian Walls.* Built by Greek masons from Sicily, they comprised 11 kilometres of wall with

* The name comes from the mistaken supposition that the walls were originally built by one of Rome's kings, Servius Tullius, who was said to have reigned in the sixth century BC (see page 9).

21 gates enclosing an area of 426 hectares. On the plateau of the Esquiline hill the wall was further protected by a wide ditch and a huge earth rampart. These massive defences, some of which survive to this day, are a reminder that, as early as the fourth century and long before it acquired an empire, Rome was already a great city.

As the years passed, the walls became overgrown with buildings and beyond them lay unguarded suburbs. In the third century AD the risk of barbarian invasions grew, and between the years AD 270 and 282 the emperors Aurelian and Probus refortified the much enlarged city with a new set of walls built in brick-faced concrete. This time they were 19 kilometres long; there were 383 towers, 18 main gates and many posterns; and 1,372 hectares were enclosed. The walls ran along the riverbank and, for the first time, the Janiculum hill on the far side of the Tiber (above today's Trastevere) was defended.

These fortifications are remarkably well preserved. They were modified during the Renaissance and formed part of the city's defences as late as the nineteenth century, although the development of artillery made them ineffective.

111

WATER, WATER EVERYWHERE

WITHOUT aqueducts to bring fresh water in and a drainage system to take dirty water out, the city of Rome could not have grown from a medium-sized town into a megalopolis by the end of the first century BC.

As early as the time of the kings of Rome, it was clear that the marshy Forum would have to be drained if it was to become the city's political, religious and business centre. A stream running through the square was covered over and construction began on the Cloaca Maxima ('biggest drain'). Over the centuries it was enlarged and improved.* A copious supply of used water from

* Some of the drain's stone-clad tunnels survive and are in use today, and its mouth—a stone arch on the banks of the Tiber—can still be seen.

public bath-houses flowed through the sewer, swilling away sewage deposited from public buildings and latrines, and perhaps also from private cesspits. The Cloaca even had its own special goddess, Venus Cloacina—Venus of the Sewer.*

Aqueducts were the necessary twin of the drainage system: without the one you could not have the other. By the first century AD nearly 300 million gallons of clean water, collected from the Apennine mountains, gushed into the city every day by means of eleven aqueducts. They fed the city's thirsty bath-houses and public fountains, where people collected water for their own use. The aqueducts were not meant to serve private houses, although senators were said to filch water from nearby pipes (or to have paid bribes to have them run under their houses, into which they could illegally cut a spur).

The sewers of Rome were much imitated throughout the Roman empire, especially when combined with aqueducts. The drainage system in Eboracum (the modern-day English city of York), part of which was excavated in the 1970s, is an especially impressive example.

iv

FLUSHING OUT THE CITY'S HUMAN GARBAGE

THE CLOACA Maxima wasn't Rome's only means of waste disposal. Near the Forum stands the little church of San Giuseppe dei Falegnami, which used to be the ancient city's official prison. A shaft from an upper room leads to a small circular subterranean chamber where a spring rose through the floor and flowed down a chute into the Cloaca. It was in this wet, dark, cramped space that important prisoners were detained and sentences of death carried out. The victim was strangled and his body pushed into the sewer, whence it would be flushed into the Tiber and carried downriver to the sea. This was not only a simple and

* The goddess was responsible not only for waste disposal but also, oddly, for sexual intercourse within marriage.

practical means of disposal, but also a token of the state's disgust with its enemies: they were no more than garbage.

v

BRIDGES BUILT TO LAST...

ROMAN ENGINEERS built arch or pillar bridges over all the major rivers of the empire except for the Euphrates and the Nile. Typically made from stone and concrete, a good number of them are still in use today. Two of the most famous are in Rome.

The Ponte Sant'Angelo, now open only to pedestrians, was completed in AD 134. Originally called the Pons Aelius, it was commissioned by the emperor Hadrian (whose family name was Aelius) to connect the city of Rome with his colossal tomb. This was converted into a fortress in AD 401 and is now known as the Castel Sant'Angelo.

The Ponte Milvio or Milvian Bridge (originally Pons Milvius) was erected by the consul Gaius Claudius Nero in 206 BC following his victory over the Carthaginians at the river Metaurus during the Second Punic War. It was completely rebuilt in 115 BC. It was here, in 63 BC, that the statesman and orator Cicero, consul for that year, intercepted some damning letters and exposed a planned coup d'état. And it was at the battle of the Milvian Bridge, on 28 October, AD 312, that the emperor Constantine saw a vision that converted him to Christianity.*

* For the story of Constantine and the Milvian Bridge, see page 266. Today the bridge is popular with young lovers, who attach 'love padlocks' to a lamp-post and throw away the keys, as a symbol of their affection. Rust from thousands of padlocks and their sheer weight threatened the integrity of the structure and, to protests, the authorities removed them in September 2012.

[vi]

... AND NOT TO LAST

ROMAN LEGIONS employed talented engineers who constructed and deconstructed temporary wooden bridges in a very short space of time. In 55 BC Julius Caesar had a timber bridge built across the river Rhine in ten days, led his army across it for a brief campaign against some Germanic tribes, and destroyed it on his return eighteen days later. The most remarkable of these ephemeral creations was a bridge crossing the river Danube built by the emperor Trajan in AD 104. It was 2,205 feet long and had 21 arch spans, each of which measured about 105 feet.

[vii]

HADRIAN'S PLACE IN THE COUNTRY

HADRIAN'S VILLA (Villa Adriana in Italian) is not really a villa at all. It is more of a township and occupies hundreds of acres of land below the hill town of Tivoli some 20 miles northeast of Rome. The 'villa' was commissioned by the emperor Hadrian, who reigned from AD 117 to 138. He wanted a perfect setting that doubled as a holiday retreat and a centre of government.

The setting is perfect indeed—the loveliest of places. The ruins of thirty-five elaborate stone and brick structures stand among cypresses, maritime pines and olive trees. Renaissance polymaths were fascinated. As well as stealing its architectural ideas, they stripped the walls of their marble facings and the floors of their mosaics, to adorn the *palazzi* of cardinals. They also removed numberless statues. But what remains is still one of the wonders of European civilization.

Beneath the grand edifices where the emperor Hadrian and his guests lounged or held their committee meetings lay a hidden world of tunnels, store-rooms and windowless sleeping areas. Here servants and slaves lived and laboured—out of sight, out of hearing and out of mind—to provide all the necessary services for those in the light above ground. Some of these corridors in the cellarage survive, just as they were.

A curious aspect of the complex is that it gives a representation in miniature of the Roman world as Hadrian saw it, especially those parts of it that held a special meaning for him. It was his metaphor in brick and stone for the empire itself. So, for example, there was a symbolic evocation of the Academy, the grove outside Athens where the philosopher Plato taught. Canopus, a tourist resort in the Nile delta, was represented by a long, statue-lined pool and a monumental half-domed open-air dining room. Apparently a version of Hades was constructed—the underworld to which all human beings descended after death—but we do not know where it was located or what it looked like.

[*viii*]

A PUZZLE BENEATH THE EARTH

As well as representing a microcosm of the world, Hadrian's Villa conceals a subterranean mystery. To the south of the imperial estate rises an upland, with only a few buildings on it. Here the emperor Hadrian and his companions could ride or hunt. However, below rough fields one of the villa's most astonishing features is to be found: four uniform passageways, 800 metres long in all and wide enough for a chariot to clatter along, join to form a rough rectangle.

A huge amount of labour went into their creation—20,000 cubic metres of rock had to be cut out and removed. At intervals holes in the ceiling let in light and air. The tunnels look and feel much as they did in Hadrian's time. The air in them is decidedly chilly, even on hot days. So far as can be judged, these unseen corridors had no practicable exits except for one link to an open-air stone theatre. So what on earth were they for?

Such a major engineering project must have had an important function. Some scholars say that it could have had something to do with religious ceremonial. We know that Hadrian was attracted to cults which offered an out-of-body spiritual experience. Perhaps initiates were brought down here to take part in chthonic rituals, not unlike the terrifying mysteries at Eleusis near Athens, where darkness and sudden bright light induced ecstatic visions of truth. Or the solution of the conundrum may be that the tunnels represented Hadrian's vision of the afterlife, the Hades of his imagination. This explanation fits the evidence, such as it is, but we cannot be sure. The villa keeps its secrets.

TRAVEL AND TRANSPORT

1

ROME'S SPREADING TENTACLES

All roads lead to Rome? Not at all. From the Roman point of view, they all led *from* Rome. They enabled the army, provincial governors, tax farmers and countless others to march or ride off from the city to govern the world. Like a vast spider's web, they spread across the empire. There were more than 250,000 miles of high-quality Roman highways, of which 50,000 were paved. At their greatest extent, they would have girdled the earth thirty-one times.

Roman roads were less to do with business and tourism than with *control*.

They existed, in the first instance, to serve the legions. Communications in the ancient world were very slow, and the Romans would have found it next to impossible to manage their expanding empire if they had not found a way to speed them up.

Rome's road network had a symbolic as well as a practical value. The Greek-born historian, biographer and essayist Plutarch wrote in the first century AD:

> [The] roads were carried straight through the country without deviation, and were paved with hewn stone, and supported with masses of tight-rammed sand. Depressions were filled in, all intersecting torrents or ravines were bridged over, and both sides of the roads were of equal and corresponding height, so that the work had everywhere an even and beautiful appearance.

The effect was one of conquest over nature. No natural feature—neither hill nor valley—was allowed to get in the way. Where the Roman wanted his roads to go, there they went. And they were built to last: two millennia after they were laid down, we still travel on some of them today.*

* When driving in Europe, you can often tell you are going over what was once a Roman road by the way it rolls on and on without a curve. In many cases the original paving stones lie beneath the tarmac.

ii

INTO THE LANDS OF ALEXANDER

ROMAN ROADS allowed the legions to get where they needed to get to—fast. The Via Egnatia is a fine example. To reach it from Rome, you travelled down the Appian Way to the port of Brundisium (modern Brindisi) and sailed across the Adriatic Sea to the port of Dyrrachium in northern Greece (now Dürres in Albania), where the road started. Built in the second century BC when Rome was busy conquering Greece and the Middle East, it ran for nearly 700 miles to the strategically placed town of Byzantium on the Bosphorus.

The road drastically cut the time it took to reach the provinces of the Middle East. If there was trouble—say, a rebellion—the legions could march post-haste along the Via Egnatia and into the lands once owned by the Persian King of Kings and then Alexander the Great.

iii

CROSSING THE POND

THE ROMAN EMPIRE was a field around a pond. This meant that the tourist or the businessman had the singular advantage of being able to take ship from Ostia, Rome's port, and sail in one direction or another across the Mediterranean to almost any provincial destination. It was quicker, cheaper and more convenient than travelling by land on grindingly uncomfortable roads.

This is not to say that sailing was, in itself, especially quick. Ancient ships moved slowly through the water, powered by a large square-rigged mainsail, a small, triangular topsail, and (to help manoeuvrability in confined waters) a bowsprit sail.

Nor was travelling by sea all that convenient. It was, in fact, quite risky. Ships were vulnerable to storms and gales, and shipwrecks were frequent. Sailing was impractical during winter months. Sea-captains set a course by the sun in the day and by the stars at night, so in cloudy weather they were lost. For safety they tended to hug the coastline and rely on landmarks; inevitably, rocks and reefs—to say nothing of pirates—were never far off.

There were no passenger liners, and the traveller had to go to a port and hitch a lift from a merchantman. Unless he was a VIP, he would be allotted a space on deck, for cabins were few and far between. He would sleep in the open or under some sort of rigged-up tent. He had to provide his own food, which he could cook in the galley. It was best to have a servant or a slave to help out—if you could afford it.

[iv]

DON'T SNEEZE ON THE GANGPLANK!

THERE WAS no question of Roman ships running on time: timetables were out of the question. Ships had to wait for a fair wind before setting off. Then there were the omens. Sailors were (and are) very superstitious, and they would refuse to move on the numerous officially unlucky days, which were scattered throughout the calendar. Before departure animal sacrifices were held and unfavourable signs in the carcass (say, an anomaly in the liver) inevitably meant a postponement.

Even after clearance to sail, problems could still arise. A nightmare might deter a voyager or a ship's officer. It brought bad luck to sneeze on the gangplank. A crow croaking in the rigging was an ill omen too, but once a ship was underway birds were auspicious. If the weather was fine, no one on board should cut their hair or nails; but a storm god could be appeased if you threw clippings or locks into the sea.

In 51 BC it took more than a fortnight for the orator and statesman Cicero to cross the Aegean Sea from Athens to Asia Minor, where he was to take up his duties as a provincial governor. He was delayed by a troublesome wind and battered by a savage gale. A cautious man, he took care to go ashore at night, where he could eat a proper meal and sleep undisturbed. He noted: 'Travelling by sea is no light matter, even in July.'

[v]

A MIGHTY MERCHANTMAN

Rome's merchant fleet needed to carry large amounts of goods, and large ships were required to do it. A standard Roman cargo ship could be more than 180 feet long—about 30 feet longer than the *Mary Rose*, Henry VIII's flagship, which sank more than a millennium later.

Lucian, a Greek author of the second century AD, once saw a giant grain ship stopping off at Piraeus, the port of Athens. This vessel was probably able to transport 1,000 tons of cargo—three times as much as any ocean-going merchant ship before the early nineteenth century. His amazement is palpable when he describes the crew as a 'small army' and stares in awe at the amount of cargo the ship held. He writes excitedly how the grain being transported 'could feed Attica [the national territory of Athens] for a whole year'.

'I say, though, what a size that ship was!' writes Lucian. 'It was more than 45 feet wide, and there was a depth of 44 feet from the deck to the keel. And then the height of the mast, with its huge yard! And what a forestay [rope] it took to hold it!... As to the other ornamental details, the paintings and the scarlet topsail, I was more struck by the anchors, and the capstans and windlasses.'

But Lucian does display some concern about the ship's steering system: 'Everything depends for its safety on one little man, who controls the great rudder with just a broomstick of a tiller. He was pointed out to me, and called Heron, I think—he was a woolly-haired guy with a receding hairline.'

[vi]

AN EVENTFUL JOURNEY

Poet, sensualist, lover of the quiet life, Horace was a friend of Octavian, later to be the emperor Augustus and already a leading man in the state. In 38 or 37 BC he went on an official trip to Brundisium (today's Brindisi), accompanied by Octavian's minister of culture, Maecenas, and an even greater poet than he,

Virgil.* Horace has left a light-hearted record of the journey in verse, which gives an idea of the travails of travellers.

The party left Rome, probably in a carriage, and after 16 miles put up at a modest inn. 'The Appian Way is best taken slowly.' The next stage was through the Pomptine Marshes, which were endemic with malaria.† Night was falling when Horace and his friends boarded a barge. He writes:

> Our slaves shout angrily at boatmen, boatmen at the slaves.
> 'This way with the boat.' 'You're jamming three hundred people
> on board,
> Hey, that's enough.' What with collecting fares and harnessing
> The barge-mule, a whole hour slips by. The bloody mosquitoes and
> The marsh frogs banish sleep. The boatman, soused in stale wine,
> Sings of the girl he's left behind, and a passenger joins in.
> At last the passenger gives up and nods off. The boatman turns
> out his mare
> To graze, ties the reins to a stone and lies on his back snoring.
> Day dawns and we find we're not moving. A furious passenger
> Jumps out and wallops mule and boatman on the head and back.

Next stop was Capua (north of Naples), well known for its enthusiasm for gladiators and its splendid amphitheatre. Horace had an eye infection and rested while Maecenas went out to take some exercise. Days later, when the dry hills of his native Apulia (today's Puglia) came into view, Horace escaped from the heat in a roadside villa. His sore eyes were irritated by a smoky stove, but he had high hopes of an amorous encounter. He was out of luck:

> Here, like an utter fool, I stayed up till midnight
> Waiting for a liar of a girl. Then, eventually, sleep
> Carried me off, but still keyed up for sex.
> A wet dream spattered my tunic as I lay on my back.

At last, Brundisium. A fortnight had passed and 375 miles had been covered. Horace, Maecenas and Virgil, exhausted by their journey, needed a day or two to recover from their tribulations.

* For more on Horace, Virgil and Maecenas, see page 160.

† The marshes were not drained until the time of Mussolini, and malaria was only finally defeated in the 1950s.

MAGIC

1

OVER TO THE DARK SIDE

ROMANS were fascinated by magic and astrology, which they saw as part of the fabric of everyday life, the dark side of religion. Spell books were published and 'magical papyri' have been unearthed from the bone-dry sands of Egypt which reveal the lengths to which people were willing to go to unleash the powers of darkness. Although magic had long been illegal, it became increasingly popular under the emperors. It was employed for many purposes, such as healing illnesses beyond the reach of conventional medicine; hurting, even killing, one's enemies; and improving one's sex life and compelling the object of one's affections to respond in kind.

One of magic's key principles was *sympatheia*, or 'fellow feeling', which allowed the part to be taken for the whole. So, for example, the removal of some hair or nail clippings from a barber's shop gave the spellbinder power over their original owner. Alternatively, and more ambitiously, the principle of 'like for like' explained the use of wax dolls which, when pierced with a needle, communicated pain, or even death, to their human originals. Another version of this same principle involved human sacrifice, where one living person was killed to save another, or volunteered his or her own life in an act of self-immolation (like Alcestis handing herself over to Death in place of her husband in the play by Euripides).

The best way of countering magic was to seek protection. Amulets, for example, worn on the body prevented demons from taking it over. One of them reads: 'Save Esther from evil tormentors, the evil eye, spirits, demons and night ghosts.'

ii

BLABBERMOUTHS BEWARE!

ARCHAEOLOGISTS have unearthed a spell in London anathematizing a woman who seems to have betrayed the secrets of a cult: 'I curse Tretia Maria and her life and mind and memory and liver and lungs mixed up together, and her words, thoughts and memory; thus may she be unable to speak what things are concealed.'

iii

STAR-GAZING INTO THE FUTURE

THE PUBLIC AUTHORITIES believed in astrology and other arcane means of foretelling the shape of things to come, and took a very dim view of them. Because astrology depended on complicated mathematical calculations, reading the stars was felt to be more of a science than spells and incantations, and—despite its inherent implausibility—was bracketed with astronomy as a legitimate form of inquiry.

It was precisely because the authorities were convinced that astrologers genuinely opened a door into the future that they frowned on it. It seemed to give humankind a god-like knowledge compared to which even kingship was insignificant. Casting an emperor's horoscope was high treason, for it might predict the time and manner of his death.

iv

HOW TO FIX A CHARIOT-RACE

THERE WAS PLENTY of passion and money in chariot-racing, so many were tempted to try and fix a race.* And what better way than by casting a curse spell? A favourite method was to incise a message on a lead tablet, roll it up and pierce it

* For the wild world of Roman chariot-racing, see page 173.

with nails; it would then be buried or dropped into a well or pool. Alternatively a tablet might be melted down.

One remarkable example has been discovered in which the curser sought the defeat of a charioteer at the races. It still conveys a strong stench of hatred after two millennia. It demands of a powerful spirit (*daimon*) 'from this day, from this moment that you torture the horses of the Greens and Whites [chariot teams]. Kill them! The charioteers Glarus and Felix and Primulus and Romanus, kill them! Crash them! Leave no breath in them!' Another tablet reads: 'May everyone who rejoices at my expense about the loss of my money become like the lead which is now being liquefied.'

[v]

TWO FOR THE PRICE OF ONE

PROFESSIONAL prophets had to be on their toes. When a traveller consulted one of them and asked how his family was back home, the clairvoyant replied that they were all well, especially his father. 'But he's been dead these ten years.' 'It's obvious you don't know who your real father is,' answered the quick-witted seer.

[vi]

ROMAN VAMPIRES

IN HIS encyclopedic *Natural History*, Pliny the Elder commented disparagingly on medical magic:

> The blood of gladiators is drunk by epileptics as though it were an elixir of life... But (would you believe it?) patients think it extremely effective to suck warm, living blood from a man. They press their lips to the wound to drain the victim's very life, despite the fact that it is not the custom for human beings to apply their mouths to injuries of any kind. Other sick people extract bone marrow from legs, and infants' brains.
>
> Apollonius writes that scraping sore gums with the tooth of a man killed by violence is extremely effective, and Meletus says that a

human gall-bladder heals cataracts. Antaeus made pills from the skull of a hanged man to cure bites from rabid dogs.*

But I don't believe life should be so highly prized that it should be prolonged by any and every possible means.

[vii]

A DYING CURSE

THE POET Horace wrote about a witch called Canidia, who seems to have been a real person, or at least the caricature of one. His horrific evocation of the witch at work as she slowly murders a young boy is one of the nastiest poems in the Latin language.

Canidia and two female companions have buried the boy in the ground, alive and with only his face protruding—like 'someone afloat in water, his chin touching the surface'. Two or three times a day, plates of food are placed in front of him, but he is only allowed to look:

> Once his eyes, on the unattainable food,
> have withered away, his marrow and liver,
> extracted and dried, will serve
> for a love potion.

At last the boy accepts that he is doomed. Instead of trying to pacify his cruel captors, he curses them. When he is dead, he says,

> I'll drive sleep out with terror.
> The mob will crush you, you obscene, senile hags,
> They'll surround you and pelt you with stones.
> No one will bury you. Wolves and birds in the gardens
> Of the Esquiline will scatter your limbs,
> And my parents, who will survive me, alas,
> Won't miss a moment of the spectacle.

* Apollonius, Meletus and Antaeus were well-known medical authorities.

XXI

SEVEN WOMEN

i

A WOMAN'S LOT

Being a Roman woman was not recommended. She was a second-class citizen. She could not vote, and throughout her life she fell—at least in theory—under the guidance of her father, her husband or (in the absence of either of the former) a specially appointed guardian. To be widowed was a stroke of luck, for only then could a woman live freely and be, to all intents and purposes, unsupervised.

The very idea of 'woman' was deeply ambiguous. She was seen throughout the classical world, in the ancient Greek poet Hesiod's much repeated phrase, as a 'beautiful evil', necessary for the propagation of the human race, but at the same time as a wild and sexually insatiable member of what many men saw almost as a different species.

This bleak picture does not tell the whole story. We should not be surprised, for it was painted by men. We only catch glimpses of Roman women; it is as if we are snatching a quick chat with some guests at a half-open door through which the hubbub of a party can be heard—and which we cannot join. The sketchy accounts that have survived suggest vigorous and lively personalities who managed to do far better in a patriarchal society than the traditional record implies. There were surely many other equally remarkable women whose names are lost.

ii

AN INDEPENDENT WOMAN

A very grand lady who knew her mind, Cornelia was a personality in her own right who showed how intelligence, money and class could empower a woman. She was a daughter of Scipio Africanus, the Duke of Wellington of his day—the man who had defeated Rome's fiercest enemy, Hannibal (see page 148). Scipio was an unrepentant lover of Hellenic culture. He enjoyed following Greek fashions and gave his sons a good education in the Greek language and literature. He probably did the same for Cornelia, for she grew up to be a highly cultivated woman and an intellectual. She always had literary people about her.

Born in 191 BC, Cornelia was happily married to a much older husband, Tiberius Sempronius Gracchus. He died when their two sons, Tiberius and Gaius, were small, but she made sure they were as well educated as she had been. Once she was entertaining a woman friend from Campania, a wealthy region where fancy trappings were *de rigueur*. Her guest drew particular attention to some showy jewellery she was wearing. Cornelia waited till her two sons came home from school and said to her: 'These are *my* jewels.'

Cornelia was the nearest thing the Roman Republic had to an international royal celebrity. The pharaoh of Egypt, Ptolemy VIII, offered her his hand in marriage. Nicknamed 'Physcon' (Greek for 'sausage' or 'bladder'), he was a deeply unappealing prospect, and Cornelia politely declined. She decided not to marry again but to manage her estates and devote herself to the education of her children.

Her jewels grew up and became political reformers. Tiberius was elected a tribune of the people and assassinated by reactionary senators in 133 BC. Ten years later, Gaius decided to run for office too. Cornelia was displeased. She sent him a strong letter, telling him to change his mind: 'As my only surviving son, you should have taken trouble and care that I should have the fewest possible anxieties in my old age.' Gaius didn't listen and, another energetic activist, he met a violent fate as his brother had done.*

The mother of the Gracchi left Rome after her second son's death. She settled in Misenum (modern Miseno), a pleasant resort at the northern end of the Bay of Naples that had beautiful views and was off the beaten track. However, she did not hide herself away and made no alteration to the brilliancy of her lifestyle. The Greek author and biographer Plutarch reports: 'She had many friends and because of her love of visitors kept a good table. She always had Greeks and intellectuals as guests, and all the reigning monarchs exchanged gifts with her.'

* For more on the careers and violent ends of the Gracchi, see page 28.

Cornelia was happy to reminisce about her father's life and character. She spoke of her sons, whom she survived by more than ten years, without any tears or displays of emotion, discussing their careers and tragic ends as if she were referring to some long-ago statesmen from Rome's early centuries. She lived the blameless life of a Roman matron, while at the same time running her own affairs as a fully independent person: a rare combination in the ancient world.

iii

THE LYRIC POET

SHAMEFULLY, Sulpicia is the only woman poet from ancient Rome whose work has survived to this day. It is hard to believe that there were no others like her, but they have not come down to us.

Almost nothing is known of her, but luckily a few of her verses survive. She lived during the reign of Augustus (27 BC to AD 14) and came from a good family. Her uncle was a leading statesman, Marcus Valerius Messala Corvinus. He believed in the old republican constitution, which Augustus had neutered, but the two men got on well together and Messala took care not to ram his political views down the emperor's throat. Messala was a generous patron of the arts, and he seems to have encouraged Sulpicia's literary aspirations.

All that is left of her work are six love poems. They are written to a not altogether reliable young man she calls Cerinthus (not his real name, though he must have been a real person). It was unusual for a woman to admit publicly her feelings for a man; most marriages were arranged between the father and the husband-to-be. Feelings were neither here nor there. Sulpicia is aware that she is treading on thin ice, but brazens it out:

> Let people talk, especially those
> Who haven't found joys like mine.
> I want to send my letters to my love
> Unsealed, so anyone can read them first.
> I love my sin, to hide it for fear of disgrace is bitter.

Her watchful uncle Messala sends Sulpicia to celebrate her birthday in a family villa in the countryside. She is displeased:

> You are too zealous.
> Journeys, dearest uncle, aren't always welcome.
> I leave my heart and soul behind me
> Since your insistence trumps my wishes.

Messala gives way and the trip is cancelled. She complacently tells Cerinthus:

> An unexpected stroke of luck for you.

But Cerinthus turns out to have a roving eye. Sulpicia is furious that 'any tart is dearer to you than Sulpicia, Servius' daughter'. By mentioning her father she is reminding her lover that she is a respectable woman. Her family will take a dim view of their intended marriage if he misbehaves.

The last poem is the most touching. It records a quarrel, at the end of which Sulpicia walks out on Cerinthus:

> I've never done anything so stupid in my young life,
> That I've confessed to regretting more,
> Than leaving you by yourself, as I did last night.
> I was wanting to hide how much I love you.

And that is all. We are not given the end of the story. Whether or not the couple married and lived happily ever after or split up is anyone's guess. What we do know is that Sulpicia was not afraid of breaching convention. She meant to live her life as *she* intended, not as her male relatives, however distinguished and well intentioned, might have meant her to.

iv

THE AMATEUR PROSTITUTE

CLODIA WAS AS GRAND a lady as Cornelia, but no one ever accused her of domestic virtue. Born about 95 BC, she was a member of the Claudian clan, the origins of which reach back to the monarchy. The Claudians had a reputation for arrogance. Whether persistent genes or a desire to live up to people's expectations were the cause, every generation threw up disagreeable specimens of the family type. Clodia was very close to her youngest brother, Publius Clodius Pulcher, a populist politician —so close, according to gossip, that they committed incest—and they both changed their patrician names to a more plebeian, or working-class, spelling. Both of them were typical Claudians.

Clodia had an affair with the poet Catullus. He was infatuated with her and wrote her love poems, giving her the pseudonym 'Lesbia'. Things started well but soon went badly, as these two quotations show:*

> Lesbia, let us live and love
> And not care tuppence for old men
> Who sermonise and disapprove.
> Suns when they sink can rise again,
> But we, when our brief light has shone,
> Must sleep the long night on and on.

The scream of hate that follows was written to a friend of his, Marcus Caelius Rufus, a handsome and clever young politician:

> The Lesbia, Caelius, whom in other days
> Catullus loved, his great and only love...
> Now hangs about crossroads and alleyways
> Milking the cocks of mighty Remus' sons.†

Clodia's dull husband died in 59 BC and she took a string of young lovers. One of these was Catullus' friend Caelius, and after the affair was over, there was bad blood between them. Clodia accused Caelius of trying to poison her, and this led to a trial for attempted murder. She seems to have been present in court.

Clodia had made a bad mistake. Caelius' defence counsel was the great orator Cicero. The speech he made was a comprehensive and comedic demolition of her reputation. He drew a portrait of a woman overwhelmed by 'sheer uncontrollable lust', who was, in effect, an amateur prostitute.

Referring to Clodius, he addressed her: 'He loves you very much, and when he was a little boy, suffered, I presume, from

* The translations given here are by the poet James Michie; see Further Reading for bibliographical details. For more on the poet Catullus, see page 159.

† 'Remus', here, is a reference to Rome's founders, as in Romulus and Remus.

nerves and nightmares since he always went to bed with you, his older sister.' In another reference to Clodius, the barrister mentioned 'the woman's husband—so sorry, I mean brother. I'm *always* making that mistake.' It is not hard to imagine the laughter which greeted these sallies. To nobody's surprise, Caelius was acquitted.

Little or nothing is heard of Clodia from then on. We do not even know when she died. But the date is immaterial, for her life as a respected Roman noblewoman had come to an end in court, at Cicero's hands. Was the picture he drew of her fair? We don't know that either, for her own account of herself, if she ever gave it, has long been forgotten.

v

THE PARTNER IN EMPIRE

SEPTIMIUS SEVERUS assumed the purple in AD 193. He was an able and strong ruler who reasserted Rome's military preeminence. In this he was helped by an able wife, Julia Domna.

By this stage in the empire's history having Roman blood was not a necessary qualification to become its ruler. Luck and talent in varying proportions were enough. Severus came from northern Africa and may have been of Carthaginian stock. We are not sure of his ethnic origins, but some have speculated that he was Rome's first black emperor. His family was not fully Romanized and his sister was unable to speak Latin.

Julia Domna was a remarkable woman. There was little Roman about her, too. Probably Arabian, she was the daughter of the high priest at a temple of the Sun at Emesa, in western Syria. Severus first met her when he was serving in Syria as a legionary commander, but nothing came of the encounter. Julia was not especially good-looking, although she more than made up for this by her intelligence and courage.

Sometime later she came to Severus' notice again, in a curious manner. He was very superstitious and a believer in astrology. He learned that Julia had a horoscope which predicted she would marry a ruler. This matched his ambitions, so he sent for her and they were married. It was a good decision. She was trustworthy and became the most influential of Rome's empresses. She accompanied Severus on his campaigns and was given the special title of *mater castrorum*, Mother of the Army.

Unfortunately, Julia fell foul of a certain Fulvius Plautianus, commander of the Praetorians, the imperial guard. He had her accused of adultery, a charge equivalent to treason, and for a while Severus distanced himself from her. She did not allow herself to be down-hearted, however. She set herself up as a patron of the arts and philosophy and established a lively salon. Her fall from grace lasted no longer than three years.

Meanwhile Plautianus' daughter married the emperor's eldest son, Caracalla. He loathed her and threatened to kill her and her father once he inherited the throne. Unsurprisingly, this prompted the guard commander to plot the deaths of Severus and Caracalla, but he was betrayed. The imperial family tricked him into meeting them on his own. Severus reproached him for his disloyalty, and when he tried to defend himself, Caracalla punched him and then ordered attendants to kill him. Someone plucked a few hairs from the dead man's beard and took them to Julia, saying: 'Here is your Plautianus!'

Caracalla and the emperor's other son, Geta, were on very poor terms. Before his death in York in AD 211, Severus tried and failed to reconcile them, leaving the problem to Julia. At Caracalla's suggestion, she invited the two young men to discuss their differences with her. They came alone, but Caracalla had arranged for some junior army officers to wait outside. They rushed in and attacked Geta, who ran to his mother. He hugged her and begged her to save him, but there was nothing she could do. He was stabbed to death, and in the confusion Julia herself was wounded.

Although she was grief-stricken at her son's murder, Julia remained loyal to the dynasty and stayed on good terms with Caracalla (so much so that whispers of incest began to circulate). She helped him run the empire, as she had Severus. Despite her best efforts, though, she could not persuade her son to take the job of emperor seriously. After a short reign, he was assassinated in AD 217.

The next emperor, Macrinus, was of Berber descent. He had no use for somebody else's dowager empress. Julia could not envisage life away from the imperial court and took her own life.

[vi]

EGYPT'S BEGUILING PHARAOH

WHO IS history's most famous Egyptian? Well, it isn't Cleopatra. She may, arguably, be Egypt's most famous pharaoh, but she wasn't herself Egyptian. Born in 69 BC, she was Macedonian, a descendant of Ptolemy, one of Alexander the Great's commanders, who grabbed Egypt as his kingdom when Alexander's empire broke up after his death. Cleopatra was, in effect, a foreigner in her own country, living the life of a Greek aristocrat in her capital, the port of Alexandria, and seldom wearing Egyptian dress.

Most of what we think we know about Cleopatra is myth. The beautiful Egyptian siren who used her sexual wiles to entrap unwary Romans; her passionate love affair with Mark Antony; her dramatic suicide by snakebite: all this and much else besides was exaggerated, embroidered or simply invented by fanciful historians, propagandists or romantics. What we do know about her, however, paints no less fascinating a picture.

Cleopatra was in fact no beauty—the coins she had minted show the portrait of an ugly woman with a large hooked nose—but she was a delightful conversationalist. According to the historian Plutarch, her 'personality, which pervaded her actions in an inexplicable way when meeting people, was utterly spell-binding. The sound of her voice was sweet when she talked.' She was highly intelligent and spoke many languages fluently, including Ethiopian, Hebrew, Arabic, Syrian, Babylonian and Parthian. Most of her predecessors on the throne only spoke Greek, but Cleopatra took the trouble to learn Egyptian.

Egypt was a rich and independent kingdom, on which Rome, the Mediterranean's sole superpower, cast a greedy eye. Cleopatra's mission in life was to keep Egypt free. The best way to do this, she thought, was to persuade a leading Roman to be her ally. Her first choice was Julius Caesar, victor in Rome's civil war, who visited Alexandria in 47 BC when the queen was twenty-two. The couple soon embarked on an affair. But the best-laid plans... On 15 March 44 BC Caesar was assassinated and Cleopatra was once more without a protector.*

Next along was Mark Antony, one of the three men, or triumvirs, who ruled Rome after Caesar's death. In 40 BC, they struck a business deal: Cleopatra agreed to bankroll Antony, who was in charge of the eastern half of the empire, and to keep his army supplied; in return, Egypt would retain its independence. Sex sealed the deal, but Antony was soon off on his travels and it was four years before the pair met again. These were no passionate lovers. In fact, although they had children, Antony, now well into middle age, seems to have preferred the tavern and the dinner table to the bedroom.

Antony's great rival for control of the empire was Octavian, Caesar's adopted son and the future Augustus. Civil war broke out again, and by 30 BC the game was up—Antony and Cleopatra were the losers. For a brief moment Cleopatra wondered whether Octavian might become her third Roman patron, but quickly guessed that he wanted nothing from her except her humiliating presence in his triumphal procession in Rome. The death of Egypt's queen quickly followed, though whether by her own hand or by that of another is not certain.†

vii

THE TOMBOY QUEEN

CLEOPATRA was not the only oriental queen who made a nuisance of herself to the Romans. Zenobia of Palmyra (AD 240 to *c.* 275) claimed to be a descendant of Cleopatra and Rome's other female menace, Dido of Carthage. Legend paints her as a physically super-fit tomboy who loathed sex. Largely

* For more on Caesar and his assassination, see page 35.

† The story of Cleopatra's death is told more fully on page 143.

forgotten now, she was a legendary figure in the Middle Ages. Chaucer writes:

> She was a wrestler and could win a fight
> Against a stripling of whatever might.

Zenobia succeeded to the throne of Palmyra (in what is now Syria) on her husband's death and conquered much of the Middle East, crowning herself pharaoh of Egypt. The good times soon came to an end, however, and she was defeated by the emperor Aurelian. She starred in his triumphal parade in Rome, fettered hand and foot in shackles of gold—a fate which Cleopatra is supposed to have avoided by taking her own life. But that was her only punishment. The ex-queen was given a luxurious country house near Tivoli, where she ended her days as a respectable Roman matron and hostess. A happy ending of sorts.*

viii

A LOVING WIFE

NEITHER noble nor notorious, Turia was an ordinary person who survived extraordinary times: a loyal wife who was ready to stand up for what was hers and what she believed in.†

A wealthy young woman, Turia married her husband at some point in the 40s BC. Civil war had broken out; opposing factions in the Roman state, one of them headed by Julius Caesar, were fighting it out across the empire. Forty-one years later she died and her widower wrote a long, grieving epitaph on her gravestone. At some point in antiquity the stone was broken up for reuse. Bits of it have been found all over Rome, and from time to time new fragments are unearthed. About half the original text has survived, but this is enough to tell a remarkable tale.

Turia lived in troubled and lawless times. The day before her

* Zenobia was stolen from history by opera composers. Her romanticized career was much admired in the eighteenth and nineteenth centuries; she is the heroine of operas by Albinoni and Rossini among others, and of a late offering in 2007 by the Lebanese composer Mansour Rahbani.

† Unfortunately, the names of this admirable woman and her husband are missing; the name 'Turia' has been borrowed from another woman with a similar history.

wedding, her mother and father were murdered at their country house, perhaps by their slaves. While her husband was away at the wars, she pressed for justice and eventually obtained the conviction of the assassins. Some distant relatives tried to challenge her father's will. They wanted to be appointed her official guardians, and thereby to control (and doubtless spend) her fortune. Turia was having none of it. 'They gave way,' her husband writes, 'before your firm resolution and did not pursue the matter further.'

The battle of Pharsalus, the decisive battle of the civil war, was fought in Greece in 48 BC. Julius Caesar was the victor and men like Turia's husband, who had been on the other, republican side, were forbidden to return to Italy without special leave. He seems to have been under sentence of death and Turia talked him into going into hiding. During this time of exile she looked after his finances, secretly sending him cash, servants and provisions. Her efforts saved his life, and once things had settled down, he was allowed to return home.

This was not the end of her troubles. A political gang-leader called Milo had sold his home to Turia's husband before going into exile after a conviction for murder. He had his mob go round to the house and plunder it, but Turia's husband reports that 'you beat him back'. Frustratingly, he gives no details, but she was obviously able to muster her household to repel the attack.

In 44 BC Caesar was assassinated and the civil wars broke out again. A troika took power: Octavian, Caesar's adopted son (the future Augustus); Mark Antony; and a third, lesser figure, Marcus Aemilius Lepidus.* They published a 'proscription'—an official list of their enemies, who were condemned to death and whose estates were confiscated. Anyone who killed a named victim qualified for a generous reward.

Turia's husband was one of those proscribed, and true to form she did all she could to persuade Octavian to take his name off the list. A year later, when the need for the proscription had ended, he issued a pardon, but Lepidus disagreed. Turia arranged to meet him. She begged him to recognize the pardon and prostrated

* In Shakespeare's words, Lepidus was a 'slight unmeritable man'; for more on the second triumvirate, see page 36.

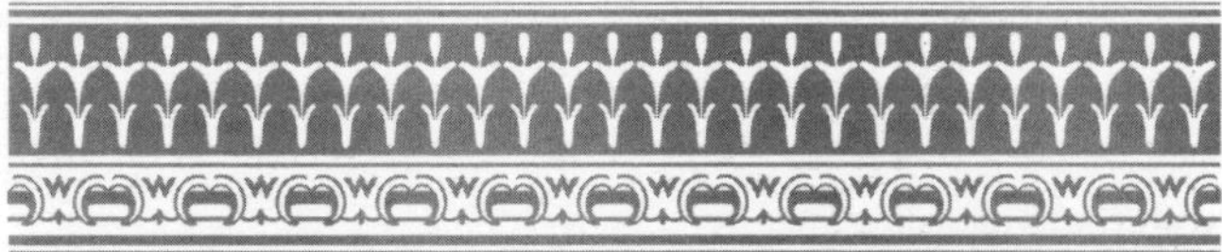

MONEY MATTERS

i

A QUESTION OF VALUES

It is difficult to be precise about the value of money in ancient Rome. The basic unit of account was the *sestertius* (sesterce), a small silver coin, four of which made a *denarius*, also usually of silver. Goods and services had different relative values when compared to similar ones today, and we only have a very vague idea how these values changed over time. So it is sensible to consider a range of specific instances of income and expenditure rather than suggest a single rate of exchange.

In the first century BC the fortune of Rome's (reputedly) richest man, Marcus Licinius Crassus, was reported as 200 million sesterces. The wealthy Pliny the Younger, around the turn of the first century AD, was worth about 20 million sesterces. In the same period a legionary soldier's annual pay was 1,200 sesterces. A Roman citizen could live decently on an annual income of 20,000 sesterces; this modest affluence would presuppose capital worth 400,000 sesterces.

Graffiti at Pompeii show that a modius of wheat (rather more than 14 pounds) in the mid-first century AD cost 3 sesterces and a loaf of bread weighing just over 1 pound cost less than 1 as, or ¼ sesterce. A measure of wine, a plate or a lamp could each be purchased for 1 as; ¼ as, called a quadrans, was the price of admission to the public baths. The minimum wage—whether in cash, or in cash plus keep—will seldom have fallen below 4 sesterces a day.

ii

ROME'S SERVILE BANKERS

In 1959 an archive of bankers' accounts was discovered in the remains of a Roman building near Pompeii.* The documents are wooden tablets with inscriptions in ink or scratched onto wax. They throw fascinating light on the banking industry

* The discovery was made during the construction of a motorway between Pompeii and Salerno.

in the first century AD. A group of ex-slaves, the Sulpicii, conducted their business in the important port of Puteoli (today's Pozzuoli). They provided credit for merchants and shippers, accepted deposits and made short-term loans. The peculiar thing is that the majority of providers of financial services were—like the Sulpicii—freedmen; some were even slaves who set up shop with their owners' permission.

The explanation is that those with wealth did not like to be seen increasing it. This was not just snobbery. Senators were not allowed to engage directly in trade or financial business. But they possessed large amounts of capital and wanted it to be put to work. As well as lending to trustworthy friends and relatives, they would often give their former slaves, whom they knew and trusted, start-up capital that enabled them to develop careers as bankers or traders in goods such as grain and olive oil.

iii

THE NOT SO NOBLE ROMAN

SENATORS may have been supposed to keep their noses out of business, but greed tempted some to ignore the ban. Astonishingly, one of these was Marcus Junius Brutus—'the noblest Roman of them all', according to Shakespeare, famous as the leading assassin of Julius Caesar.

Brutus had a reputation for virtue and disinterestedness. He was something of a philosopher and, both in politics and in his personal life, made a point of acting from the highest possible motives. But there was more to him than met the eye. Caesar, who knew him well, said of him: 'What he wants is hard to say, but when he wants it he wants it badly.' On this occasion he was after cash, at the risk of soiling his good name.

In 51 BC Brutus went to the Middle East on a government posting as quaestor, an elected official with special responsibility for financial matters. While there he loaned money to a town in Cyprus at an extortionate interest rate of 4 per cent per month (i.e. 48 per cent compound interest per year). To enforce the debt, his agents shut up the town's senators in their senate house, as a result of which five of them died of starvation. The impecunious king of Galatia was also in Brutus' debt and found it almost impossible to keep up repayments.

Brutus' friend, the statesman and orator Cicero, who discovered the scandal, said he was sorry 'he is not the man I thought him'. In the event his friends and colleagues sighed and turned a blind eye, but Brutus would have been wiser to have kept himself above such matters.

iv

SPINNING COINS

COINS were not simply for getting and spending; for imperial publicists, they were a unique means by which an emperor could communicate with his far-spread peoples in an age before radio and television, newspapers, telephones and computers.

In the first century BC Julius Caesar issued coins which bore his portrait, the first time a living individual was featured in this way. Their purpose was simple: to tell the world who was now in charge at Rome.

When Trajan died in AD 117, the succession was unclear and nobody knew what the dead emperor's wishes had been. This did not stop Hadrian from immediately taking power. For the avoidance of doubt, he issued a gold piece which showed Trajan handing over the globe to him.

Coins acquired a moral value and the public came to identify them with the image they carried. After Caligula's welcome murder, the Senate ordered the coins that carried his portrait to be withdrawn from use and melted down. Hadrian's friend, the philosopher Epictetus, jokingly observed: 'Whose image is on this sesterce? Trajan's? Give it to me. Nero's? Throw it away, it is unacceptable, it is rubbish.'

It is no surprise that emperors used the coinage to mislead. In AD 244 Philip the Arab declared victory over the Persians and issued coins that boasted of his having made peace. In fact, he had had to pay a huge indemnity of 500,000 gold denarii.

[v]

QUANTITATIVE EASING, ROMAN STYLE

In the second half of the third century AD, the Roman authorities were issuing a million coins a day, a rate not surpassed until the Industrial Revolution, more than a millennium-and-a-half later. What was going on?

During their first two-and-a-half centuries the emperors maintained a tri-metallic system with coins in bronze, silver and gold. The system failed when a shortage of silver and endless frontier wars led the state to debase the coinage to as little as 1 or 2 per cent silver. This had two consequences: bronze coinage became unviable and was no longer issued, and the debased coinage was issued in ever greater numbers.

So to all the troubles of the later Roman empire (see page 293) can be added massive price inflation.

FASHION

1

NOT SO HAUTE COUTURE

WALK THROUGH a gallery of statues of Roman worthies and their wives and you will come away with the impression that this was not a civilization with an interest in fashion. For century after century Rome's leading ladies seem to have dressed in the same unchanging uniform.*

The basic female outfit comprised an under-shift and a bra. Over this a respectable woman wore a floor-length *tunica* (or *stola*).† This was a one-piece garment with kimono sleeves. The front and back were made up from two lengths of cloth sewn together along their edges from the bottom for about three-fifths of their length. The unjoined portions at the top were folded beneath the neck into a cuff or apron and ruched.

If there was no talk in ancient Rome of different hem lengths or cutting on the bias or the New Look or hobble dresses or the *petite robe noire*, there was still room for novelty. But this was largely restricted to colour and new fabrics.

As early as the third century BC, well before Rome could boast an empire, the comic playwright Plautus was sending up women who found 'names for each new fashion—the Loose-knit Tunic, the Close-knit Tunic, the Blue Linen Tunic, the Lined Tunic, the Marigold or Saffron Tunic, the Petticoat or Chemise, the Little Pink Dress, the Veil, the Royal Look or the Foreign Look'.

Indian cotton was much in demand during the years of the early empire. Alternatives were linen and wool, or silk imported mysteriously from the distant undiscovered East. White and black, or bright colours such as purple, yellow and blue, were popular. Scarves could be worn, tied at the neck, and a *mappa* or kerchief dangling from an arm could be used to wipe dust or perspiration from the face.

* A tour around the marvellously comprehensive Palazzo dei Conservatori in Rome, for instance, will be sufficient for this purpose.

† A toga, by contrast, was a male citizen's official outfit; if a woman wore one, it signified that she was a prostitute.

II

COMPLETE MAKEOVER

HIGH STANDARDS of dress and appearance were expected of the wealthy noblewoman. She would employ dressers (*ornatrices*) as well as staff to look after her wardrobe. One person was responsible for her formal garments and accessories; another, a *calciator*, made her shoes; while a masseuse (*unctrix*) helped keep her physically in good shape. Many women enjoyed wearing flashy jewellery and would use the services of a *margaritarius*, or pearl-setter. Others thought it smarter to dress plainly and liked to be, in Horace's phrase, *simplex munditiis*, 'simple in their elegance'.*

As manager of the domestic household, the Roman matron was not only responsible for turning herself out decently; she was also in overall charge of the family's clothes. For this purpose she employed members of staff with titles such as wool-weighers (*lanipendi*) and sewing men and women (*sarcinatores* and *sarcinatrices*).

III

HOW TO TIE A TOGA

THE TOGA, the formal costume of a respectable Roman male, must be the most inconvenient item of clothing ever invented. It was made from a large length of unbleached woollen cloth, was stifling in summer and draughty in winter, and could not be put on without someone else's help. It was draped over and around the body, and considerable skill was required to stop it from slipping off. For decency's sake a tunic and loin-cloth were essential.

This is how to wear a toga:

Obtain a very large semi-circular cloth made from heavy white wool and about 20 feet in length along the straight edge (a bed

* Prime examples of such understated Roman ladies are Cornelia and Livia, for more on whom see pages 221–22 and 139–40.

sheet will not be long enough and is the wrong shape).

Drape the cloth over the left shoulder with the straight edge next to your neck and the curved edge to your left hand. The point should fall nearly to the ground. The rest of the fabric hanging down your back must be folded across the back, beneath your right arm, across your chest and, finally, up to and back over the left shoulder.

If you lift up your left arm, there will be enough fabric both to cover it and to pull out at the front a small fold or lap, in which you can place a document or other small item (a dagger to stab Julius Caesar at a Senate meeting, say). Fabric can also be pulled over the head, which has to be covered if the wearer is conducting a sacrifice.

[iv]

THE ART OF DISHEVELMENT

ONE AREA in which Roman women could express themselves was in elaborate coiffures, and, to judge by coins and busts, hair styles changed regularly over the years.

Broadly speaking, there were two basic approaches. The first featured two partings with a raised tuft or forelock above the brow. The second involved a single parting with the parted hair drawn in close waves across the temples.

The poet Ovid advises pretty girls to look in the mirror and choose the hairdo that matches their appearance. He could be writing for *Vogue*:

> ... the Neglected Look suits many girls: quite often
> You'd think it untouched since yesterday, though in fact
> It's fresh combed. Art simulates chance.

[v]

HOW COULD YOU TELL A ROMAN FROM A GREEK?

FOR CENTURIES Romans of the ruling class shaved regularly.* The fashion had been set at the beginning of the second century BC by Scipio Africanus (see page 148). His adoptive grandson, Publius Cornelius Scipio Aemilianus Africanus Numantinus, the general who besieged and sacked Carthage, liked to shave once a day. Julius Caesar hated going bald, but could not stand facial hair: he attached the greatest importance to appearing freshly shaved every day.

Shaving, or more often among the affluent, being shaved, was a grisly experience, as soap was not used to soften the bristles.† Perhaps understandably, the lower classes did not bother to copy their betters in this regard. Romans had a way, then as now, of kissing each other socially, and the poet Martial writes disgustedly of the 'whiskery farmer with a kiss like a billy-goat's'.

In the twilight of the Republic gilded young men sported goatees to irritate their elders. The orator and statesman Cicero called them *barbatuli* ('beardy boys'), but the tradition of beardlessness persisted into the empire.

Boys took as long as possible before having their first shave. There was even a special ceremony for it, the *depositio barbae*, in which a man dedicated his whiskers to his household gods. In most cases the ceremony took place when he was about sixteen or seventeen, not long after he had come of age. Octavian, however—Julius Caesar's adopted son and the future Augustus—waited until he was twenty-four, when he was already a leading figure in the state. He had been captivated by a beautiful young woman, Livia Drusilla, whom he married soon afterwards. She would have been forgiven for being put off by the long wispy hair on her lover's cheeks.

In the first century AD the emperor Hadrian changed the

* In civilian life, at any rate. They often let their beards grow when on military campaign, as the reliefs on Trajan's Column clearly show.

† There was in fact a Latin word for 'soap', *sapo*, which was a mixture of tallow fat and ashes, but it was employed, bafflingly, as hair pomade and not for washing.

fashion: he grew a beard. Some said that he wanted to cover some natural facial blemishes, but that would not have been his only motive. Doubtless he listened to his favourite philosopher and teacher, Epictetus, who claimed that facial hair was nature's way of distinguishing men from women and was more beautiful than a cock's comb or a lion's mane.

More to the point, though, Hadrian was very pro-Greek and it was his policy (like Nero before him) to promote Hellenic culture. The Greek adult male always wore a beard, so when Hadrian had himself shown with a beard on his coins, he was making a political point. It did not take long for all who wanted to get into his good books to cancel their appointment at the barber's.

[vi]

CLEOPATRA'S HAIR TONIC

CLEOPATRA, queen of Egypt and the most glamorous personality of her age (see pages 228–29), was credited with writing a handbook on cosmetics in the first century BC. It includes a recipe against baldness:

> The following is the best of all, acting for fallen hairs, when applied with oil or pomatum;* acts also for falling-off eyelashes or for people going bald all over. It is wonderful.
>
> Of domestic mice burnt, 1 part;
> of vine-rag burnt, 1 part;
> of horse's teeth burnt, 1 part;
> of bear's grease, 1;
> of deer's marrow, 1;
> of reedbark, 1.
>
> To be pounded when dry, and mixed with lots of honey till it gets the consistency of honey; then the bear's grease and marrow to be mixed (when melted), the medicine to be put in a brass flask, and the bald part rubbed till it sprouts.

* Pomatum was what is now termed a 'hair-styling product'—a kind of ancient Brylcreem.

The queen had no need herself of a cure for baldness, but her celebrated lover, Julius Caesar, certainly did. He was very sensitive about his thinning hair and, rather than resorting to an embarrassing comb-over, used his laurel wreath to hide a naked scalp. If he tried Cleopatra's concoction, nothing is reported to have sprouted. Then as now, there was no permanent remedy for capillary deficiency.

vii

MAKE-UP TO DIE FOR

ROMAN WOMEN, especially prostitutes and the rich, used make-up. In the pursuit of beauty they often risked their lives —and they also created a terrible stench while they were about it.

The main aim was to whiten the skin of the face. This was done by applying white lead, a poisonous substance used in modern times by artists and applied in the eighteenth century as waterproofing to the hulls of naval ships. Today white lead is banned in most countries.

Romans liked black eyebrows that almost met in the centre. Women darkened them with antimony, another poison, and soot. Coloured eye-shadow was used, green being derived from the equally lethal malachite. Various plants, including seaweed and the juice of the mulberry, offered different shades of rouge.

Before cosmetics were applied, the skin was prepared with an unpleasantly smelly substance made from the sweat in sheep's wool. Perfume was liberally deployed to mask the odours emanating from many of the components of face cream. These might include excrement of kingfisher, animal urine, placenta, bile and sulphur.

Ovid, the poet of sexual love, advised caution. 'The best make-up remains unobtrusive,' he said. 'That goo from unwashed fleeces—from Athenian sheep, maybe, but my dear, the *smell*—which is used for foundation make-up: avoid it.'

viii

UNDER THE KNIFE

How one looked meant as much in the ancient world as it does today, and cosmetic surgery was popular. Treatments included operations to heal pierced ears that had become infected, to lift slack eyelids and to redirect eyelashes that had grown into the eye.

Such operations may have been all the rage, but they were dangerous, and no proper antiseptics or anaesthetics were available. The poet Martial wrote sarcastically of one man:

> You have become a gladiator. You used to be an eye specialist.
> What you're doing now as a gladiator, you were very good at as a doctor.

One particular area of cosmetic treatment concerned former slaves. When (as happened quite often) slaves received their freedom or bought it with their savings and became Roman citizens, they were keen to remove the visual evidence of their servitude. Members of chain-gangs might carry brands to display who owned them, while slaves who ran away or stole were branded on the forehead. Surgeons who offered to obliterate these marks enjoyed a thriving trade.

ix

IN SEARCH OF A FORESKIN

The aim of one fashionable kind of cosmetic surgery was to remove the effects of circumcision. Jews who had come to terms with the Greco-Roman world did not want to arouse comment when naked in the baths or the open-air gym. They had somehow to restore their foreskins.

This could be done by surgery. What was left of the prepuce was cut round with a scalpel and the skin of the penis yanked back as far as its base. Celsus, writing in the first century AD, reported, not reassuringly, that 'this is not so very painful… nor is there any bleeding'. The skin was then pulled forward beyond the glans and tied in place, only to be released when the wound had healed.

This would take some time and the patient was instructed to fast, in order to reduce the risk of an untimely erection. Still, the probability of inflammation and infection was high.

There was a non-surgical alternative, though the procedure was equally unappealing. Weights could be attached to the skin of the penis to extend it over the glans. It could take months for the appearance of a foreskin to be created and, we may suppose, seriously incommoded the patient's daily life.

[x]

JUST DON'T GRIN AND BARE IT

LOOKING AFTER one's teeth could be a major concern, as the sharp-eyed and acid-tongued Martial suggests:

> Thais' teeth are black, but Laecania's snow-white.
> How is that? The one has bought hers, the others are her own.

Gold was used for dental repairs. A loose tooth was attached by gold wire to its neighbours. A missing tooth could be replaced by an ivory copy or by a real one (with the root sawn off), and bridged to the teeth on either side.

Tooth decay was comparatively rare, for the Roman diet did not include sugar and finely milled flour. Those who wished might use toothpicks. Mastic, a natural resin, was chewed and sweetened the breath. Ashes from dogs' teeth mixed with honey was the recipe for one disagreeable dentifrice.

Toothaches could be almost unbearable. The active ingredient in a pain-killing mouthwash was a decoction from a plant in the deadly nightshade family. A doctor noted: 'The patient should carefully avoid swallowing the fluid.' Indeed.

Perhaps the most realistic advice for the young person about town with dental problems came from the poet Ovid in his handbook on love-making, *The Art of Love*: 'If you have a black tooth, just take care not to smile.'

EMPERORS
GOOD, BAD
& UGLY

i

ASSUMING THE PURPLE

THE PEOPLE of Phoenicia, especially those from the city of Tyre, manufactured a colour-fast dye extracted from the murex sea mollusc. It stained cloth a reddish-purple. It was sold around the Mediterranean from at least the fourteenth century BC and may even have been used by the ancient Cretans as early as the eighteenth century BC. The dye was a very costly product and could only be afforded by the wealthiest people. It tended to be used by rulers and on ceremonial occasions.

Victorious Roman generals were sometimes hailed as *imperator*, a title of honour meaning 'commander-in-chief'. An *imperator* was entitled to wear a purple cloak. In time the title became the monopoly of Roman emperors, and so did the cloak. In this way the colour purple became associated with imperial rule and the phrase 'to assume the purple' means to become emperor. 'Born in the purple' refers to members of an imperial (or a royal) family born during the reign of their parents.

ii

LITTLE BOOTS

CALIGULA is the very model of the mad, bad emperor. He committed incest with his sisters, had a noisy argument with a statue of Jupiter, king of the gods, ordered his legions to fight the North Sea and celebrated his 'victory' by collecting sea-shells as booty. Most ridiculous of all, he proposed a favourite horse for Rome's highest elective post, that of consul. But these stories are stories and do not tell the truth.

In AD 12 Gaius Julius Caesar Germanicus was born in an army camp, son of a glamorous general and member of the imperial family. As a little boy he was popular with the soldiers, who nicknamed him 'Caligula' (Little Boots) after his baby-sized military footwear.

From childhood he suffered from epilepsy. He may have had mental health problems and suffered a serious illness shortly after inheriting power, but these difficulties should not be exaggerated. At the beginning of his reign he was well liked, but soon fell out with the ruling class and its institutional embodiment, the Senate.

Caligula was not barking mad. Although he was certainly no administrator, his real weakness was that he was rude, arrogant and high-handed. What else would one expect from an almost completely untrained and overconfident young man of twenty-five who had become absolute ruler of the known world overnight? As emperor, he liked testing the limits of the tolerable. He was extravagant, enjoyed dressing up in drag and was, to put it mildly, sexually promiscuous, but the anecdotes about his horse, his row with Jupiter and the sea-shells were almost certainly distortions of flip remarks or jokes.

Caligula knew he could get away with murder, but that meant being outrageous rather than literally massacring the hapless courtiers and grandees around him. Although he liquidated a young cousin and potential rival for the throne, there are few other reliable tales of extrajudicial executions.

In the end, though, the people who looked after him grew weary of the young emperor's tiresome japes. An officer of the Praetorian Guard, whose task was to protect the emperor, was furious with Caligula for regularly giving him a sexy daily watchword, which provoked gales of laughter at court. The soldier headed a successful conspiracy to assassinate the 29-year-old emperor, who was struck down on his way to a bath and lunch, after attending a gladiatorial show.

iii

THE WIT AND WISDOM OF CALIGULA

WHATEVER ELSE he may have been, Caligula was not stupid. He was intelligent and had a sense of humour—albeit of a rather twisted kind. Testimony to these characteristics are the stories, tall and not so tall, that were told about him and the various pithy comments that he was supposed to have made.

- ‘Remember that I have the right to do anything to anybody.’
- When discussing somebody’s execution: ‘Strike him in a way that makes him *feel* he is dying.’
- When the two consuls asked him at dinner why he was chuckling to himself: ‘What do you think, it just occurred to me I only have to give the nod and both of you will have your throats cut, just like that.’
- ‘I wish the Roman people had a single neck.’
- For his entertainment, Caligula used to hold auctions at which he forced up prices to the point where bidders bankrupted themselves. At a sale of gladiators and items from a gladiatorial show, a senator called Aponius Saturninus dozed off on a bench. The emperor told the auctioneer: ‘Keep an eye on the gentleman who keeps nodding his head to you.’ The bidding was not stopped until Aponius had unknowingly bought thirteen gladiators for the fabulous sum of 9 million sesterces.
- Caligula liked to quote a tag from a well-known Latin play: ‘Let them hate me, so long as they fear me.’
- Caligula fell seriously ill and many people prayed for his recovery. One supporter offered to sacrifice his life if the emperor recovered. Caligula duly did so. When he found that the man was still alive, he had him thrown over the embankment into the river Tiber.

iv

WHAT AN ARTIST!

LIKE CALIGULA, Nero is held up as a model of the bad ruler. He had sex with his mother, Agrippina, and later arranged her murder. He wrote poetry and performed it at Greek festivals, rather than concentrating on running the empire. He was alleged to have lit the great fire of Rome in AD 64 and to have fiddled while the city burned, unfairly blaming the Christians for his crime. He had a habit of putting senior politicians to death (or forcing them to commit suicide). When at last the legions rose in revolt in AD 68, he decided to kill himself, but he lost his nerve and his private secretary had to help him drive a dagger into his throat. His last words were: 'What an artist the world is losing!' And like Caligula, Nero has been the butt of a great deal of bad publicity.

Nero was a fat, rather plain boy who assumed the purple at the age of seventeen. He was spotty and smelly, with a thick neck, prominent stomach and thin legs. Somehow his ugliness seemed appropriate, for there is little doubt that some of the criticism was well founded; Nero was not a good man and he had his little ways.

Life at court was precarious, for the teenaged emperor was cruel and capricious. He quarrelled with the Senate. His personal life was disreputable. His first marriage to his half-sister Octavia was one of convenience only, and he compelled her to cut open her veins. Nero had a number of mistresses, but the woman he really cared for, Poppaea Sabina, died after he lost his temper and kicked her when she was pregnant. He fell in love with a young freedman called Sporus, who was the spitting image of Poppaea. He arranged for his castration and then married him.

While he may have had his quirks, Nero was not all bad. Most agree that he did not start the great fire and he certainly did not fiddle while the city burned. Apart from anything else, the violin had not been invented; his instrument was the lyre. It is clear that he was popular with the masses. He seems to have used tax policy to encourage productivity and his many public works helped revive a deflated economy. His encouragement of Hellenic culture was very well received in the eastern half of the empire, where Greek was the *lingua franca*.

When Nero died, the Senate and the ruling elite in Rome were delighted. They had suffered the most. But ordinary people, especially in the Middle East, were upset. For years anonymous admirers laid flowers on his grave. A belief grew that Nero had not died, but had fled to Parthia. A contemporary observer wrote: 'Even now everybody wishes [Nero] were still alive. And the great majority do believe that he is.' At least three impostors, who looked like the emperor and, of course, played the lyre, led (unsuccessful) rebellions. The years rolled by and Nero became a kind of King Arthur, who, said St Augustine of Hippo four centuries later, 'will live until he is revealed in his own time and restored to his realm'.

[v]

THE MOTHER-KILLER

AGRIPPINA, second wife of the emperor Claudius, long schemed that Nero, her son by a first marriage, should succeed her husband—and not the son of his own blood. When astrologers told her that Nero would become emperor but kill his mother, she replied: 'Provided he becomes emperor, *let* him kill me.'

She changed her tune when it became clear that her son was tiring of her bossiness. Fearing for her life, she took particular care of her personal security, so ensuring that any assassination would need to be very carefully planned.

Her son rose to the challenge. A special ship was built with a section designed to collapse when at sea; it would then sink and everyone would imagine that a tragic accident had occurred. In AD 59 Nero invited his mother to dinner at a seaside villa of his, at which he allayed her fears by behaving with unusual affection. To return to her own country house, she boarded a splendid new boat which Nero said he had specially chosen for her.

On a signal the roof of Agrippina's cabin fell in, and she and her companions were flung into the water. Suspicious, Agrippina did not cry out for help (others did and were knocked on the head), but swam off silently to another boat and eventually made her way home.

She realized she had been the victim of a plot, but decided that her only hope was to profess ignorance. Meanwhile word reached Nero that the attempt had failed. In a panic, he decided to invent a conspiracy against himself. When a messenger from Agrippina arrived to report the 'accident', Nero dropped a sword at his feet and had him arrested for attempted murder of the emperor.

Soldiers were sent to his mother's house. The captain cracked her skull with a truncheon. When another officer drew his sword to finish her off, Agrippina, plucky to the last, pointed to her womb and shouted: 'Strike here!'

Unrepentant, Nero told the Senate: 'Her death is a national blessing.'

[vi]

THE DEVIL'S BANQUET

IT WAS the dinner party from hell. The host was Domitian, emperor from AD 81 to 96, a man whose command of mental cruelty anticipated the imaginative brutalities of twentieth-century despots. And an invitation from Domitian was not something to be taken lightly.

A room had been prepared with walls, ceiling and floor all covered or painted in pitch-black, and black dining couches had been installed. The senators and other guests were invited to come in on their own, leaving their attendants outside—an unusual break with custom. Beside each couch a stone slab like a gravestone was brought in, from which a small lamp hung as in a tomb. Then attractive boys, naked and painted all over in black, entered and performed a dance. After this, sacrificial offerings to departed spirits were laid before the guests, all of them black and placed in black dishes. Afterwards the apparatus of religious ceremonies for the dead was set out. By this time, the historian Dio Cassius writes,

> every single guest was in a state of fear and trembling, and expected to have his throat cut any moment. The effect was accentuated by a dead silence as if everyone had already expired – except for the emperor who chattered on about topics exclusively concerning death and slaughter.

The company was then dismissed, but each guest, to his alarm, was handed over to slaves he did not know who escorted him to his home. Hardly had each caught his breath before a messenger from the emperor arrived. This was potentially sinister, for perhaps he was bringing instructions to commit suicide, a regular punishment for senior politicians suspected of treason, or even just of opposition. In the event costly gifts were delivered, plus the pretty boys, now with the black paint scrubbed off.

It is difficult at this distance of time to be quite sure what Domitian was up to. One is left with the impression of an over-the-top practical joke rather than of a real ceremony. One thing is clear, though. The emperor indubitably did intend to scare the wits out of his guests. And in this he succeeded.

[vii]

THE FLY-KILLER

THE EMPEROR Domitian was a highly competent administrator, but he did not trust the senatorial class and launched a reign of terror, in which many senior politicians lost their lives. A youngest son, he was neglected in childhood in favour of a glamorous older brother, Titus, and seems to have been psychologically damaged. At the beginning of his reign he is reported to have spent hours alone teasing flies and despatching them with a keenly sharpened stylus (a pointed implement for writing on wax tablets). On one occasion, when someone asked if anyone was with the emperor in his room, an official wittily replied: 'No, not even a fly.'

Eventually Domitian's wife and domestic staff lost patience. They suspected that they were next on the list of victims during his reign of terror. According to Suetonius, Domitian was stabbed to death as he read a paper at his desk by a steward, a subaltern, a freedman, a decurion and a gladiator.

[viii]

LETTING BYGONES BE BYGONES

AFTER THE assassination of Domitian, a civilized, sixty-five-year-old senator and poet called Nerva succeeded him to the purple. He freed political prisoners, but vetoed the prosecution of the dead emperor's henchmen. It was an astute but unpopular decision.

One evening at dinner in the palace the conversation turned to Catullus Messalinus, a notorious former consul under Domitian who had made a career by laying capital charges against innocent senators. Nerva asked: 'I wonder what his fate would be if he were alive to-day.' A guest snapped back: 'He would be dining with us.'

[IX]

WHEN HARD WORK IS NOT ENOUGH

TO BE A GOOD ruler was hard work, and Hadrian, emperor from AD 117 to 138, was certainly hard-working. But sometimes the job got to him.

One day a woman stepped forward as Hadrian walked by and made a request. 'I haven't got the time,' he said crossly. 'Well, stop being emperor then!' she replied. The blow struck home. Hadrian relented and gave her a hearing.

He lost patience on another occasion, with a less happy outcome. He struck one of his attendants with a pen. When he realized that he had blinded the man, he told him to request any gift he wanted, to make up for what he had suffered. Silence. Hadrian repeated the invitation. The man refused to ask for anything, except to have his eye back.

[X]

AN EMPEROR'S FAREWELL

ALTHOUGH Hadrian was in fact a success as an emperor, he died in his early sixties, ill, lonely and bitter. He wrote his own elegy. Glum and wry, it is a minor masterpiece:

animula vagula blandula
hospes comesque corporis
quae nunc abibis? In loca
pallidula rigida nudula
nec ut soles dabis iocos

[My little soul, you charming little wanderer,
my body's guest and partner
where are you off to now? Somewhere
without colour, savage and bare;
you'll crack no more of your jokes there.]

THE PHILOSOPHER EMPEROR

VERY FEW Romans talk to us directly, person to person, across the gap of ages. The emperor Marcus Aurelius is a remarkable exception. He wrote a jumble of notes and queries that we call the *Meditations*, although the book's real title, in Greek, means 'things spoken to himself'. These were private jottings and anxious self-communings, never meant for publication. Somehow they survived.

In AD 121 the future ruler of the Roman world was born Marcus Annius Verus into a wealthy family from Spain. The emperor Hadrian met him when he was about four and found him 'a solemn child'. He came across Marcus again when he was a promising teenager and was impressed by his intelligence and honesty of mind. Verus happens to be the Latin for 'true', and Hadrian nicknamed the boy Verissimus, 'most true'.

Hadrian took a completely unexpected decision to nominate Marcus as his second heir. Antoninus Pius, a little-known but sensible senator, was to inherit the empire after Hadrian's death, and Marcus would follow Antoninus, who was obliged to adopt him. The arrangement went as planned, and Marcus eventually acceded to the imperial throne in AD 161. He proved to be a capable ruler, but it is clear from his notebook that he took little pleasure in power. 'Take care,' he advised himself, 'not to be Caesarified, or dyed in purple.' He served from a sense of duty and insisted on being treated, so far as possible, as if he were a private citizen. He admired men who argued for an end to emperors and a return to the Republic. 'It is possible,' he wrote, 'to live in a palace and yet do without bodyguards or gorgeous uniforms, candelabra, statues and all that kind of pomp.'

Marcus did not have much of a sense of humour, and he took a dim view of the human condition. 'Man's time is a passing moment, his existence a flux, his perception misted over, the fabric of his body rotting away, his mind a spinning top.' He agreed with Stoic philosophers that a rational principle governed the universe and that all things were meshed together. The closer one kept to the laws of nature, the happier one would be. Virtue resided in self-control, prudence, bravery and justice.

Frontier wars took up much of the emperor's time and attention, and he died exhausted on campaign against a Germanic enemy in AD 180. The succession was not decided according to Hadrian's wise policy of adoption, and an heir of his own loins took over: the idle and useless Commodus (see page 261).

Marcus Aurelius was much respected in his lifetime, and after his death much missed. 'The only harm he ever did us,' said one admirer, 'was to have a son.'

xii

OF MEMBRANE AND MUCUS

PERHAPS fortunately, given the quality of his offspring, the joys of love passed the emperor Marcus Aurelius by. Sexual intercourse was 'no more than the friction of a membrane and a spasmodic spurt of mucus'. As a young man Marcus preserved his virginity well into his twenties, most unusually for a Roman, and made a point of refusing to sleep with good-looking slaves. When he did have sex, he didn't think much of it—and gave it up as a bad job.

xiii

WHEN LIFE IS CHEAP...

ON ONE occasion the emperor Marcus Aurelius muses: 'The endless repetition and monotony of the gladiatorial spectacle bores you.' It is a telling comment on the relativity of values between then and now that this good, if somewhat priggish, man was silent about the morality of the arena itself.

[xiv]

MAD, BAD AND DANGEROUS TO KNOW

It doesn't often happen, but sometimes Hollywood is outdone, or at least equalled, by reality. The emperor Commodus, who reigned in the second century AD, has a starring role in two movie epics—*The Fall of the Roman Empire* (1964) and *Gladiator* (2000). Fictionally he is a nasty piece of work, but the real Commodus was no better. He assumed the purple at just eighteen and immediately showed himself in his true colours. Inexperienced and lazy, he left the business of government to officials and favourites and devoted himself to pleasure.

And that meant chariot-racing and playing at being a gladiator. He knew he had to be careful of public opinion, which took a dim view of elite members of society competing on the racecourse. He drove chariots from time to time on moonless nights and dressed in the colours of the Greens, his favourite team, but he longed to drive a chariot in front of a crowd.

A physical coward, he was obsessed with violence against both man and beast. On two successive days in the arena, all alone and with his own hands, he dispatched five hippopotami, a couple of elephants, some rhinoceroses and a giraffe. On another occasion he killed a hundred bears, shooting down at them from the safety of a balcony in the amphitheatre.

Once Commodus cut the head off an ostrich and, with a grin on his face, wagged it threateningly at the assembled senators, where they sat in their reserved seats in the arena. The historian Dio Cassius, who was present, observed:

> We were overcome by laughter rather than fear, and many of us would have been put to the sword for laughing at him, if I hadn't chewed some laurel leaves which I got from the wreath I was wearing. I persuaded other colleagues sitting next to me to do the same thing, so that our continual chewing could hide the fact that we were cracking up.

But the historian judged that Commodus was naïve rather than cruel:

> He was not naturally wicked, but, on the contrary, as guileless a man as ever lived. His great simplicity, however, together with his cowardice, made him the slave of the people around him.

Commodus was born in the purple. He could not have been more different from his father, the austere philosopher Marcus Aurelius (see page 259), and we can guess that the boy reacted against a gloomy, duty-bound upbringing.* Is it permissible to have a smidgeon of sympathy for a man so manifestly unequipped for his destiny? Probably not, but his life is a salutary reminder that misfortune can be gold-plated.

Offending the emperor Commodus was dangerous indeed. He was so incompetent that a number of conspiracies were laid against him. All but the last were discovered and led to many executions. People close to Commodus began to worry for their safety. On New Year's Eve AD 192 his mistress, Marcia, gave him poison, but he vomited it up. Eventually his wrestling partner was brought in to strangle him while he was in the bath.

[xv]

THE HOLLOW CHAMPION

IN LIVING OUT his gladiatorial fantasies, Commodus liked to play the part of the heavily armed *secutor* ('follower'), whose opponent was the lightly armed *retiarius*, with net and trident. When doing this in the privacy of a palace, his opponents had to look to themselves. The emperor had to be allowed to win, but this was often at the cost of a sliced nose or ear. He seems not have been all that good at fighting, but every now and again he managed to kill a man or two. In the amphitheatre he fought as a gladiator but with wooden weapons. No blood was allowed to flow. He won every bout. Of course.

* A modern parallel, in this respect alone, is the way in which the future Edward VII –'Bertie'—resisted the strict education Albert and Victoria gave him.

[xvi]

REFUSING THE PURPLE

ROMAN SOLDIERS had a habit, when they were angry with the authorities in Rome, of offering the imperial throne to a popular general. This would put him in an extremely difficult position. If he said yes, he was launching a civil war he might very well lose. If no, he would infuriate his men, who might lynch him.

Some commanders allowed themselves to be bullied into power. Priscus, a plain-speaking lieutenant, was an exception. When the legions in Britain chose him for emperor in place of the hopeless Commodus, he put them firmly in their place: 'I am no more an emperor than you are soldiers.'

[xvii]

THE CROSS-DRESSING SUN-WORSHIPPER

THERE WERE many wicked Roman emperors, but the youthful Elagabalus (or Heliogabalus) was not among the maddest or the most cruel. He assumed the purple as a teenager who had recently entered puberty, and behaved as if, by some magic, he had been given the power to realize his every fantasy. At this time the boy was the high priest of a religious cult dedicated to the sun god Elagabal, in the Syrian city of Emesa (today's Homs), and he was nicknamed Elagabalus after the divinity he worshipped and perhaps embodied. Despite the fact that he achieved nothing in his short reign (AD 218–222), he has had an extraordinary life after death.

Elagabalus was encumbered by a surfeit of domineering female relatives—great-aunt, grandmother, mother, aunt. The first of these, Julia Domna, married the highly successful emperor Septimius Severus. He died in York in AD 211, and some years later, after the murders of his two sons and a brief usurpation, there was no obvious successor to the imperial throne.* The grandmother, Julia Maesa, cast an eye over her grandson. He was the best available choice for emperor, but hardly an ideal one. Not only was he young and green, but he was obstinate and obsessed with sex. The 'aunts' soon found that they had taken on a handful.

The boy made his way to Rome to claim his inheritance. If we are to believe the contemporary sources (and some modern historians do not), he married a number of women in quick succession, including, scandalously, one of the six Vestal Virgins, on whose chastity depended the safety of the state.† He used to dress up in drag and prostituted himself in brothels. When he was addressed as Lord Emperor, he replied: 'Don't call me that. I'm a lady.' The emperor 'married' a blond charioteer, one Hierocles. He also had an affair with a chef called Zoticus, whom he singled out not just for his good looks but for the immense size of his private parts.

All this was too much for the Praetorians, the emperor's special force of bodyguards, not to mention the women of the family. Julia Maesa acted, locating a young cousin for promotion to the purple. The guards approved and proceeded to hunt down Elagabalus. They found him hiding in a public convenience and on 11 March AD 222 put him to death. His mother shared his fate. A disgusted Senate erased the memory of Elagabalus from the public record.

And that, one might have thought, would have been that. But in the late nineteenth century Elagabalus was rediscovered by the Decadent movement and presented as an amoral aesthete, an antique Dorian Gray. In 1881 Sir Lawrence Alma-Tadema portrayed him in his painting *The Roses of Heliogabalus* (the emperor was supposed to have killed his dinner guests by smothering them with rose petals released from the ceiling). He inspired a monochrome banquet in J.-K. Huysmans' novel *À rebours*, and in the 1930s reappeared as a cultural anarchist in Antonin Artaud's *Héliogabale ou l'anarchiste couronné*. Alfred Duggan made of Elagabalus a naïve and ill-advised lad in his 1960 historical novel *Family Favourites*. His most

* The story of Julia Domna and Septimius Severus' troubled succession is told on pages 226–28.

† The Vestal Virgins are treated more fully on pages 91–2.

recent incarnation is in *Roman Dusk* (2006) one of Chelsea Quinn Yarbro's Count Saint-Germain series of vampire stories.

[xviii]

THE CREATIVE IMPULSE

GORDIAN II was co-emperor with his father, Gordian I. They only lasted a few weeks on the throne in AD 238, the Year of the Six Emperors. In his *Decline and Fall of the Roman Empire* (1776–88), Edward Gibbon memorably summarizes his personality:

> His manners were less pure, but his character was equally amiable with that of his father. Twenty-two acknowledged concubines, and a library of sixty-two thousand volumes, attested the variety of his inclinations, and from the productions which he left behind him, it appears that the former as well as the latter were designed for use rather than ostentation.*

[xix]

IN PRAISE OF THE CABBAGE

DIOCLETIAN, who ruled at the end of the third century AD, was the first of Rome's emperors to abdicate.† He retired to a luxurious compound in Split, where he spent much of his time gardening.

People begged him to return to the throne, but he refused. Instead, he devoted his time to the cabbage.‡ Like a proud allotment-holder, he pointed to the cabbages he had planted with his own hands and wondered who would 'replace the peace and happiness of this spot with the storms of a never-satisfied ambition'.

* Gibbon explains: 'By each of his concubines, the younger Gordian left three or four children. His literary productions, though less numerous, were by no means contemptible.'

† His full nomenclature was Gaius Aurelius Valerius Diocletianus Augustus.

‡ Fuller treatment of this venerable vegetable is given on page 192.

[xx]

THE THIRTEENTH APOSTLE

On 28 October AD 312 the emperor Constantine and his army met a rival for the imperial throne just outside the city of Rome, at the Milvian Bridge over the river Tiber. As they marched into battle, he and his men saw a strange sight in the sky: a cross of light and with it a phrase, in Greek, reading 'With this sign, win!' It was an unambiguous message that the risen Christ was on his side, and indeed the forty-year-old emperor routed his enemy Maxentius, who was pushed into the Tiber and drowned. Constantine converted to Christianity in gratitude.

Are we to believe this story? A memorable *son et lumière* effect, one would accept, but not altogether plausible as a historical event. And was Constantine's conversion sincere or political? The odd thing is that three years previously it had been given out that the then pagan Constantine had had a similar experience—a vision of his guardian divinity, the pagan sun god Apollo. He ran the risk of becoming a serial seer. Perhaps we don't need to take the tale too literally. The political advantage of a conversion was substantial. Christians were still a minority in the Roman empire, but a growing one. Their refusal to venerate emperors and practise the state religion made them a divisive force, and Constantine wanted to promote unity. So his decision made sense.

However, it did not mean that the state was now officially Christian. Pagans lived their lives as before. But the emperor removed legal disabilities against Christians, gave the church some tax breaks and financed the building of many Christian places of worship, especially in Rome and at his new foundation, Constantinople (today's Istanbul).*

So was Constantine a cynic? Not really. He took a great interest in church affairs; in fact he pioneered the overlapping of church and state of which today's Church of England is a living example. He even saw himself as a thirteenth apostle. He gave

* Constantine did not intend, as many suppose, to move the capital of the empire from the river Tiber to the shores of the Bosphorus. Over time Constantinople did become the New Rome, but that was later. For Constantine the city was no different from other imperial residences such as Milan and Trier.

sermons to his court, lowering his voice, pointing upwards to heaven and threatening divine punishment. The courtiers clapped but paid little attention.

So can we add hypocrisy to the charge of cynicism? Well, there is one completely convincing piece of evidence that the emperor *was* a true believer. In the spring of AD 337 he felt unwell, and soon he realized that his illness was terminal. So he asked to be baptized. In those days, adult baptism was the rule, and men holding public office whose jobs often entailed criminal or unethical behaviour waited till the last possible moment before accepting a sacrament that wiped out all their sins up to that point. Constantine would not have forgotten that, for instance, he had put his wife and eldest son to death for reasons of state.

The emperor was absolved and purified by full immersion. He exchanged his imperial robes for a simple white shift and took no further part in government. In a fortnight he was dead—but (he evidently expected) saved.

[xxi]

RETURN OF THE GODS

JULIAN was an intelligent young man in a hurry. He wanted to turn the empire on its head and rescue it from the austere mercies of Christianity. Its stranglehold on the state had been growing relentlessly since Constantine the Great had legalized the religion and, even more shockingly, announced his conversion to the faith in AD 313. When Julian became emperor in AD 361 as Flavius Claudius Julianus Augustus, he meant to reverse the trend and change the course of history.

Constantine's family may have been Christian, but it had little of the milk of human kindness in it. The old emperor died when Julian was only six. He was barely in his grave before his son Constantius II shored up his power by massacring most of his male relatives. The only ones still alive, apart from Constantius himself, were his two brothers, who became co-emperors—together with a couple of little boys whom no one had the heart to put to death. The younger of these was Julian.

Julian had a horrid childhood, locked away in remote corners of the empire with his disagreeable half-brother Gallus. After the deaths of his brothers, Constantius found himself sole emperor. There were now no family members left to share the heavy burden of running the empire—except for the boys. Gallus was promoted to be Constantius' deputy, but he proved unpredictably bloodthirsty and was executed. At the age of eighteen Julian was recalled from exile. He was the only surviving relative capable of helping the emperor, and when he was twenty-four he was appointed to govern the empire in the west, while Constantius prepared for war with Persia in the east. Julian did extraordinarily well—unnervingly well, thought Constantius, who scented a rival for the purple. He was not wrong. Julian's troops acclaimed him emperor, and civil war was averted only by Constantius' death from natural causes.

Until then Julian had pretended to be Christian, but now he became openly pagan. He inveighed against the Christians (whom he called Galileans), withdrawing the church's privileges and attempting to engineer a renaissance of the Olympian gods. Julian dabbled in odd cults and was obsessed with the religious importance of animal sacrifices, which in that era many of his subjects felt to be in poor taste at best.

In AD 363 the emperor fell in battle against the Persians, so we will never know whether his pagan revival could have succeeded. In the event history marched on regardless and the Galilean was victorious.

However, Julian has not been forgotten, and he is the hero of a number of modern novels. He would surely have thrilled to the Victorian poet Swinburne's rhythmical, rhyme-rich *Hymn to Proserpine*, in which a pagan very like him laments Christianity's irresistible rise and defies the Son of God:

> Sleep, shall we sleep after all? for the world is not sweet in the end;
> For the old faiths loosen and fall, the new years ruin and rend...
> O lips that the live blood faints in, the leavings of racks and rods!
> O ghastly glories of saints, dead limbs of gibbeted Gods!
> Though all men abase them before you in spirit, and all knees bend,
> I kneel not neither adore you, but standing, look to the end.

POMPEII

I

WHEN DAY TURNED INTO NIGHT

THE ERUPTION of Mount Vesuvius started on the morning of 24 August AD 79 and lasted for more than twenty-four hours. It left the towns of Pompeii and Herculaneum, in Campania, south of Rome, smothered in up to 20 feet of hot ash, pumice and rock fragments. They had disappeared from the landscape and were never rebuilt.

This was one of the greatest natural disasters ever to strike the ancient world. Day turned into night and it seemed to inhabitants of the area that the end of the world had come.

II

DARKNESS AT NOON

THE STORY of one Roman's experience evokes the horror of what happened on that fateful day in AD 79. He was a very fat man, but endowed with untiring energy. He was nosy and fearless. This was the 55-year-old Gaius Plinius Secundus, known to us as Pliny the Elder.* He was admiral of the Fleet of Naples and high in favour with the emperor Titus, but he wasn't just a statesman and public administrator. He was also the copious author of a multi-volume encyclopedia, *Natural History* (see page 217), and other reference books.

Pliny was on duty at the big naval base at Misenum (modern Miseno) on the northern tip of the Bay of Naples. In the early afternoon of 24 August his sister drew his attention to a large, oddly shaped cloud. It was like an umbrella pine with a tall, thin trunk which then split off into branches. Soon afterwards a desperate message arrived from a woman friend of his whose seaside villa stood at the foot of Mount Vesuvius. It was clear that the long-dormant volcano was erupting. She begged him to come

* So named to distinguish him from his identically named nephew, Pliny the Younger (see page 100).

and rescue her. He did not hesitate. He ordered warships to be launched and went on board himself. His plan was to pick up his friend from the beach and anyone else who wanted to leave. He sailed straight into the danger zone.

His nephew, Pliny the Younger, described in a letter to a friend, the historian Tacitus, what happened next. He had been with his uncle at Misenum, but had decided not to accompany him on his errand of mercy. He learned the details from survivors of the expedition. The admiral, he writes,

> was now so close to the mountain that ash mixed with pumice stones and black bits of burning rock fell on the ships, and grew thicker and hotter the nearer he approached.

The sea suddenly ebbed and the flotilla was at risk of running aground. To add to the peril, the shore was blocked off by large stone fragments which had rolled down from the mountain. The ship's pilot advised Pliny to turn back, but that was not the Roman way: '"Fortune favours the brave," he said, and told the man to press on.'

The ships eventually moored at Stabiae, a seaside resort not far from Pompeii, where another of Pliny's friends, Pomponianus, had a villa. He was in a state of panic, and so the admiral displayed his usual sang-froid by insisting on having a bath and dining. His nephew wrote: 'He was quite cheerful, or at least pretended he was.'

Sheets of flame could be seen flaring on the mountainside, but Pliny went for a rest and was heard snoring. Meanwhile the courtyard that led to his room was filling up with ash and pumice stone. Soon he would not be able to get out, so he was woken up. It was decided to leave the house, which was swaying from ground shocks. The admiral and his companions protected themselves from falling objects by tying pillows to their heads. There should have been daylight, but it was still pitch-dark. They went down to the beach to see if it was possible to sail away, but the waves were too wild and dangerous.

Pliny felt unwell and lay down on a sailcloth. He frequently asked for drinking water. Flames and sulphurous gases drove the group away. Two remaining servants helped Pliny to his feet, but suddenly he collapsed, overcome by the fumes. According to his nephew:

> as soon as it was light again, which was not till 26 August, two days after he had last been seen, his body was found unharmed, and without any signs of violence on it, still in the clothes he had been wearing, and looking as if he was asleep rather than dead.

[111]

PISO'S LIBRARY

THE GREAT VILLA with its cascading terraces stood on the slopes of Mount Vesuvius. It belonged to Julius Caesar's father-in-law, Lucius Calpurnius Piso Caesoninus. Destroyed in the eruption of AD 79, it is now only partly excavated. But the ruins of what was a vast building allow us to dream of lost masterpieces of the ancient world—vanished tragedies of Aeschylus, Sophocles and Euripides, say—which may have survived and only await the archaeologist's shovel.

This is because Piso had a large library, the only one to have survived in its original format to the present day. When disaster struck, the books were being stored in wooden cases for transport to a safe place. It was too late. A pyroclastic surge—superheated gas mixed with rock and flowing down the mountain at nearly 70 miles an hour—overwhelmed the villa. It was a disaster, but with a silver lining, for the air was so hot that paper and wood were carbonized rather than burned—and so preserved.

Unfortunately, Piso's country house was discovered in the eighteenth century, long before the science of archaeology had been properly established. Attempts, eventually successful, were made to open up and read the surviving documents. Modern technology is now making it possible to 'unwrap' them digitally, although further advances will be necessary before texts can be fully recovered.

Piso's library specialized in Greek philosophy, but maybe he was interested in other topics. How many more books remain to be discovered we do not know—more of the villa needs to be dug up, but the will to do so is currently lacking.* It looks as if we will have to wait a long time before we get to read any 'new' classics of Greek and Roman literature.

iv

FIGURES FROZEN IN TIME

UNDERNEATH a staircase near the two garden rooms in the House of the Golden Bracelet, with their luxuriant horticultural murals, a family—a man, a woman and two children—took shelter on that terrible day when Pompeii was destroyed.† They had with them jewellery and other valuables. Among them was the eponymous and very beautiful bracelet, or more precisely armlet, with snakehead terminals holding a medallion of the goddess of the moon. These were evidently very wealthy people and are likely to have been the owners of the house.

Nineteenth-century archaeologists discovered that, by pouring plaster of Paris into voids in the volcanic ash that had smothered Pompeii, they could recover three-dimensional replicas of people who had been overwhelmed and were now no more than bones. In a letter of 1863 to the director of excavations, Giuseppe Fiorelli, who thought up the idea, a correspondent wrote:

> So far they have discovered temples, houses and other artefacts that take the interest of educated people [but you] have uncovered human suffering and whoever has an ounce of humanity will feel it.

The technique has revealed the final moments of many inhabitants of Pompeii, including those of the luckless group under the stairs. They seem to have died from sudden and extreme heat. The adults have fallen backwards and have their arms raised like boxers, an effect caused by high temperature contracting their tendons. One child can be seen on the mother's lap and the other, whose facial features are finely preserved, is lying on the ground.

* The Italian government is refusing to permit any further work, apparently preferring conservation to exploration. A feasibility study is in slow preparation.

† More detail on the House of the Golden Bracelet is given on page 130.

The family committed a fatal mistake by not making their escape sooner. Perhaps they could not bear to be parted from their lovely home with its gardens, both the real one outdoors and those that had been painted within.

v

SOCIAL MEDIA, ROMAN STYLE

GRAFFITI were the social media of the Roman era. Many handwritten messages have been discovered among the excavated ruins of the town of Pompeii, victim of the erupting Mount Vesuvius in AD 79. All kinds of people penned graffiti and, more than any other evidence from the remote classical past, their scribbles and brush-strokes evoke what it was like to be alive in those days.

Local elections spawned copious campaign messages. Cuspius Pansa, a local worthy, was standing for *aedile*, a public post. 'All the goldsmiths recommend Gaius Cuspius Pansa for aedile,' wrote some friendly campaigners, only to be contradicted by the supporter of another candidate: 'Please, I beg you, unguent-makers, make Verus aedile, I entreat you.' Cuspius was less hospitable than was wise in a candidate for office; a visiting civil servant scrawled on the wall of the entrance to Cuspius' house: 'The finance officer of the emperor Nero says the food here is poison.'

Public notices abounded and, local authorities being much the same down the ages, they often dealt with planning permission:

> Gaius Vulius son of Gaius and Publius Aninius son of Gaius, Duoviri [town mayors, literally the 'two men'], let the contracts for the Public Baths and the Robing Room and for the refurbishing of the Portico and the Gymnasium, in accordance with a Decree of the Town Council, out of the money which the law requires them to spend for games or public works. The same officials oversaw the construction and inspection.

A wall could also be used for a commercial break. All kinds of services and wares were advertised. A small hotel sets out its offer: 'Guest House. Dining room to let, with three couches and furnishings.' Gladiatorial fights are heavily publicized. A sports promoter, accompanied by his right-hand man, a former slave and probably one-time fighter in the arena, arrives in town. He announces:

> Twenty pairs of Gladiators, belonging to Aulus Suettius Antenio and to his freedman Niger, will fight at Puteoli [not far from Pompeii] on 17, 18, 19 and 20 March. There will also be a beast hunt and athletic contests.

Individuals expressed their personal feelings with directness and candour: 'Samius says to Cornelius—bugger off.' A reactionary releases steam: 'I detest beggars. If somebody wants something for free, he is an idiot; let him pay his cash and get what he wants.' Poignantly, a runaway slave leaves a parting message which encapsulates an almost unbearable mixture of pride, fear and excitement: 'I have escaped. I have fled. Hope and fortune, farewell!'

Many of the graffiti deal with sexual desire—already satisfied, to be satisfied or unsatisfied. 'Nobody is cool till he has had sex with a young girl,' boasts a paedophile. On the wall of a bar-cum-brothel a bisexual customer writes: 'Weep, you girls. My penis has given you up. Now it penetrates men's behinds. Goodbye, the eternal feminine!' A sufferer warns of the risks of sexually transmitted disease: 'The man who buggers a fire burns his prick.'

The vertical surfaces of Pompeii are nothing other than a stone-and-plaster red-top. As the *News of the World* used to brag, all human life is here.

XXVI

SLAVERY

1

OF HUMAN BONDAGE

HERCULANEUM, the small town that was destroyed by the eruption of Vesuvius at the same time as Pompeii in AD 79 (see page 271), had about 5,000 inhabitants. Some 1,500 are estimated to have been freedmen and their families; slaves and their families probably added up to 2,250 people. This left the free-born population standing at only about 1,250 souls. These numbers probably reflect the fact that Herculaneum was an upmarket resort for wealthy families which were likely to own more slaves and have more dependants than ordinary people; but they do suggest that slaves and freedmen made up a substantial fraction of the overall population of the Roman empire (unfortunately, we do not have census records).

Every aspect of life, all its institutions, were scarred by the fact that Rome was a slave society. The nearest modern equivalent was the American South before the Civil War, but there are significant differences, the most important of which is that Romans were not racist. 'Slavery is a human invention and not found in nature,' wrote the jurist Gaius in the second century AD. 'Indeed, it was that other human invention, war, which produced the majority of slaves.' In addition to warfare, slaves were procured by piracy and brigandage, and by reproduction within the existing slave population. They were often bought at auction or in trade, and became the absolute property of their master or mistress, who by law could do with them whatever they wanted—even kill them. The antiquarian Varro, who lived in the first century BC, called them 'tools that can speak'.

If you had to be a slave, it was best not to be deployed as a farm labourer or (even worse) a miner. Life in those cases was exhausting, brutal and brief. Another unpleasant fate if you were good-looking (and of either sex) was to be billeted in a brothel. Working in the master's household as a domestic servant was much more comfortable. Many slaves were hired for their specialist skills. A slave was not only employed in a family business; often he ran it. Some even had their own seals inscribed with their names so that they could act on their master's behalf.*

Of course, there were awkwardnesses. A master might well expect sexual favours. 'I know of a slave who dreamed that his penis was stroked and aroused by his master's hand,' wrote Artemidorus, a well-known interpreter of dreams in the second century AD, adding ominously that this meant he would be bound to a pillar and 'receive many strokes'. In this analysis the dream fused many slaves' two recurring fears: sexual and physical abuse.

The single most important fact about the 'peculiar institution' of slavery (to borrow an American term) was that free-born citizens could easily end up in a minority. The inevitable consequence was perennial paranoia and fear of slave revolts, indiscipline and violence. Incorrigible slaves were sold off as gladiators, while country houses were often equipped with subterranean prison cells for the unruly. At the Villa of the Mosaic Columns just outside Pompeii, the skeleton of a slave was found in such a room with manacles on his legs. No one had thought to free him at the time of the eruption.

11

THE MULTICULTURAL METROPOLIS

THE GREAT PRIZE for the household slave was the likelihood of emancipation and Roman citizenship. Freedom was a reward for good service. Some slaves became close friends of the family that had owned them, and after liberation they adopted the family name and were expected to continue in their old jobs. The Romans had no concept of racial purity, and over time their capital became the most culturally diverse of cities; its population, filled with ever greater numbers of freed slaves, mirrored the ethnic composition of its vast empire and indeed of the lands beyond its frontiers.

* One area of business where slaves played an important role was banking; on this, see pages 235–36.

GUILT BY ASSOCIATION

If the master of a household was murdered, the law required that all his slaves were executed, whoever was actually guilty of the crime.

In AD 61 the City Prefect, Lucius Pedanius Secundus, was murdered by one of his slaves. The motive was unclear; he may have asked his master to sell him and been refused. There was talk that he and Pedanius were both infatuated with the same young man, and the slave could not endure the competition. In any event, Pedanius was a rich man and owned 400 slaves, all of whom were condemned to death according to the law.

When news of this got out, there were riots in Rome. The authorities had not taken into account the fact that much of the city population was of slave descent. A debate on the subject was held in the Senate. Some members felt the law was too harsh, but one speaker, a certain Gaius Cassius Longinus, argued that it was essential to good order and made a comparison with the military practice of decimation.* 'None of the murderer's fellow slaves prevented or betrayed him,' he said. 'Our huge households are international. They include every religion—or none at all. The only way to keep down this scum is by intimidation. Innocent people will die, you say. Yes, and when in a defeated army every tenth man is to be flogged to death, the brave have to draw lots with the others.'

The mass execution was confirmed and great crowds ready with stones and torches gathered to prevent it from taking place. The emperor Nero was forced to call out troops to make sure that the law was carried out.

* For more on the military punishment known as decimation, see page 66.

iv

RUN—BUT YOU BETTER NOT GET CAUGHT

A SLAVE could always run away, but the risks were great. Punishments were severe if he was caught, and he very likely would be. Regular runaways could be branded or tattooed on the forehead, or they had to wear an iron collar around the neck embossed with the initials TMQF (*tene me quia fugio*—'take hold of me because I am a runaway'). It was a crime to harbour fugitive slaves, and professional slave-catchers were hired to hunt them down. Notices were posted with detailed descriptions of escaped slaves, and rewards were offered for their return. Owners who had lost patience with a recaptured slave might put him to death, by crucifixion if he liked, or cut off his hands or feet.

v

SEARCHING FOR SPARTACUS

'I AM SPARTACUS!' shouted his defeated followers in Stanley Kubrick's movie (1960), each of them determined to prevent their leader from handing himself in to the hated Roman general Crassus. To modern eyes, Spartacus could be a spokesman for oppressed workers, even a campaigner for the abolition of slavery; a modern socialist. In Karl Marx's opinion, he was 'the most splendid fellow in the whole of ancient history. Great general (no Garibaldi), noble character, and a real representative of the ancient proletariat.' Although we know little about the man, this can hardly be right.

Spartacus was a Thracian slave in the first century BC who became successively a mercenary, a Roman soldier, and then a deserter and robber. Presumably the authorities then caught him, and because of his great physical strength he was enrolled as a gladiator at a high-security training school in Capua. In 73 BC he and about seventy others grabbed choppers and spits from the kitchens and broke out.

Many thousands of slaves and free poor joined Spartacus' revolt. Roman army after army met with disaster. Spartacus was a good tactician, but it is unclear what his and his comrades' long-term intentions were. They marched up towards northern Italy, where they were to disband and disperse to their original homes. But then there was a change of mind, and the rebels, now an army of about 70,000, marched back to the south and spent their time counterproductively ravaging the countryside. After failing to find ships to transport them to Sicily, doubtless for more looting, the slave forces were cornered in southern Italy and destroyed. All survivors were crucified.

What was missing in this great uprising was a final objective or plan. One thing is clear, though: Spartacus and his men had no intention of abolishing slavery; they merely wanted to stop being slaves themselves. They were not quite the models of virtue Marx thought them to be.

[*vi*]

THE SELLING HABIT

CATO THE ELDER was not a sentimental man, as he makes clear in his book on agriculture, written in the second century BC. Many labourers in the fields were slaves and Cato had little or no interest in their welfare. What he expected from them was unremitting hard work; if they could not deliver that, they were to be got rid of. He advises farmers:

> Sell worn-out oxen, blemished cattle, blemished sheep, wool, hides, an old wagon, old tools, an old slave, a sickly slave, and whatever else is superfluous. The master should have the selling habit, not the buying habit.

ROMAN WIT

i

LAUGHTER DILUTED BY TIME

A JOKE is like a cut flower—it soon withers. The Romans liked to think they had a sense of humour, but it is hard to appreciate it at this distance in time. A number of popular jokes have come down to us. Here are two which may have raised a belly laugh during a liquid evening in a *taberna*, though they would doubtless get a rather less enthusiastic reception today.

> A young man said to his lusty wife, 'What should we do, darling? Eat or have sex?' She replied: 'Whatever you want. But there isn't a crumb in the house.'
>
> * * *
>
> An astrologer casts a horoscope for an ailing boy. He assures the boy's mother that he will have a long life, and then asks her to pay his fee. She says she will bring him the money the following day. 'But what if he dies in the night?' asks the astrologer.

ii

THE WITTIEST MAN IN ROME

THE GREAT orator and lawyer Cicero, who lived in the first century BC, was held to be the wittiest man of his age. His political enemy Julius Caesar was one of his fans. He got his staff to report the great man's latest *bons mots* on a daily basis and one of them published a collection. Cicero had a weakness for puns, which do not travel well. Here is one of the better ones:

Cicero was defending a man on a murder charge. The victim had been a riotous politician and had for a long time been cordially disliked by respectable people. At sundown one day he was set upon by enemies and killed. 'When did he die?' the prosecutor asked. '*Sero*', replied Cicero—to loud guffaws around the court. The word he used had two meanings—'late in the day' and 'too late'. Those present enjoyed the suggestion that the disreputable figure should have been got rid of long ago.

At another trial, a young man accused of having given his father a poisoned cake said he wanted to give Cicero a piece of his mind. 'I'd prefer that to a piece of your cake!' came the response.

Cicero specialized in the brutal put-down. When he met a man with three ugly daughters, he quoted a well-known verse: 'Apollo never meant him to have children.'

He is at his best ad-libbing during a meeting of the Senate. Caesar had proposed a controversial bill that state-owned land in Campania should be distributed to his veteran soldiers. Lucius Gellius, one of the oldest members of the Senate, protested that this would only be done over his dead body. 'Well, let's wait then,' quipped Cicero, 'since Gellius isn't asking us to postpone things for long.'

[iii]

AUGUSTUS' DOUBLE

POWER attracts humour. Jokers enjoyed pulling the emperor Augustus' leg—although they took care not to be too subversive.

> A youth from the provinces has come to Rome and everyone stops and stares at him as he walks through the streets, for he is Augustus' double. The emperor has him brought to the palace, looks at him and then asks: 'Tell me, my boy, did your mother ever come to Rome?' He replied (casting some doubt on the virtue of Augustus' mother): 'No, she never did. But my father was often here.'

[iv]

AUGUSTUS' RAVEN

AFTER his great victory at Actium over Mark Antony and Cleopatra, Octavian (soon to become Augustus) returned to Rome in state. Among those who welcomed him back was a man with a raven, which he had taught to say: 'Greetings to Caesar, our victorious commander.' Octavian was delighted by the compliment and gave the man 20,000 sesterces for the bird—a substantial sum of money.

The bird-trainer had a partner, and when he wasn't given a share of the reward, he informed Octavian that the man had a second raven and suggested that he should be made to bring that out as well. The bird was duly produced and repeated the words it had been taught to say: 'Greetings to Mark Antony, our victorious commander.'

Luckily for the owner, Octavian laughed.

THE FALL OF ROME

i

TOO MUCH FOR ONE TO BEAR

THE ADMINISTRATIVE burden of running the Roman empire efficiently was far too much for one man. The first emperor, Augustus (see page 43), understood this when he shared his authority with his old school friend Marcus Vipsanius Agrippa and later with his stepson Tiberius.

Those who followed Augustus usually ruled alone, but they were only able to do so because they could take advantage of the benign inertia created by the Roman system of imperial government. Despite the fact that the Romans had won their empire through bloodshed, for centuries they enjoyed the consent of their subject peoples. This was because, after conquest, they brought peace, the famous *pax Romana*, and with it prosperity. Provincials were elected to the Senate and emperors took power who did not have a drop of Roman blood in them.

ii

EAST IS EAST AND WEST IS WEST

DURING the third century AD the Roman empire staggered under two handicaps. First, there was rising pressure from barbarian invaders along the Rhine and Danube frontiers and from the Parthians (and later the Persian Sassanids) in the east. And second, a quick-fire succession of military rulers meant that an emperor would last no more than a few years or even months in office. More than twenty-five emperors came and went in this period, and there were frequent civil wars on their deaths.

When Diocletian assumed the purple in AD 284, he was determined to re-establish order. On the principle that the empire could not be governed by a single emperor, he introduced a system according to which there were two senior rulers, each given the title of Augustus, and two junior rulers, each called Caesar. When an Augustus died or retired, the idea was that he would be succeeded by a Caesar.

The system was too complicated to last and single emperors returned (although they often shared their powers in the interest of imperial defence). In AD 364 Valentinian I appointed his brother Valens to govern the empire's eastern half. Eventually, in AD 395, two permanent imperial courts were created, one at Ravenna in north-east Italy (which was more defensible than Rome) and the other at Constantinople, and they were headed by different emperors, Honorius and Arcadius. The theory was that, while there were two administrations, there was still one empire. But the courts gradually drifted apart and co-operation between them was minimal. When the disunited west faced extinction, it did so alone.

iii

WHY DID THE ROMAN EMPIRE FALL?

ALL SORTS of reasons have been advanced to explain the fall of the Roman empire, and many or all may well have played a part. Scholars have spoken of climate change and population decline, plagues, corruption and administrative breakdown, civil wars and incompetent emperors, even something as wispy as moral decline. Some have blamed Christianity for weakening Rome's imperial resolve.

There had been pressure on the frontiers for centuries, and as far back as the reign of Marcus Aurelius emperors had recruited barbarian invaders into the legions to fight their fellow tribesmen and allowed them to settle inside the empire.

But if we are looking for a single cause, we can safely point to the Huns. Their arrival on the scene was the crucial factor in Rome's decline. They were nomads who had their origins in northern China, where they were called Xiongnu (pronounced roughly 'Hunnu'). Their mounted archers were lethally effective fighters. Active in Siberia, Mongolia and Manchuria, they moved slowly westwards and arrived in central Europe around AD 370.

The Huns attacked the Germanic tribes on the far side of the Rhine and Danube rivers—among them, the Goths, whom they drove out of the territory they were occupying. The barbarian populations fled before the oncoming Huns and poured into Gaul and the Balkans. Over the course of the next century they roamed around the western empire. The Franks ended up in what is now France and Germany, the Visigoths ('good Goths') in Spain, the Ostrogoths ('bright Goths') in Italy and the Vandals in northern Africa.

In AD 378, the Goths defeated and killed the eastern emperor Valens in a great battle at Adrianople (today's Edirne, in European Turkey), an event that shook the empire to its core and marked a decisive moment in its decline.

[iv]

CLOSING TIME

ONE BY ONE, during the western empire's last centuries, its great institutions began to disappear.

The celebrated pagan oracles were religious shrines that gave guidance to anyone who came asking questions about the future. The world-famous oracle of Apollo at Delphi shut up shop during the reign of Julian (AD 361–3). In her last message in verse, the priestess of the god, intoxicated (it was said) either by chewing bay leaves or by breathing fumes from a sacred spring, prophesied the end of the old order of things:

> Apollo has no chapel left, no prophesying bay,
> No talking spring. The stream is dry that had so much to say.

In AD 379 Theodosius I became the last Roman emperor to rule both the eastern and the western halves of the empire. He made Christianity its official religion and outlawed paganism. He abolished the Vestal Virgins and brought an end to the Olympic Games in Greece, which were not to reopen on a continuous basis until 1896.

Fanatics attacked and destroyed Roman temples. Holy sites and images were vandalized. Blood sacrifices were banned and so was the practice of determining the will of the gods by examining animals' entrails. An old legion of gods and goddesses gave way to another of saints and martyrs.

[v]

THE CONQUEROR BROUGHT LOW

'A DREADFUL rumour reaches us from the west. Rome is occupied... My heart is choked with sobs as I dictate these words. The city that has conquered the universe is now herself conquered.'

Such was the reaction of the Christian writer and theologian St Jerome in AD 410, when the city of Rome fell to a barbarian invader. The empire's long-lasting peace—the *pax Romana*—had depended on the prowess of the legions that guarded the frontiers from invasion from without. Now these had failed.

The invading Visigoths were a Germanic tribe that, like many others, had been pushed westward by the Huns in the 370s and had muscled their way inside the imperial borders south of the river Danube. Their leader, Alaric, was ambitious and busy making a name for himself. For ten years he had been a lurking threat. However, he had no intention of overthrowing the empire. Quite the reverse; he approved of it and merely wanted to be part of it. (As a matter of fact, the so-called 'barbarians' were often rather more civilized than Romans were willing to admit.)

Alaric was repeatedly bought off with promises of land and money—promises that were usually broken. Twice he had marched south through Italy and angrily threatened Rome. He wanted to force the emperor to give his people a large permanent homeland and to appoint him as the official defender of the empire. Eventually Alaric lost patience with a regime that could not decide whether to fight him or give him what he asked. So he attacked Rome, captured it and allowed his soldiers to burn, kill and loot at will. The sack went on for two or three days.

The impact of Alaric's victory on the Mediterranean world was colossal. Many blamed Christianity, the empire's new official religion, for the debacle—hence Jerome's alarm. The old pagan gods were taking their revenge, it was said, for the apostasy. Another saint and one of the greatest church fathers, Augustine of Hippo, went to the trouble of writing a book, *The City of God*, in rebuttal.

The ordinary citizen, meanwhile, had more to worry about than theological debates. Within sixty years the empire in the west had broken up into lawless kingdoms. The centuries of peace and prosperity were ending.

vi

THE DEATH OF ALARIC

THE SACK of Rome in AD 410 by Alaric and his Visigoths may have been a decisive event in the decline of Rome, but he himself gained nothing from it, since he died soon afterwards in southern Italy, probably from a fever. For his funeral, a river in Calabria was dammed and temporarily diverted. Then his followers buried their great leader in the riverbed, broke the dam and allowed the river to return to its course. The slaves who had done the work were all killed so that the secret of Alaric's final resting place would never be known.

vii

THE SCOURGE OF GOD

BY THE FIFTH century AD the Huns controlled a vast territory that stretched from the Rhine to the Caspian Sea. Despite their being the cause of massive and inconvenient barbarian incursions, Rome was on good terms with them and, as it had short-sightedly done with other tribes and peoples, hired Huns as mercenaries.

Attila and his brother acceded to the Hunnish throne in AD 434 as joint kings (the brother died after some years, perhaps killed by his sibling). They ran an extremely aggressive foreign policy. They attacked the Sassanid Persian empire but were repelled. They had better luck when they invaded the eastern Roman empire, but failed to capture its capital Constantinople. They also campaigned in the west around the Danube. To stop their marauding, the Romans handed over a large quantity of gold and a substantial annual tribute. For a time there was peace.

Attila could not keep still, though, and in AD 450 his acquisitive eye fell on the Visigothic kingdom of Toulouse. He also claimed the hand of the western emperor's sister, Honoria, impertinently demanding half the western empire as her dowry. The request was poorly received. In AD 451 a huge battle was fought near Châlons in France between Attila and the Roman general Flavius Aetius, assisted by Theodoric, king of the Ostrogoths. The Romans won in what was to be their last great military campaign.

Attila withdrew from view for a year or two, but he returned, like a bad penny. He was still chasing Honoria and now he invaded Italy, ravaging the land as he marched south. Men feared that Rome would fall. Pope Leo I met Attila and begged him to abandon his campaign. The king agreed to leave Italy, not so much out of respect for Leo as for logistical reasons.

Then the Scourge of God, as European Christians called him, suddenly died. On the night of his marriage to a new wife, a young Ostrogothic beauty, he drank too much, burst a blood vessel and was gone. To the civilized world it appeared to be a narrow escape, for Attila's kingdom quickly collapsed. The Huns were no longer a threat.

So was Rome saved? Not really, for the immigrant multitudes whom the Huns had chased into the empire were now emboldened by their absence. They advanced the process of dismantling Roman rule and setting up their own independent kingdoms. The bright day was nearly done.

[viii]

THE BIRTH OF VENICE

THE HUNNISH cloud had a silver lining. One consequence of Attila's attacks on Italy was that people fled in terror to some small islands in a lagoon on the north-eastern coast. It was an ideal spot for self-defence and there they stayed. The panic-stricken settlement grew into the Venetian Republic. So Venice began in peril. Lovers of *La Serenissima* owe a debt to the Scourge of God.

ix

A KING OF SIMPLE TASTES

We have a unique insight into the personality of Attila, for a detailed account of a Roman embassy to the Hunnish king in AD 448/9 has survived. The author was a diplomat and historian called Priscus.

After a long and uncomfortable journey through woods and wasteland chasing after a quarry who was always on the move, the embassy at last arrived at one of the king's numerous palace settlements. This consisted of a series of circular wooden buildings, each surrounded by elegant wooden walls.

The ambassadors were invited to dinner in the king's living quarters. Priscus writes:

> All the seats were arranged around the walls… Right in the middle of the room Attila sat upon a couch. Behind him was another couch, and behind that steps led up to Attila's bed, which was screened by fine linens and ornamental hangings.

The king was short, with a broad chest and large head. He had a sparse, grey-flecked beard; his nose was flat and his complexion dark.

Although surrounded by the luxury that honour demanded of a famous ruler, he himself had simple tastes:

> While for the other barbarians and for us, there were lavishly prepared meals served on silver plates, Attila ate a simple meat dish on a wooden platter… Guests at the feast were given gold and silver goblets, but his cup was made from wood. His clothes were plain and differed in no way from what others were wearing—except that they were clean. The sword at his side, the fastenings of his boots and his horse's bridle were not decorated with precious stones as were those of the other Huns.

Priscus makes it clear that Attila dominated his court and had the respect and admiration of his entourage. He was self-confident, charismatic, ruthless and shrewd, yet capable of moderation. Like the best leaders, he trusted his subordinates.

[x]

GIVE A DOG A BAD NAME...

ALARIC was not the last barbarian invader to capture Rome. In AD 455 the Vandals took the city. They have had a bad press. There appears to have been little bloodshed and no buildings were burned, but they looted large amounts of treasure and removed gold and bronze roofing tiles from the great temple of Jupiter Optimus Maximus on the Capitoline hill.

The word 'vandalism' was coined in their honour—a blow to their reputation from which they have never recovered.

[xi]

THE LAST EMPEROR

ROMULUS was the founder of Rome and Augustus the 'second' founder, in that he was the first emperor and created the imperial system. It is a bizarre coincidence that the last emperor, who assumed the purple on 31 October AD 475, was a fourteen-year-old boy known as Romulus Augustulus (or 'little Augustus'—a nickname, for his *ex officio* name as emperor was, of course, Augustus). He was put on the throne by his father, a Germanic general called Orestes. Perhaps Orestes had a sense of humour. He could see that the end was nigh and may have thought it would be amusing, or at least neat, to have his son called by Latin names that echoed Rome's origins.

Anyhow, the youth lasted less than a year before being deposed by a warlord called Odoacer, who proclaimed himself king of Italy. He was not put to death, however, but given a pension and lived out his days quietly in a country villa in Campania.

Life did not change overnight. Romulus Augustulus' ousted predecessor, Julius Nepos, still asserted his title to the imperial throne and the court in Constantinople maintained its territorial claims. But, for good or ill, the empire in the west had given way to a confusion of jostling lands and kingdoms. There was no call for any more emperors. The way lay open to the Middle Ages.

XXIX

AVE ATQUE VALE

My thanks are due to the emperor Claudius, for conquering the island of Britannia, and to his successors for subjecting it to a thorough-going Romanization. This little book is the product of 2,000 years of native familiarity with both the virtues and the vices of Roman culture.

But just as the stories, language and imagery of the Bible are fading from our secular consciousness, and even from our memory, so too are the stories, language and imagery of the classical world. They (or at least the decent bits) no longer reside at the heart of the school curriculum. There are good reasons to give children the new skills necessary to navigate the future; but something is being lost. That something is our old, easy access to the past from which we grew.

In AD 410 the feeble emperor Honorius withdrew Rome's legions from Britannia and abandoned its civilized inhabitants to the uncertain mercy of foreign invaders. Today the legions of the Roman mind are marching off.

In these pages I wish them hail and farewell—*ave atque vale*.

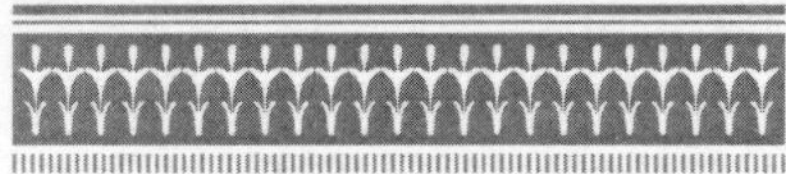

A CHRONOLOGY

BC

---

c.800	• First village settlement on the Palatine hill.
753	• Traditional date of the foundation of Rome (probably a century too early). Rome is ruled by kings. These are, in order: Romulus, Numa Pompilius, Tullus Hostilius, Ancus Marcius, Lucius Tarquinius Priscus, Servius Tullius and Lucius Tarquinius Superbus. They begin the process of Rome's territorial expansion. Rome is already an important city on the southern edge of the Etruscan empire, by which it is culturally influenced.
509	• Rape of Lucretia. Fall of the monarchy; creation of the Roman Republic, headed by two annual consuls with an advisory committee, the Senate.
494	• Rivalry between the common people (plebeians) and the aristocracy (patricians); the latter monopolize government, military and religious posts. First of a series of general strikes, or secessions, by the people. Gradually over the coming centuries the patricians give ground.
451–450	• Publication of the Twelve Tables, Rome's first published legal code.
395	• Rome captures the Etruscan city of Veii after a long siege. The goddess Juno, in her Veian incarnation, is persuaded to side with Rome in an evocatio.
390	• Gauls sack Rome, but not the citadel; they are raiders and leave. The city soon recovers, but the threat from the barbarian north continues on and off throughout Rome's history. The Servian Walls are built.

366 • First plebeian, or non-patrician, consul elected. A plebeian nobility joins the patrician ruling class.

358 • Lucius Quinctius Cincinnatus appointed dictator. He symbolizes an ideal Roman—plain-living, unconcerned with money, patriotic and brave.

338 • Rome has been fighting its neighbours since the age of the kings; now its conquest of central Italy is completed. The Latin League of Italian tribes hostile to Rome is dissolved. They are each given various levels of citizenship or bilateral treaties.

326–290 • Long wars with the Samnites, hill tribesmen in the Apennine mountains in central Italy, who wish to expand down into the fertile coast of Campania. Rome is ultimately victorious.

280–275 • Greek cities in southern Italy object to Roman encroachment. Pyrrhus, king of Epirus and a mercenary general, is hired by Tarentum to fight Rome; he loses and Rome now controls all Italy south of the river Po through one-to-one alliances with subject communities, tribes and city-states. Most are given partial Roman citizenship in return for the provision of troops, when required, to join the legions.

264–241 • First Punic (Carthaginian) War. Rome and the Carthaginians, a great north African sea-power, fight for control of Sicily. To beat the Carthaginians Rome builds fleets, and wins the war. Sicily becomes Rome's first colonial province.

264 • First gladiatorial show at Rome, a sacrifice at a nobleman's funeral.

218–201 • Second Punic War. Hannibal, a military genius, seeks to avenge Carthage's defeat. He crosses the Alps and invades Italy, where he spends sixteen years on campaign. His aim is to restore Carthaginian power. He wins many battles but loses the war.

216 • Rome's greatest defeat. Hannibal wins the battle of Cannae. 70,000 Roman and allied Italian soldiers are killed.

214–205 • First Macedonian War. Inconclusive hostilities between Rome and Philip, king of Macedonia (Macedonia includes all of mainland Greece).

202 • Hannibal is finally vanquished in north Africa at the battle of Zama. Carthage surrenders and is no longer a first-class power.

200–196 • Second Macedonian War. Rome is drawn into Balkan politics and defeats Philip. Greek city-states are freed from Macedonian control.

192–189 • Rome is drawn into Middle Eastern politics. It defeats Antiochus the Great, ruler of Syria and western Asia, and becomes the Mediterranean superpower. Huge wealth pours into Rome.

172–167 • Third Macedonian War. Rome is victorious. To emasculate its potential power, Macedonia is cantonized.

147 • Macedonia, including Greece and its quarrelsome city-states, becomes a Roman province.

146 • Jealous of its economic revival, Rome razes Carthage to the ground.

133 • Beginning of Rome's constitutional breakdown. A tribune of the people, Tiberius Sempronius Gracchus, proposes a controversial land reform; he is killed by rioting senators.

121 • Gaius Gracchus, Tiberius' younger brother and also a reformer, is attacked by rioting senators and kills himself. A century of domestic disturbances and civil strife ensues.

102–101 • Mass invasion by Gallic tribes repulsed by the great Roman commander Marius. Marius reforms the army. He is elected consul for an unprecedented seven times. He is a better general than a politician.

91–88 • War of the Allies. The subject Italian communities fight for universal full Roman citizenship. Rome nearly loses the war and gives way. All Italians south of the Po become Roman citizens.

88 • Sulla, first in a series of ruthless dynasts and politically a conservative, becomes consul. Dismissed from his command in the Middle East, he marches on Rome to regain it. Because of the state's reluctance to allocate farming land to veterans, the legions transfer their loyalty from the state to their generals.

88–85 • Sulla fights a war against Rome's greatest foe since Hannibal, Mithridates of Pontus on the Black Sea. The king has organized the mass killing of all Romans and Italians found in the Middle East. Stalemate ensues.

87 • Marius, radical and populist, massacres followers of Sulla during his absence on campaign.

86 • Marius dies, old and mad.

83 • Sulla returns to Italy and takes power in Rome.

82 • Sulla is appointed dictator, with full executive powers; he launches a proscription, a state-endorsed or legal massacre of his opponents. He introduces reforms designed to strengthen the constitution against subversion by other dynasts like himself.

81 • Sulla resigns the dictatorship. He becomes consul again, then retires and dies two years later. His reforms are soon unpicked.

74–62 • Rome fights and finally defeats Mithridates, who kills himself. The Middle East is now secure.

73–71 • Slave revolt, led by Spartacus, a gladiator. After early successes, it is put down.

60 • First triumvirate. Julius Caesar and two other leading politicians, Pompey and Crassus, form an alliance, in what is in effect a temporary coup d'état. With a combination of bribery and popular policies, they take control of the political system.

59 • Caesar becomes consul.

58–49 • Caesar invades and conquers Gaul, on a slight pretext. One million are estimated killed.

53 • Crassus is killed on campaign against the Parthian empire (today's Iraq and Iran).

52 • Revolt in Gaul of Vercingetorix. It ends with Caesar's successful siege of Alesia.

49–45 • Civil war. The remaining dynasts fall out; Caesar fights Pompey and the constitutionalist party in the Senate.

48 • Caesar wins a decisive battle against Pompey at Pharsalus in Greece. Pompey escapes to Egypt, where he is murdered.

44 • After quashing resistance in north Africa and Spain, Caesar wins the civil war, but does not know how to reform the state and retain the confidence of the ruling, or senatorial, class. He decides to leave Rome for a campaign against the Parthians, but is assassinated by discontented senators, who fear the destruction of the Republic and the return of a monarchy.

43 • Caesar's adopted son and heir, the clever teenaged Octavian, enters into partnership with Mark Antony, Caesar's leading lieutenant, and campaigns against the assassins and constitutionalists.

• Second triumvirate. Rome is governed by three men in a state-endorsed arrangement that consists of Octavian, Mark Antony and (for a time) Lepidus. The triumvirs launch a second proscription; many lose their lives, among them the famous statesman and orator Cicero.

42 • Brutus and Cassius, the leading assassins of Caesar, lose to Mark Antony at the battle of Philippi.
The Republic is dead.

41 • Octavian besieges Perusia and defeats Lucius Antonius, Mark Antony's brother. He enters into a new concordat with Mark Antony and, respectively, they rule the western and eastern halves of the Roman empire.

• Antony meets Cleopatra, pharaoh of Egypt. Over time they set up a political and personal partnership.

31 • Civil war breaks out between Antony and Octavian. Antony and Cleopatra lose the battle of Actium; they commit suicide in Alexandria the following year. Octavian, the last triumvir, is now master of the Roman world.

27 • Octavian is given the title of Augustus, or 'revered one'. He claims to restore the Republican constitution, but in fact establishes a covert autocracy backed by the army. He is modestly referred to as *princeps*, or 'first citizen'. His reign is marked by administrative competence, decentralization to local communities, and aggressive frontier wars along and across the Rhine.

2 • Julia the Elder, Augustus' daughter, is exiled for immorality.

AD

---

8 • Julia the Younger, Augustus' grand-daughter, is exiled ostensibly for immorality, but probably also for political reasons. The poet Ovid is banished.

9 • Annihilation of three legions in the Teutoburg Forest in Germany; Augustus is deeply shocked. He drops his policy of imperial expansion and the Rhine becomes a permanent frontier of the empire.

14 • Death of Augustus. Tiberius, his stepson, becomes emperor; he is efficient but depressive.

?29 • Crucifixion of Jesus Christ.

• Death of the influential dowager empress Livia.

37 • Death of Tiberius. Caligula, young, bright but somewhat unhinged, succeeds him.

41 • Caligula is murdered. Claudius, disabled probably by polio, becomes emperor and proves to be an unexpectedly good ruler.

43 • Conquest of Britannia.

54 • Death of Claudius, probably by poison. Nero, self-indulgent but no fool, becomes emperor; he promotes Greek culture.

59 • Nero murders his interfering mother Agrippina.

61 • Defeat of Boudica, queen of the Iceni.

64 • Great fire at Rome; not Nero's doing. Christians are wrongly blamed and persecuted.

68 • Faced by army revolts, Nero commits suicide.

69 • Year of the Four Emperors—namely, Galba, Otho, Vitellius and, finally, the able and witty Vespasian.

70 • A great Jewish revolt is quashed.

79 • Vespasian dies. His son Titus becomes emperor. Eruption of Mount Vesuvius. Destruction of Pompeii and Herculaneum.

81 • Titus dies. Domitian, Vespasian's youngest son, becomes emperor; he is able but despotic.

89 • Domitian launches a 'reign of terror' against the Senate.

96 • Domitian is murdered by his wife and household staff, alarmed for their own safety. Nerva, an elderly senator, succeeds him.

98 • Trajan, a leading general, becomes emperor. He is a well-wishing and effective public administrator; he has an expansionist military policy.

101–6 • The Dacian Wars extend the empire northwards to the defensible frontier of the river Danube.

113 • Unsuccessful (and unnecessary) invasion of Parthia, which is Rome's only political and military rival but does not pursue expansionist policies. A quick victory is followed by an insurgency.

117 • Trajan dies. Hadrian becomes emperor; his reign is the Roman empire's high point. He withdraws from Trajan's contested Parthian conquests and bans further imperial expansion. He promotes Greek culture as an essential part of the empire's identity, especially in the east.

118–38 • Hadrian's Villa near Tivoli is built.

128 • Hadrian's Wall is largely completed.

130 • Unexpected death of Antinous, Hadrian's lover; he is deified.

131–3 • A Jewish revolt is quashed, and Jerusalem sacked with much loss of life. The new province of Palestine replaces Judaea and Syria.

138 • Hadrian dies after adopting Antoninus, a senator, who succeeds him. Simultaneously, it is arranged that

Antoninus adopts the young Marcus Aurelius.

161 • Antoninus dies after a quiet and prosperous reign. Marcus Aurelius, philosophical author of the *Meditations*, becomes emperor.

162–6 • Successful war with Parthia, but the army returns with the plague.

168–80 • German wars; the Romans have hard work defending the empire's frontier from external attack.

180 • Marcus Aurelius dies. His foolish son Commodus becomes emperor.

192 • Commodus is murdered.

193 • Septimius Severus becomes emperor. An able and tough ruler, he stabilizes the empire, assisted by his intelligent wife Julia Domna.

194 • Septimius Severus invades Parthia.

---

211 • Death of Septimius Severus. Caracalla, Severus' cruel and unpopular son, becomes emperor. He murders his brother and co-emperor Geta.

212 • Roman citizenship is granted to all free men in the empire.

217 • Caracalla is murdered. Empress Julia Domna, widow of Severus, commits suicide.

218–22 • Teenaged Elagabalus (also known as Heliogabalus) becomes emperor.

227 • The Parthian empire, weakened by constant Roman attacks, is overthrown by the more aggressive Persian Sassanids.

235–84 • Period of the 'Soldier Emperors', a succession of short-lived military rulers.

267 • Zenobia becomes ruler of Palmyra after the deaths of her husband and stepson.

269 • Zenobia conquers Egypt.

271–5 • The Aurelian Walls are built at Rome.

272–3 • Aurelian defeats Zenobia.

284 • Diocletian becomes emperor. One of the few emperors of the third and fourth centuries to die in his bed (aged sixty-six), he restores stability and reforms

Rome's system of government; he establishes two co-emperors, each titled Augustus, and two deputies, each titled Caesar.

303–11 • Major persecution of Christians.

305 • Diocletian and his co-Augustus abdicate, the first emperors to do so voluntarily. Diocletian retires to Split in Croatia.

306 • Constantine the Great becomes emperor.

311 • Death of Diocletian.

312 • Battle of the Milvian Bridge. Constantine is the first emperor to convert to Christianity.

330 • Constantinople is founded on the site of Byzantium. It becomes the main imperial residence, and over time the eastern 'Rome'.

337 • Death of Constantine, also in his bed.

360 • Julian 'the Apostate' becomes emperor; he re-asserts paganism as the state religion.

362 • The oracle of Delphi closes, a symbol of the decline of paganism.

363 • Death of Julian on campaign against the Sassanids.

364 • Valentinian I becomes emperor; he divides the empire with his brother Valens into western and eastern halves. A successful general, he defends the frontiers.

c. 370 • The Huns, aggressive nomads, appear in Europe and fight other barbarian tribes.

375 • Death of Valentinian I, the last great ruler of the western empire.

378 • Battle of Adrianople: the Goths defeat and kill the eastern emperor Valens.

• Theodosius I becomes the last sole emperor.

391 • Theodosius makes Christianity the official state religion. State support for other religions and cults ends.

395 • Death of Theodosius I. His weak and ineffectual sons Arcadius and Honorius rule the east and west, respectively.

408 • Death of Arcadius.

410 • Alaric, king of the Visigoths, a group of Germanic nomadic tribes, frustrated in his wish to lead the empire (not to destroy it), sacks Rome. Rome is fortunate in the death of Alaric soon afterwards.

• Honorius tells Britannia to look to its own defence, marking the end of Roman rule in the province.

423 • Death of Honorius.

429 • The Vandals, an east Germanic tribe, settle in north Africa after ravaging Gaul and Spain.

434 • Attila becomes king of the Huns.

451 • Attila is defeated in Gaul and withdraws to regroup. He becomes one of the empire's most feared enemies.

452 • Attila invades Italy, but is persuaded to leave.

453 • Death of Attila from natural causes (even luckier for Rome).

476 • Rome's last emperor, the teenaged Romulus Augustulus, is deposed. Odoacer becomes king of Italy. End of the western empire.

1453 • The eastern (Byzantine) empire lasts for another 1,000 years. Constantinople eventually falls to the Muslim Ottoman Turks.

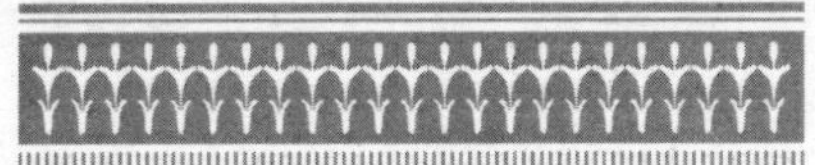

FURTHER READING

Here are some ideas for those who would like to read more about ancient Rome. The general histories, written by scholars for students, are informative if a little dull. The ancient historians in translation bring you close to the action, but are not always reliable. The versions of poets I recommend are, in their different ways, intelligent and imaginative re-creations. Most of the translations of quotations in this book are my own, except where I indicate otherwise in the text (in those cases full publication details are listed below).

GENERAL HISTORIES OF ROME

CAMERON, Averil, *The Later Roman Empire*, Fontana Press, 1993

GRANT, Michael, *The History of Rome*, Weidenfeld & Nicolson, London, 1978

SCULLARD, H. H., *A History of the Roman World, 753* to *146* BC, Routledge, London and New York, 1935 (4th edition 1980)

SCULLARD, H. H., *From the Gracchi to Nero: A history of Rome, 133* BC *to* AD *68*, Routledge, London, 1988

WELLS, Colin, *The Roman Empire*, Fontana Press, 1984

No one should read up on Rome without consulting this literary masterpiece:

GIBBON, Edward, *The Decline and Fall of the Roman Empire*, 1776, 1781 and 1788 (many modern editions)

ACCOUNTS OF DAILY LIFE

BALSDON, J. P. V. D., *Life and Leisure in Ancient Rome*, Bodley Head, London, 1969

BALSDON, J. P. V. D., *Roman Women: Their history and habits*, Bodley Head, London, 1962

Hopkins, K. and Beard, M., *The Colosseum*, Profile Books, London, 2006

Toner, Jerry, *Popular Culture in Ancient Rome*, Polity Press, Cambridge, 2009

THE ROMAN ARMY

Keppie, Lawrence, *The Making of the Roman Army*, Batsford, London, 1984

MEDICINE

Jackson, Ralph, *Doctors and Diseases in the Roman Empire*, British Museum Press, London, 1988

CLASSICAL WRITINGS

Penguin Classics have published many translations of poets and ancient historians of the Roman world. The following are particularly recommended (unless otherwise stated, they are published by Penguin):

[Anon.], *Lives of the Later Caesars*, trans. Anthony Birley, 1976

Ammianus Marcellinus, *The Later Roman Empire*, trans. Walter Hamilton, intro. and notes Andrew Wallace-Hadrill, 1986

Appian, *The Civil Wars*, trans. John Carter, 1996

Catullus, *The Poems,* trans. James Michie, Rupert Hart-Davis, 1969

Horace, *Odes*, trans. James Michie, 1967

Julius Caesar, *The Conquest of Gaul*, trans. S. A. Handford, intro. and revised Jane F. Gardner, 1951 and 1982

Julius Caesar, *The Civil War*, intro. and trans. Jane F. Gardner, 1967

Livy, *The Early History of Rome, Books 1–5*, trans. Aubrey De Selincourt, intro. R. M. Ogilvie, revised ed. 2002

Livy, *Rome and Italy, Books 6–10*, trans. Betty Radice, intro. R. M. Ogilvie, 1982

Livy, *The War with Hannibal, Books 21–30*, trans. Aubrey De Selincourt, intro. Betty Radice, 1972

Livy, *Rome and the Mediterranean, Books 31–45*, trans. Henry Bettenson, intro. A. H. McDonald, 1976

Ovid, *The Erotic Poems*, trans. and intro. Peter Green, 1982

Plutarch, *The Makers of Rome*, trans. and intro. Ian Scott-Kilvert, 1965

Plutarch, *Fall of the Roman Republic*, trans. and intro. Rex Warner, revised Robin Seagar, 1958 and 2005

Polybius, *Rise of the Roman Empire*, trans. Ian Scott-Kilvert, intro. F. W. Walbank, 1979

Suetonius, *The Twelve Caesars*, trans. Robert Graves, revised with intro. and notes J. B. Rives, 1957 and 2007

Tacitus, *Annals of Imperial Rome*, trans. and revised Michael Grant, 1959 and 1996

Tacitus, *The Histories*, trans. Kenneth Wellesley, revised and new intro. Rhiannon Ash, 1964 and 2009

Tacitus, *Agricola and Germania*, trans. Harold Mattingly, revised J. B. Rives, 1948 and 2009

Virgil, *Aeneid*, trans. Cecil Day-Lewis, intro. and notes Jasper Griffin, Oxford World Classics, Oxford University Press, 1952 and 1986.

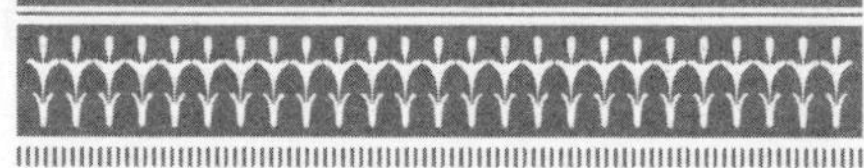

ACKNOWLEDGEMENTS

My chief debt of gratitude is to Roddy Ashworth, who came up with the idea for this book, advised me throughout and wrote a number of the items.

Richard Milbank of Head of Zeus and Ben Dupré edited the text with assiduous care and imagination, greatly improving my original draft. I have been much heartened by the enthusiasm and encouragement of Anthony Cheetham, Head of Zeus' chairman.

As ever, my literary agent, Christopher Sinclair-Stevenson, has been my invaluable guide.

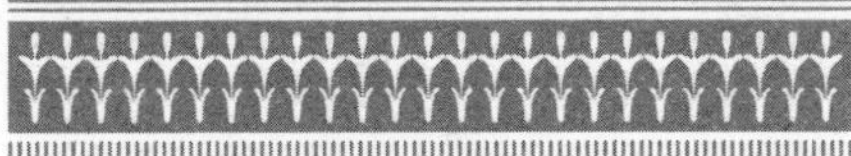

INDEX

Birth and death dates, when known, are only offered for completely historical figures. Romans are usually given their full names, except for emperors, who are cited under the names by which they are best known today.

A

B

C

D

H

J

K

L

M

N

O

P

Q

R

S

T

U

V

W

Z

A note on the types

THE TEXT TYPE is
10.5/12.5pt Bembo Book,
a digital recutting of
the last of Stanley Morison's
much admired Monotype
'revivals' of the 1920s
(which also included Garamond,
Fournier and Baskerville).
Originally designed for hot metal
composition, the face is,
broadly, based on a type cut
for Venetian printer-publisher
Aldus Manutius (1450–1515)
by Bolognese punchcutter
Francesco Griffo, who,
in his turn, looked to the formal
humanistic scripts of the
Renaissance writing masters
for his basic model.
Aldus' first use of the type was
in Pietro (later Cardinal) Bembo's
De Aetna, published in 1495,
which is considered as one of
the milestones of printing history.
Griffo's types of this period
mark a subtle shift away from
an essentially imitative *calligraphic*
approach to type design
towards a more *typographic,*
which is to say 'drawn', letter,
and have subsequently exerted
a profound influence on
typographic development
down the centuries.

THE DECORATIVE INITIALS
are set in Castellar, drawn by
John Peters (1917–89)
and issued by
Monotype in 1957

★